Under the Cedars and the Stars;

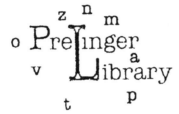

Under the
Cedars and the Stars

BY THE
Rev. P. A. Sheehan, D.D.

AUTHOR OF

"*My New Curate*," "*Luke Delmege,*" "*Geoffrey Austin;*"
"*The Triumph of Failure;*"

Etc , etc.

NEW YORK   CINCINNATI   CHICAGO
BENZIGER BROTHERS
PRINTERS TO THE   PUBLISHERS OF
HOLY APOSTOLIC SEE | BENZIGER'S MAGAZINE

94

CONTENTS.

PART I.—AUTUMN.

SECTION I

SECTION II

SECTION III

PART II —WINTER.

SECTION I

SECTION II.

SECTION III

PART III.—SPRING.

SECTION I

SECTION II

SECTION III

CONTENTS

PART IV.—SUMMER.

SECTION I

SECTION II

SECTION III

UNDER THE
CEDARS AND THE STARS

PART I

AUTUMN

UNDER THE CEDARS AND THE STARS.

" Mio picciol orto
A me sei vigna, e campo, e selva, e prato."
—*Baldi.*

PART I.—AUTUMN.

SECTION I.—I.

THIS is its great, its only merit. It is a *hortus conclusus, et disseptus.* Three high walls bound it, north, south, and west; and on the east are lofty stables, effectually shutting out all possibility of being seen by too curious eyes. It is a secluded spot, and in one particular angle, at the western end, is walled in by high trees and shrubs, and you see only leafage and grasses, and the eye of God looking through the interminable azure   The monks' gardens bound it on the northern side; and here, in the long summer evenings, I hear the brothers chaunting in alternate strophes the Rosary of Mary. The sounds come over and through my garden wall, and they are muffled into a sweet, dreamy mono- tone of musical prayer. But the monks never look over my garden wall, because they are incurious, and because there is not much to be seen   For I cannot employ a professional gardener, and it is my own very limited knowledge, but great love for flowers—" the sweetest things God has made, and forgot to put a soul in "—and the obedient handiwork of a humble laborer, that keeps my garden always clean and bright, and some are kind enough to say, beautiful. And we have sycamores, and pines, and firs; and laburnum, and laurel, and lime, and lilac; and my garden is buried, deep as a well, beneath dusky walls of forest trees, beeches and elms and oaks, that rival in sublimity and alti- tude their classic brethren of Lebanon, leaving but the tiniest margin of blue mountain, stretching sierra-like between them and the stars.

II.

But my garden is something more to me. It is my *Stoa*—my porch, where some unseen teacher ever speaks, as if with voice authoritative. It is to me the grove of Academe. Here, under the laburnum, or the solitary lime or sycamore, I walk with spirits quite as wise as those who trod the ancient groves with Plato, and questioned him sharply, and drew out his wonderful dialectical powers But my spirits question not. They are no sophists, weaving subtleties out of the web and woof of dainty words; nor do they ask *why* and *wherefore*. They only speak by their silence, and answer my interrogations. For I am an inquisitive being, and the mystery of the world weighs heavily upon me. I have the faculty of wonder strangely developed in me. An ephemera, floating in the summer air; a worm creeping from cave to cave in the warm, open earth; the pink tips of a daisy's fingers make me glad with surprise. Miracles are all around me, and I take them literally, and wonder at them *Omnia admirari !* is my motto; I have not steeled myself into the stoicism, that can see worlds overturned—with a shrug. I have a child's wonder, and a child's love.

III.

For example, I want to know who is the time-keeper and warden and night-watchman of my flowers. It is not the sun, because they are awake before the sun, and after his rays slant high above their heads. It is not light, because whilst it is yet light, light enough to read with ease and pleasure, behold, my little flowers close their eyes ever so softly and silently, as if they feared to disturb the harmonies of Nature , and as if they would say . "We are such little things, never mind us ! We are going to sleep, for we are so tiny and humble, why should we keep watch and ward over the mighty Universe ?" And again, who has bidden my crocuses wake up from their wintry sleep, whilst the frost is on the grass, and the snow is yet hiding in the corners of the garden beds ? And here, my little snowdrop, so pure and fragile, braves the keen arrows of frost and sleet, and pushes its pure blossoms out of the iron earth ! This is the bulb of a hyacinth; this the bulb of a gladiolus or a dahlia. But the former wakes up in early spring, and hangs its sweet bells on the pure virgin air; while the latter sleep on through the cold of Spring and the blazing heat of Summer, and only wake up when all Nature is dying around them, and seems to be calling, calling for another proof of its immortality. Who is the watchman of the flowers? Who holds his timepiece in his hands, and says: "Sleep on, O dahlia! Sleep, though Spring should call for universal allegiance, and Summer winds challenge thee to resurrection; but awake, Narcissus, and tremble at thine own beauty!" It is not the atmosphere. The Spring might be warm, and the Autumn chilly; or *vice versa*. It is not temperature, for the most fragile things flourish in the cold. What is it? Who hath marked their times and seasons, and warns them when their hour hath struck? Who but Thou, great Warden of the Universe?

IV.

Yet, whatever be said of times and seasons, which the Father has placed in His own power, I perceive that there is implanted in all being, even in these tiny flowers, a principle, a law, which appears to be universal. That law is what may be called the centrifugal force of being, or the power and tendency to expansion Wherever it is focalized, there it is—the universal and uniform impulse of everything to get outside itself, to enlarge its sphere of being, to develop its potencies, to become other than it is. It is true of the nebula, which is ever broadening and deepening, until by perpetual accretions it grows into a sun; it is true of the acorn, that yearns to become an oak; of the bulb that is ambitious to become a flower. And again is there a counter law, that by some hidden, irresistible force is equally bent on repressing this impulse, and destroying it. Expansion means repression. For the solitary, innate force that seeks to develop or reproduce, there are a hundred external forces that try to suspend or check that evolution. When my beautiful gladiolus comes forth, painted in all lovely colors,—saffron tinged with red, or purple streaked with gold, everything around will conspire to destroy the loveliness And the moment a nebula rounds its sidereal fires into a central sun, all its sister suns will seek to drag it into the cauldrons of their own terrific fires; it will be pelted by vagrant comets, and stoned with fiery meteors; and that Hercules of the heavens, that invisible giant, Gravitation, will drag it hither and thither, and force its centrifugal and expansive powers into the training circles of the Universe.

V.

And weep not, O thou child of genius, if obeying the universal law, and driven on, not by ambition, or other unworthy impulse, thou seekest to cast at the feet of men the vast and beautiful efflorescence of thy own mind, shouldst thou find all things around thee conspiring to check and destroy thy imperative development. Thou wilt expand and grow and put forth beauty after beauty; and lo! men will wonder at thee, but seek to destroy thee. Harsh winds will blow their keen arrows into thy face; the crystals of ice will nestle in thy bosom to chill thee unto death; winged demons will probe thee with their stings, and steal away thy perfections. Weep not, and murmur not! It is the law—the law of the star and the flower; of the clod and the nebula. If thou seekest thy own peace and comfort, hide thyself in the caves of the mountains, or the caverns of the ocean; repress all thy longings, check nature in its flight after the ideal; be content to live and not to grow; to exist but not to develop. But canst thou? No, alas! Nature is not to be repressed. Thou, too, must go into the vortices; and in pain and suffering, in mortification and dissolution, pass out to the Unknown!

VI.

What then? Well then, imitate Nature in its work, and—its indifference! Keep on never minding. If thou tarriest to pick up the stones flung at thee, or to scrape the mud from thy garments, thou wilt never accomplish thy destiny! The energies thou dost waste in fretting or philosophizing about human waywardness or malevolence, had better been spent in wholesome work. The time and thought thou expendest in answering the unanswerable, or explaining the inexplicable, would help thee to give the world out of the storehouse of wholesome thought, new vitalizing principles, fresh forces for wellbeing and welldoing. Well said the poet :—

> Glory of virtue to suffer, to right the wrong ;
> Nay, but she aims not at glory, no lover of glory she ;
> Give her the glory of going on, and for ever to be !

Aye, so it is ! Life is for work, not for weeping. Thou, too, hast thy life-work before thee, mapped for thee by the Eternal. It may be the merest drudgery, physical or intellectual; and the results are not to be foreseen. Thou must work in the dark, and there is no door outward to the future. But work steadily on! There is thy vocation and redemption :—

Nil actum reputans, si quid superesset agendum ! [1]

VII

What if some day it were found that this mighty mystery, gravitation, resolved itself into the universal law of expansion and repression ? The theory of Le Sage that the Universe is filled with infinitely minute particles that are continually colliding with larger masses, pushing them forward; but that two large contiguous masses, shielded from the bombardment, are driven irresistibly toward each other, really resolves itself into this. Or, the more recent theory of the vortex atom, whirling around and creating suction in the ether, thus dragging great inert masses toward each other, is not this the same ? Why is a column of smoke allowed to ascend and expand into rings or plumes until it is lost in the ether? And why is a column of water from its fountain allowed to expand but a little, and is then thrown back violently on the ground? And why is a stone not allowed to expand at all, but is flung back peremptorily to the earth ? Is it gravitation, or the law of expansion, that obtains fully in the case of smoke, partially in that of water, not at all in the solid matter, unless, as in the case of meteors, the propulsion is so great that it overcomes the resisting and repel-

---

[1] Considering nothing done so long as there remains ought to be done !

lent forces, and following its natural or rather the universal tendency, expands into flame, thence into vapor, and is lost? And
what a parallel with the meteoric flame of genius!

VIII.

I think Schelling, that most poetical of German philosophers,
pushes this idea too far. He makes the usual mistake of poets,
of passing from the abstract to the concrete, and lowers a great
idea by making it subservient to a whim. One can understand
his theory of Creation as being the attempt of the Infinite to embody itself, or rather to expand its supreme energies in the Finite;
and also his conception of Mind as the second movement of the
universal law, by which the Finite, driven back and seeking absorption in the Infinite, unfolds itself in Mind. A Catholic philosopher might seize the idea, to explain the existence of the Trinity,
as the eternal expansion of the Divine Intellect in the contemplation of its own perfections in the Word; and the continuous
expansion of the Father and Word in the procession of the Spirit
from both. When Schelling, driving his theory to extremes,
explains the fall of Adam by the tendency to break away from
law and expand into individualism, and the Incarnation as the
reunion or contraction of the vagrant human will into the Divine,
one cannot help feeling that truth is being distorted into ingenuity,
and that freedom is sacrificed at the shrine of " universal and
imperative law."

IX.

Is it not singular how that idea of the soul's emanation from
God, and its subsequent absorption in God, has always haunted
the human mind with its splendid suggestion of a divine origin
and a divine destiny? I can never understand how Novalis
could call Spinoza a "god-intoxicated man," for the latter elim-
inated God from the Universe, making Him a mere substance, if
universal. Schelling would have better earned the description, for
he preached at first God as the eternal, self-existent, omniscient,
and creative mind. But in very truth the epithet might be applied

to every mystic, for all have seemed to be so filled with the idea of
the great Supreme Being, as to lose themselves in the contemplation, and to have passed into that sublime trance, where they have
leaped beyond the finite conditions of time and space, and to have
touched that which is known as the Absolute. This is the *Potenz
der Subsumption* of Schelling, the "uncreated deep" of Tauler
calling to the created, and both becoming one; it is what Denis
the Carthusian calls "the plunging in and swallowing up of the
soul in the Abysm of Divinity"; what Richard of St Victor calls
"the passing of the soul into God"; what Cardinal Bona describes
when he says: "Thou art I and mine; my whole essence
is in Thee." Somehow it has always seemed to me that, with
this strange tendency towards Catholic truth manifested by the
wandering intellects of philosophy, some day there will be a reconciliation; or rather these cometary lights, which also have
derived whatever is luminous in them from the great uncreated
Light of lights, will be drawn into their right orbits in that mighty
system of which Christ is the Eternal Sun. For whatever far
spaces they have illumined, they manifest a tendency of an invincible attraction towards Him, whilst they wander afar, some
unseen power seems to draw them toward itself, and to hold them
from being lost in space, their light, though they believe themselves self-luminous, is an emanation of the light of the Gospel;
and it is the *candor lucis aeternae* that fills their extinguished lamps.
How eternally true is the apothegm: *Veram philosophiam esse
veram religionem, conversimque veram religionem esse veram
philosophiam.*

X.

And yet, an ingenious thinker could construct a theory of the
Universe out of this simple law. For what is evolution but a
new name for expansion, and the interchanges of species, and
the systole and diastole of human history; and the expansion of
kingdoms and their destruction; and the processes of suns; and
the revolutions of seasons; and the eternal strivings of the just
and perfect ones; and the aggressions of the wicked; and the
growth of genius, and all the many other changes and vicissitudes

by which God conserves the equilibrium of His Universe—what are all these secret yet unerring forces but modifications of the universal law: increase and multiply, and—pass! Or, rather: expand, contract, and return!

XI.

There never yet was a Moses without a Miriam, a Socrates without a Xanthippe, a Cæsar without a Cassius, a Napoleon without his Moscow. The law is universal and inexorable. Every expansive power in Nature and Man, in history, in philosophy, in poetry, has its enemy. Kingdoms do not crumble to pieces from within. It is the outer enemy that destroys. Babylon fell through Cyrus; Jerusalem through Titus; Rome through Vandal and Visigoth; the Eastern Empire through Mohammed; and if moribund kingdoms, like Spain, drag on their lifeless existence through centuries, it is simply because the antagonist has never arisen to attack and destroy. Similarly, every government has its opposition; every statesman, his opponent; every orator, his rival; every poet, his critic Milton had to fight for his existence; Wordsworth struggled for fifty years for recognition, reluctantly yielded at last; Shelley was hounded from England, and unrecognized for half a century after death; Gifford, the ex-cobbler, and Terry, the actor, drove Keats to a premature grave; and so on with all the brilliant and expansive geniuses of the earth. The tendency of the great is to grow; of the vile, to repress and destroy. God's prerogative of creation and development belongs to the former; man's peculiar bent toward corruption to the latter.

XII.

Hence, no one need be, or ought to be, surprised at what some call the slow expansion of the Church She has all the elements of development centered in her strong heart, or tugging at her breasts for that spiritual and intellectual pabulum which will enable them to grow, and vitalize in turn all the torpid faculties of a worn-out, effete civilization. " Lengthen thy cords, and strengthen thy stakes," said the Prophet, "for many are the children of the deserted, rather than of her who hath a husband" Yet her progress has been slow; and her vast utilities circumscribed Where she has gained, she has lost; and where she appears the loser, she gains the more. For the first three hundred years of her existence, every attempt to break her bounds, and go forth on her mighty mission, was stopped by fire and sword. When she rose above persecution from without, she was checked by rebellion from within; and her whole history has been a conflict between her own innate and immense potencies and desires for expansion and development, and the outer forces which make for destruction What she has gained in the New World she has lost in the Old, and *vice versa*; where she has won victories over kings, she has been dishonored by peoples; what she has gained in art, she has lost in science; and her very hand-maiden, Philosophy, has grown to be her rival in the affections of her children. Yet, there she pursues her immortal destiny, slowly gaining ground over humanity, every check developing her latent strength, every aggression met with indomitable valor; the mustard-seed growing, growing in spite of wind and weather, the axe and the fire, the Titan and the pigmy, the parasite and the insect, until it fulfils its promised and prophetic destiny, and overshadows all the earth.

XIII.

In a limited and sectional way, the case of the Church's growth and check in England is conspicuous. Fifty years ago, forces were let loose in that country which promised to extend the spiritual power and supremacy of Catholicism over all the land. The revival in Oxford and elsewhere seemed to promise a universal resurrection. The best moral and intellectual forces in England declared for Rome. So sudden, so important, so frequent were the conversions that it was fondly hoped that the end of the century would see the ancient Catholic land once more in union with Christendom Alas! the expansion was but temporary. It was tolerated, only to be driven back with greater force. The united energies of agnosticism, indifferentism, and open infidelity amongst the highest and lowest classes, and fierce bigotry and intolerance of the dissenting middle classes, not only stemmed, but drove back the tide of intellectual and religious thought which was tending towards Rome. The mighty fissure which the Tractarian Movement made in the Church of England, and which divided its members into the two broad sections of supernaturalism and latitudinarianism, was again closed up in a kind of common indifferentism. The time was not opportune. When education is more advanced, and toleration universal, there will be a general movement towards positive religion; and then the final reaction to Catholicism.

XIV.

I sat in my garden a few evenings ago. It was in the late summer The swallows, that had been screaming and circling round and round in ever-narrowing rings far up in the clear sky, had gone down to the eaves of my house, where, in their little mud-cabins, they now slept with their young. There was deep silence on all things—silence of midnight, or midseas. A few tendrils of white jasmine had stolen in over my neighbor's wall. The twilight had suddenly departed, and night had come down I could barely see the white stars of the jasmine, but I could feel their gentle, perfumed breath Once or twice a vagrant and wanton breeze stole over the wall and seized the top tassels of my Austrian pine, and lifted the sleepy leaves of the sycamores, which murmured and fell back to rest. Then silence again, deep as the grave ! I saw the suns of space of glinting green, and red, and yellow. I felt the throb of the Universe. As the lookout on a great steamer on the high seas, staring into the darkness, feels the mighty vessel throb beneath him, and watches the phosphorescence of the waves, and hears the beat of the engines, so felt I the thrill of Being—the vibration of existence. And as far up in the darkness on the bridge of the vessel, silent, invisible, stands the captain, who controls the mighty mechanism beneath him—dumb, watchful, with a light touch on the electric knob before him, so I saw Thee, though Thou, too, wert invisible, O my God—I saw Thy finger on the magnetic key of Thy Universe; and I feared not the night, nor the darkness, nor the grave, for I knew that the destinies of us and of Thy worlds were safe in Thy keeping.

Science shall never advance on right lines, except by imitating God. It is the wisdom of God in its infancy!

XV.

I love the science that reveals. I hate the science that explains, or affects to explain. I confess I revel in mysteries. The more profound and cryptic they are, the greater is my faith and delight. The merely natural palls on me. I see, wonder, measure, and— despise. I feel that I am its equal, no matter how stupendous it is. I measure myself with it, and lo! I am head and shoulders over it. The tiny retina of the eye of a child grasps and holds the whole dome of worlds The soul of a hind grasps the revealed universe, whilst man wonders at it. But the mightiest telescope ever invented and the all-searching eye of science cannot penetrate the impenetrable, the Universal; and the mind of a Newton or a Leibniz sinks paralyzed by Infinity. Tell me all the "fairy tales of Science." I wonder and am glad. But in a little time the wonder ceases. Weigh your suns and analyze them! Calculate your distances by billions and trillions of miles! Reveal your purple stars, and the radiant light that is flung from two or three varicolored suns upon their happy planets. I thank you for the revelation. I exult and am glad. But don't go one step further! Don't speak of Impersonal Force or Universal Motion as explanatory of such mystery! This time again I laugh, not in pleasure, but in scorn, or rather pity.

XVI.

People say to me: "Never seen Rome! or Florence! St. Peter's! The frescoes of the Sistine! The galleries in the Pitti Palace!" Never! Nor do I much care! If I were to go to Italy I would go to seek the Supernatural, because it is the only thing I could really and permanently admire. I would go to Rome, and see the Spiritual Head of Christ's Empire; I would go to Loretto, and kiss the ground once trodden by Jesus and

Holy Mary I would go to Assisi, and walk every step of the *Via Crucis* the "poor man" trod. I would make a pilgrimage to Siena; and I would visit every *stigmatica* and *ecstatica*. And there in her humble chamber, I would wonder and rejoice! I would have emotions which the grandeur of St. Peter's, and the terrors of Vesuvius, and the beauties of Naples, and the sublimity of Pompeii could never excite For I would come into touch with the Supernatural—with God; and the work of His fingers is more to me than the most stupendous creations of human hands!

XVII.

It is a good thing for men to be scientific. It makes them so humble. At least, it ought to make them so. I am quite prepared to hear that St. Thomas and Suarez were the humblest of men; that Newton and Leibniz were little children. It is only right and reasonable. When the former in their tremendous researches into some awful mystery, like the Trinity, evolved proposition after proposition, unwound as it were cerements of the awful secret, and then laid down their pens, like the scribes of old, and covered their faces, and murmured with full hearts: Sanctus! Sanctus! Sanctus! one can admire them whilst pitying them But when a sciolist, also unwrapping mystery after mystery, in search of the Great First Cause, comes suddenly upon an adamantine secret, that refuses to be broken or unweft, and lays down his pen and mutters, Unknowable! one can pity and despise!

XVIII.

God is quite right. He keeps locked the secret chambers of His knowledge and His works, because He knows that if He opened them, we would despise Him. Leibniz said, that if he had a choice he would prefer the pursuit of knowledge forever to the sudden acquisition of perfect knowledge One of the many pleasures of heaven will be the eternal, but slow unlocking of the secret cabinets of God. There must be mysteries, or man's pride would equal Lucifer's. It is God's way from the beginning. "Of all the trees of the garden, thou may'st eat; but of this one thou shalt not eat!" No one shall enter the Holy of Holies but the High Priest; and that but once a year! No wonder they tied a rope to his sacrificial vestments to drag forth his dead body, if Jehovah smote him. And yet the Lord is not in the thunder and the storm, but in the breathing of zephyrs, and the sighs of the gentle breeze!

XIX.

To a certain class of mind the doctrine of our intuitive knowledge of God has a peculiar fascination It seems so much higher and more honorable than the slow acquisition of ideas through the senses, that I am quite sure it would give unbounded gratification to this school of Catholic idealists, if it could be shown that it was not inconsistent with the most approved scheme of Catholic philosophy. Some writers deem it quite untenable, as tending to Ontologism. But it may happen that in this, as in so many other things, the confusion arises in tongues,—in different meanings and interpretations of the same word That fine thinker and metaphysician, Father Dalgairns,[2] seems to teach in his standard work on *The Holy Communion*, that the idea of God is inborn and immediately certain; that the Fathers call man, θεοδίδακτος; that man holds in himself the seeds of the knowledge of God (τὰ σπέρματα τῆς θεογνωσίας); and all this chimes in so harmoniously with all the experiences and feelings of the above-named school, that it would be an incalculable pleasure and delight to know that one might hold such beautiful and transcendent truths, and yet be at one with the great scholastics, and the most approved views of modern philosophy. There are few souls whom the lines of Wordsworth do not haunt as if with the revelation of a spirit-world :—

> " And I have felt
> A presence that disturbs me with the joy
> Of elevated thoughts ; a sense sublime
> Of something far more deeply interfused,
> Whose dwelling is the light of setting suns,

[2] Quoting Hettinger. Appendix D *Holy Communion et passim.*

And the round ocean and the living air,
And the blue sky, and in the mind of man ;
A motion and a spirit that impels
All thinking things, all objects of all thought ;
And rolls through all things "

XX.

This ethereal sense, this quick intuitive perception, which has often thrown back upon themselves the finest souls, and moved them by its swift and sudden revelation of the infinite, even to tears, is something altogether apart from mere logic or reason. Nay, perhaps, we had best interpret it as not so much a momentary penetration of the spirit behind the veils, as the sudden break in the clouds that hide God's Face ; and the swift dawning, clouded in a moment again, of that transcendent Light that makes the heaven of heavens luminous by its splendors. Hence let us say that this swift perception of the Infinite is not so much the effort of unrestrained fancy, or imagination, as the sudden revelation of God to choice spirits,—the swift and unexpected rending of the veil, the parting of the cloud for a moment ; and then, the darkness, but no longer the doubt. This is akin to the condition ἔνθεος καὶ ἔκφρων, "bereft of reason, but filled with God" ; the sense of the vision,

" when the light of sense
Goes out, but with a flash that has revealed
The invisible world "

XXI.

This intuitional principle of knowledge, although attributed in its origin to the pantheistic school of Schelling, is really the property of all poetical minds   In the German school it passed to the extreme of subjective Pantheism, just as in the Neo-Platonic schools it became a most dangerous form of mysticism   But that it is not irreconcilable with more prosaic forms of thought may be shown by the not incurious fact that the Scottish school of philosophy, essentially and professedly the school of common

sense, is also the great school where the intuitional perception of
God is unreservedly taught   The Scottish universities have, particularly of recent years, returned to the Aristotelian method, and
with it to the intuitional philosophy.   Reid, Brown, and, greatest
of all, Hamilton, have been ardent Aristotelians   The latter presented the Organon, the Nichomachean Ethics, and the Rhetoric
of Aristotle to the Oxford Examiners when presenting himself for
his degree; and it is said of him that he took up the first great
treatise, as a recreation, when wearied of kindred studies, so completely had he mastered it and so easy had its abstruse metaphysics become.   Yet he lays his greatest claim to fame to the
fact that he first affected to have bridged over the chasm that
yawned between mind and substance; and his disciples maintain
that this was his original contribution to modern thought.   What
was his secret?   What the airy bridge that he flung from the solid
basework of consciousness across the dark and unspanned gulf
that cut away that consciousness from the external world?   How
did he pass from consciousness of the Idea to consciousness of
the Represented?   By intuition !   It may, or may not, be accepted
as the final solution of the one great problem of metaphysics; and
many will be disposed to think it leaves matters just as they were.
Nevertheless, it is significant that a mind so strongly rationalistic
should seek in intuition the key of the great arcana, and yet cling
to the rigid precision of the great mediæval schools   And this
tradition, left by Scotland's greatest thinker, has passed down into
and been incorporated with the teaching of the great universities,
until the present professor in the chair of philosophy at St. Andrew's
rejects every other argument for the existence of God—cosmological, teleological, etc —and pins all his faith to the intuitional
method.   And then, perhaps, if all were known, it would be found
that the intuitions of philosophers, no matter how veiled in the
strange terminology of the science, is after all something akin to
Faith.

XXII

Strange, too, it is, that all modern agnostics seem to claim
Wordsworth as their prophet.   His vague abstractions supply the
place of religion, without binding the mind to dogma.   It is the

concrete, the defined, against which the pride of intellect persist-
ently revolts. It will not say *Credo!* but *Sentio!* It puts the
Absolute, the Unconditioned, the Non-Ego, the soul of Nature, in
place of "God, the Father Almighty, Creator of Heaven and
Earth" It puts agnosticism in place of limitation; incognizable
for incomprehensible. It declares the mystery of the universe
insoluble, because the only possible solution implicates them in
a declaration of faith But man's soul must have something to
believe in, even if it were a devil But that "something" must
not limit human freedom, nor arrogate rights over humanity, nor
disturb liberty of action and thought; and, above all, it must not
be the Arbiter and Judge of the Living and the Dead. But God
is all that in the Christian hegemony. Well, then, we must fall
back upon the Impersonal, the Uncreated, the Soul of things.

XXIII.

We shall worship in "temples not made of hands"; our
liturgy shall be poetry; our ritual, the changes of the seasons;
our sacrament, communion with Nature; our priesthood, the poet
or the philosopher; and our apotheosis, the general absorption of
all that we are, or shall be, into the universal Soul! No wonder
that Wordsworth, who wrote so bitterly against the Church, as
the enemy of all "mental and moral freedom," should be the
High Priest of the new dispensation. I think this is really the
secret of his power over moderns. It is not his poetry, which is
but a purple patch here and there on his gaberdine; nor his
philosophy, which is bald and bare enough; but this communion
with nature and worship of it, and tacit exclusion of the supernatural in the Christian sense, that makes him popular with such
writers as Matthew Arnold, or Mrs. Humphry Ward, or Emerson.
He is not a pantheist; such a term is quite inapplicable to Wordsworth. He is a Pythagorean, admitting at the same time, but
concealing, the existence of the Supreme Being, and concentrating
all his thoughts on the *Anima Mundi.*

XXIV.

And yet, though I have quoted Wordsworth here as an
example of the Intuitionist, I feel that I am somewhat in error.

He has been quoted as an apologist for Pantheism ; as a defender of Christian Theism. His friends do not seek to refute the former aspersion, his enemies are careless about the latter imputation. Yet, he is neither one nor the other. It is not the God of Spinoza he beholds and hears, for Spinoza saw nothing but dumb, irresponsive matter with its one essential of extension, neither does he address that personal God, whom we know as distinct from His universe, yet permeating in it,

Intra cuncta, nec inclusus,
Extra cuncta, nec exclusus

His appeal is to the " Presences of Nature in the Sky," " The Visions of the Hills," " The Souls of Lonely Places," the

   . . . . sentiment of Being spread
O'er all that moves, and all that seemeth still ;
" The Eternal Soul, clothed in the brook, with purer
robes than those of flesh and blood "

But all this is not the delirium of Pantheism, even in the diluted shape, called " Higher Pantheism," nor yet is it the quiet worship of God, the Creator and Consecrator. It is simply the instinct, or faculty, of Personification, the creation from his own poetic subjectivity of the *Anima Mundi*,—the soul that belongs to all inferior creation ; the response to the beauty and mystery and symbolism of the earth. And it is strange that the poet, who possessed this sensibility to a far higher degree than Wordsworth, and whose writings are one extended personification, acted upon and interacting, of all the powers, passions and sympathies of nature, is never quoted either as a Pantheist, or as a Deist. Yet he is the poet of abstractions and idealism, and he has written more poetry than Wordsworth has written prose. And this is a momentous word.

XXV.

This faculty of personification of the abstract—of casting the features of one's own mind across landscape, or human passion, or human history, is really what has given such reflective intellects a right to the title—Poet   That dogmatic and rather haughty saying of Tasso:

Non c'e in mundo chi merita nome di Creatore, che Dio ed il Poeta,

has some foundation in reason   Other artists work on rude materials, and fashion and form them according to their concepts   The poet creates his own materials, makes his own divinities, and worships them.   In a kind of Bacchic fury he calls up visions from the vasty deep, and blows them back into nothingness again.   He is the necromancer of Nature—that is, when he is a real poet, not a mere scene painter, for the greater dramatist, Nature.   Hence, too, is he priest and prophet, uttering sometimes in an unknown language the secrets of high and hidden things; and each poet has his own neophytes and disciples, who study his language, imitate his style, try to find not only the symmetry, but the symbolism of his words, and sit at his feet in life, at the foot of his statue when dead, and call him their master, their teacher, and their king.

XXVI.

And yet, strange to say, one of the greatest of these creators founds an argument for the non-existence of God in the formula: Mind can only perceive, it can never create; adding, however, the saving clause, "so far as we know Mind"   Quite so!   But man's mind is the lowest spirituality   And to argue from that to the powers of the Supreme and Sovereign Mind, is a strange fatuity. But is it true that man's mind does not create?   Where, then, O Poet of Atheism, was your Alastor, and your Beatrice, and your Prometheus, before you created them, where the "Eve of this Eden," the "ruling grace of the sweet garden"; where the "Desires and Adorations," "winged Persuasions and veiled Destinies" that wept over Adonais, where

> The legion of wild thoughts, whose wandering wings
> Now float above thy darkness, and now rest
> Where that and thou art no unbidden guest
> In the still cave of the witch, poesy?

Either there is no poet, but only a scene-painter, either there is no poetry, but word-painting, or else there is a projection over nature and man of a something which is not theirs.

A light that never was on sea or flood; and a strange reflection, where hover all beautiful forms of the Imagination, is not merely what the poet perceives or imagines, but the distinct creation of his mind!

XXVII

Some one, I am almost sure it is Emerson, has said that every great thinker must be, at one time or another in his life, an Idealist. Idealism is the land of dreams and visions, into which every new, fine spirit passes and wanders, dazed and blind, not knowing what to think, and rather inclined to believe that life and all its surroundings is a delusion—some vision painted by a sprite of evil, to torture or distress, or madden him with its beauteous unrealities Then, one day, he leaps over the bridge of Common Sense and Experience, and finds himself in the world of hard and stern realities He rubs his eyes, and wonders was he dreaming, touches and handles things without being able to prove their substance. Then reverts very often into his dream again, and murmurs this musical monologue:

> We look on that which cannot change—the One,
> The unborn and the undying. Earth and Ocean,
> Space, and the isles of life and light that gem
> The sapphire floods of interstellar air,
> This firmament pavilioned upon chaos,
> With all its cressets of immortal fire,
> Whose outwall, bastioned impregnably
> Against the escapade of boldest thoughts, repels them
> As Calpe the Atlantic clouds—this Whole
> Of suns, and worlds, and men, and beasts, and flowers.
> With all the silent or tempestuous workings
> By which they have been, are, or cease to be,
> Is but a vision, all that it inherits
> Are motes of a sick eye, bubbles and dreams;
> Thought is its cradle and its grave, nor less
> The future and the past are idle shadows,
> Of thought's eternal flight—they have no being
> Nought is but that which feels itself to be.

XXVIII

Recent researches in physiology throw considerable light on
that favorite doctrine, or rather speculation, of poets and philosophers, *Preexistence.* It has haunted the imagination of men from
the beginning of the world; and shaped itself in all kinds of
worthy and degrading assumptions   Like all other forms of
mysticism, it had its cradle in the East; thence it shadowed itself
on the great mind of Plato, under the form of *anamnesis,* or
memory of former existence, and in this shape it has become
familiar to us through Shelley, who was a professed Platonist,
and in the remarkable lines of Wordsworth, in his *Intimations
of Immortality.* —

> Our birth is but a sleep and a forgetting ;
> The soul that rises with us, our life's Star,
>   Hath had elsewhere its setting,
>   And cometh from afar
>   Not in entire forgetfulness,
>   And not in utter nakedness,
> But trailing clouds of glory do we come
>   From God, who is our home

But such hauntings as of a former existence are not limited to
poets, whose minds are supersensitive to impressions.   There are
few persons, and these of dull metal, who are not sometimes
startled by the vivid reminiscences which arise on visiting some
strange place, which certainly they had never seen before   This
feeling differs altogether from the sudden flashes of memory that
are struck from hearing some old, familiar, but forgotten strain of
music ; or from the sudden fragrance of a flower, or the grouping
of clouds at sunset, or the ashen light of an October afternoon.
It is a sudden sensation that some time in our lives we have been
here, seen those objects, just as now they are pictured to our waking vision   Nor is it the shadow cast by the vanishing skirts of a
dream, vivid in its intensity, and which the waking brain fails to
cast aside under the more imperious calls of reality   But there it
is ; and we have been here before. How can we explain it ?   By
the theory of double consciousness, and the unequal action,
therefore the unequal sensitiveness of the two great factors, or

lobes in the brain We know now that these lobes can act quite independently of each other ; that one can display the greatest activity, whilst the other is torpid; and that often, particularly under the pressure of necessity, the torpid, dormant lobe takes up its duties and emulates in its sensitiveness its more active brother If we suppose, then, a person whose cerebral power is functionally impaired by the imperfect interaction of the two lobes of the brain, coming suddenly upon a perfectly strange scene, the first impression made upon the healthy-active lobe will be of perfect strangeness and unfamiliarity But in a short time the other lobe wakes up to active consciousness, and the impressions made by the first are cast upon it, thus creating a reminiscence as of something once and long ago experienced or seen.   Alas! that science should be so ruthless ; even though it has the honor of accommodating itself to scholastic and strictly logical reasoning   It is not the only case where the conclusions of science are at one with the venerable traditions of the Church.

Section II.—XXIX.

This chain of thought which connects the conclusions of science with the traditions of the Church drags in another link out of the deep seas of speculation—the respective influences of Plato and Aristotle on the Scholastic teaching of the Church. There can hardly be a doubt that the former did hold sway through all the earlier centuries of the Church's existence, in the famous schools at Alexandria, along the Pontine shore, at Constantinople, and the cities of the Euxine Sea, until at last, after coloring with its poetry all the theology, philosophy and oratory of the East, it finally degenerated into the mysticism of the Neo-Platonists, and Rome, ever watchful of the truth, had to step in, and check the degeneration by recalling men's minds to fact and doctrine and away from dream and speculation.   Yet, it always haunted the East with its poetic splendors, until the tremendous reaction of mediæval times towards the Aristotelian method of reasoning drove Platonism back into the shades of history and tradition   And from these mediæval times downwards, the Aristotelian philosophy with its contempt for poetry, its hard, dry analysis, and the

rigid formulism of the syllogism, has been accepted informally
as the philosophic *method* of the Church. The *Summa* of St.
Thomas, the impregnable bulwark of Catholic philosophic teaching, is founded on it   The spirit of the Stagyrite passed into the
" dumb Sicilian ox," and through his mouth spoke to the world.

XXX.

There cannot, too, be the slightest doubt that, if the mission
of the Catholic Church on earth be to teach truth, and guard the
Divine Revelation, this is in reality the most effective and, we
might say, Divinely-ordained means of doing so   There must be
no question of poetry, rhetoric, or sophistry here.   The graces
of human eloquence, the lofty flights of poetry, the garlands and
the flowers of human fancy, have their own place, but they have
no place here   Truth is naked, the Clothier, Philosophy, which
has always dominated the ideas of men, has nothing to say to the
naked majesty of this heaven-sprung deity.   So far, then, as the
preservation or exposition of Truth goes, it is clear it must be
couched in the strictest terminology, and doctrine must be defined
with as close a logical accuracy as human language, expressive
of human ideas, will permit   Therefore, the syllogism and the
definition are the only rhetorical embellishments theology, in its
official form, can permit.   Hence, for six hundred years the Aristotelian method has prevailed in the schools of the Church.   And
it has been justified in its adoption by the fact that the moment the
human mind broke away from it in that first disastrous Enthy-
meme of Descartes: *Cogito, ergo sum*, it has drifted further and
further away in the endless mazes of human speculation, until at
last it completely lost itself in the visionary ideas of the German
Pantheists, or the still worse, because more contemptuous, dogmatism of French Encyclopædists   In our own days, the world,
emerging from the horrid labyrinths of rationalism and infidelity,
is rubbing its darkened eyes, and still blinded by the darkness, is
only able as yet to declare in a dazed and despairful way.

Behold, we know not anything !

XXXI

But now the question arises, whether in view of the world's awakening to the proximate and insistent issues that lie before it, it may not be well to reconsider our position, and, bearing in mind the strong prejudices that still exist against Scholasticism, try to present our truths not as dry bones, but as clothed and living realities. This suggestion, of course, only applies to our presentation of truth to the world. In our own colleges, there can be no great change from the rigid, logical method, because such method is preparatory and fundamental, and, therefore, strictly logical. But it is almost certain that we are on the eve of a tremendous reaction from agnosticism and materialism; and consequently from the inductive system of logic that led mankind into the abyss. That reaction will not take place on logical lines of thought. The world is too tired of analysis to care for more It will clamor for the poetic, for the ideal. We must do for it what the Greek Fathers and St Augustine did for the peoples who were waking out of the horrible dreams of heathenism. For men not only reason, but feel. The higher aspirations must be fed, as well as the ratiocinative faculties. Mere logic never made a saint; nor mere reasoning a convert.

XXXII.

Frederick Schlegel, I believe, says that every man is born a Platonist, or an Aristotelian There is food enough for the latter. Why should the former be starved? Goethe interprets the idea expressed in Raffaelle's famous picture of the school of Athens, where Aristotle is represented with his face bent to the earth, whereas Plato looks up to Heaven, thus: " Plato's relation to the world is that of a superior spirit, whose good pleasure it is to dwell in it for a time. He penetrates their depths, more that he may replenish them from the fulness of his own nature, than that he may fathom their mysteries." It is quite true his doctrines of emanation, preexistence, and innate ideas cannot now be held by a child of the Church; but he so far foreshadowed the cardinal doctrines of Christianity, that it is not difficult to accept the tradition that he sat at the feet of the prophet Jeremias in India; impossible to disbelieve that the whole of the Jewish or rather Judaic theology was known to him. The existence of the Word, a triune Divinity, the nothingness of life, the immortality of the soul, the rejection of Deities, the acceptance of Monotheism, the refutation of Atheism, the existence of great principles and eternal laws of right or wrong, as apart from utilitarian ideas of happiness or comfort—all these he taught with the emphasis of a Doctor of the Church   And he seems to have refuted the agnosticism of his own day, by his constant appeal to the demonstrations and axioms of geometry as certainties that can be known.   His most modern admirer, Dr Whewell, puts his case strongly

"It was these truths which really gave origin to sound philosophy, by exhibiting examples of *certain* truths.   They refuted the scepticism which had begun to cry out, *Nothing can be known*, by saying in a manner which men could not deny, *This can be known !*   In like manner they may refute the scepticism which says, *we can know nothing of God*, by saying *we know this of God, that necessary truths are true to Him.*"

Alas for Plato! and alas for Dr. Whewell!   Down come John Stuart Mill and Sir John Herschel; and shatter the theory of Necessary Truths to atoms!   And so the fabric of philosophy is Tennyson's fabled city,

> .   .   built to music,
> And therefore never built at all,
> And therefore built forever

XXXIII

There can be no doubt that whatever be said of his philosophy he has exercised a wider and deeper influence on human thought than any other seer of ancient or modern times   He was regarded as an apostle by the early Fathers.   Justin Martyr, Jerome, and Lactantius speak of him as the greatest of philosophers.   Augustine traces half his conversion to him.   The whole Eastern Church, especially the Church of Clement and Origen at Alexandria, hold him in deepest reverence.   Amongst modern thinkers, Emerson traces his direct influence in Boethius, Erasmus, Locke, Alfieri.

Coleridge, Copernicus, Newton, Goethe, Sir Thomas More, Henry More, Lord Bacon, Jeremy Taylor, etc., besides the host of minor philosophers and major poets who have taken their inspiration from him. Dante, whilst praising Aristotle as the "Master of those who know," borrows largely and without acknowledgment from Plato; for what is his famous vision of the "singing suns":

> Io vidi più fulgor vivi e vincenti
> Far di noi centro e di sè far corona,
> Più dolci in voce che in vista lucenti.
>
> . . . .
>
> Poi, si cantando, quegli ardenti soli
> Si fur girati intorno a noi tre volte,
> Come stelle vicine ai fermi poli.
>
> *Paradiso*, Canto X, 64–76.

but the "wheel with eight vast circles of divers colors, and in the circles eight stars fixed; and, as the spindle moved they moved with it; and in each circle a syren stood, singing in one note, and thus from the eight stars arose one great harmony of sound?" [3]

XXXIV.

Nor should it be forgotten that it was Averroes, the first of the European pantheists, that introduced the Aristotelian system into Europe; that if Plotinus, Iamblichus, Porphyry, and Proclus were fanatics and dangerous ones, Plutarch and Boethius were also Platonists, that many commentators in more recent times regard the Platonic doctrines of emanation, preexistence and planetary souls as poetic conceptions, not doctrinal teachings, for Plato, though he despised poets, like Homer, and would give them no place in his *Republic*, was essentially a poet himself and of a high order, and it must not also be forgotten that it was Descartes, now regarded as the parent of all modern agnosticism, who gave the deathblow to Realism, and established that Nominalism, of which Hobbes, Locke, Berkeley and Hume were subsequent exponents. The truth is that Platonism has got an evil reputation from the excesses of its interpreters, especially the Neo-

[1] *Republic*, Book X.

Platonists. Yet it is at least doubtful whether the Mysticism into which they dragged the doctrines of their Master was not a less dangerous form of heresy than that world-wide materialism, with which we have to contend, and of which Plato was, and is, the most successful antagonist.

XXXV.

But the truth appears to be that Platonism, which has an evil sound, owing to the excesses of its followers and commentators, has had at all times a great influence in the formation of thought. St. Thomas made Dante a philosopher, but Plato made Dante a poet   But, setting aside the names of founders of systems, and regarding only the development of doctrine, it would seem an opportune time to place before the world what some would call the transcendental, others the ethico-intellectual side of Catholicity. And whilst St Thomas' *Summa* reigns supreme in the schools as the *system* of sound philosophy, there can be no reason why St Augustine and the Greek Fathers in theology; Dante and Calderon in poetry, the Schlegels in literature, St Teresa, St John of the Cross, St Francis of Assisi in ascetic science; and such moderns as Balmez, Dalgairns, Faber, Gratry, etc, in popularized philosophy, should not be put forward to represent the more attractive phases of Christian science   The poorer classes have our churches and music; the artists our galleries, and all the poetry of our faith frozen in eternal marble, or frescoed in everlasting colors, musicians have all the divine delights of Mozart, Handel, Haydn, in Masses and Oratorios, but τίς φονεῖ συνέτοις in modern language and with modern adaptations?   The student who, some day, will take down Suarez's *Metaphysics* and give it to the world in strong, resonant, rhythmical English, will be one of the intellectual leaders of his generation.

XXXVI.

God holds in His hands the balance of the Universe. The Church on earth holds the balance of truth. The equilibrium of the former is disturbed by a feather's weight; that of the latter by a word, a syllable, a vowel. I cast a stone into the sea, and its fall is felt on far and unknown shores. I utter one word; it touches for good or evil souls as yet unborn or unconceived. There appears to be but a hair's breadth of difference between the *sensism* of Locke and St Thomas' theory of the Origin of Ideas The hair's breadth swells to the yawning chasm of Truth and Un-Truth The ravings of a Neo-Platonist and the mysticism of St Teresa and St John of the Cross seem the same They are as far apart as the poles And between that sense of the Infinite, the realization of God's Presence, the light touch of His hand, the breathing of the Spirit, the parting in the cloud, and the *Intellectual Intuition* of Schelling, by which reason knows the Absolute, because itself is the Absolute, and the Absolute can only exist as known by reason; how slender the verbal difference, how wide apart the faith and common-sense of one from the philosophical delirium of the other! And how necessary that infallible *magisterium* that is forever checking the turbulent and riotous waves of thought with its imperious command: "Thus far shalt thou come, and no farther."

XXXVII.

It is Vico who says :

"God is to the world what the soul is to the body ! "

As an analogy or comparison, Yes! As a fact, No! You cannot call God the *Anima Mundi* or the *Forma Mundi*. But you can mount up from the consciousness of the *Ego* and its powers, and even its limitations, by a strict, severe analogy, to the idea of God; the Finite cannot evolve the Infinite, but it suggests it. And granted the immateriality of the soul, you leap at once to the idea of the Infinite Mind—God *Cogito, ergo sum!* said the soldier-philosopher. *Cogito, et volo, ergo sum supra cognitionem et volitionem*, says the Christian thinker.

It is quite certain that no organ can command or control itself The heart, the liver, the lungs, are mostly automatic. They are beyond the power of will in their operations They work in obedience to a mysterious force, called Life. But the brain is not

automatic in its workings It is controlled from without. By
what? The *ego*, the soul, which thinks, acts, operates, controls,
subdues, excites, mollifies, or if it fails to do so, it is not so much
through lack of will, though the will is weak, but because the instrument is broken or passed beyond control How marvellous
is that power of volition to call up the faculty of memory! An
instant, and lo! the great map of the past is unrolled, and there,
in indelible ink, is the diorama of our life, or any section of our
life. Faces, scenes, works, words, touches, looks, sounds, odors—
all gleam out in the clear handwriting of the past; and, as we
will, or when the obedient instrument we command is weary, we
fold up the map again and put it away, secure that neither time
nor trial shall dim their colors, or cause their sweet associations
to cease

XXXVIII.

Frankenstein constructed a monster; but he failed to give him
a soul He gave him brain, intellect, mind; but it remained a
mere mechanical toy. It was corporeal, intellectual, sensitive,
passionate, swayed by emotions, a prey to terrors, or what is
worse than terror, the power to create it. But it was irresponsible. Its greatest crime could not be imputed to it, because it
had no soul; and no frame-builder, however skilled of hand, or
keen of mind, could ever pretend to give it.

XXXIX.

They who deny the existence of spirits deny the reality
of other than organic life. Our idea of life is limited to certain
organisms, frail and temporary, to some subtle influence that
prevents them from falling into an inorganic condition; and
which gives them faculties and powers extremely limited in
operation, yet with unquenchable aspirations after higher ideals.
But, analyze as you will, this life, even in man, is but a force, sub-
stantial in its immaterial essence though it be. To suppose that
this is the only potentiality in the Universe, exercised in this
humble and limited way, is nonsense. The same force must

be exerted in far higher and loftier ways, therefore in far higher and nobler beings, inorganic and incorporeal, but transcendently intellectual.

XL.

The automatic nerves in the spinal cord, motor and sensory, and the sympathetic nerves outside the cord are free from the operations of consciousness, and uncontrolled by them Why does not volition extend to them, if volition is a mere development of nervous power? Why is it limited to the cerebrum, and inoperative in the rest of the nervous system? If thought is only nerve-tension, and volition the same, why is thought localized in the brain, and even in different convolutions of the brain, although the physiologists have to admit the consensus of all parts of the brain to rational and consecutive thought?

XLI

I notice, too, that depression comes from dyspepsia, or solitude, or grief, or overwork It is a functional brain-disease. The blood is impure in the capillaries, or some nerve, pneumogastric or other, is irritated, and sets up in the great ganglions irritation and consequent depression. Yet I can control it, and even banish it By what? The mind But it is the mind itself that is functionally disordered and made impotent and incapable. Then, by some power beyond the mind and independent of it in existence, if not by action. This is the "spark and divine potentiality of man," as the Mystics say: "The unlost and the inalienable nobleness of man—that from which," as Pascal says, "his misery as well as his glory proceeds—that which must ever exist in hell, and be converted into sorrow there." The King in exile, warring with rebellious subjects, recalling lost royalties with pain or remorse, yet never abdicating or sacrificing the majesty of his heritage, but ever dreaming of the restoration of his kingdom and his throne—even such is, or should be, the mighty soul in its disenthronement.

XLII.

If Idealism cannot be accepted as a rational scheme, or explanation, of the phenomena of thought, sensism is still more
burdened with difficulties which admit of no explanation   For
when you have pursued its operations to their remotest end, you
have still the difficulty of *attention* to explain, and a hundred
other questions confront you that can only be interpreted by
fresh creations of the imagination   In fact, when you have
reached the terminus of physiological operations, you cannot go
further in your research after the ever-vanishing and elusive
mystery of thought, without creating or imagining a soul.   I sit
here in my garden, talking with a friend.   I am absorbed in conversation; but my eyes are fixed not on the face of my companion, but on that flower that burns itself on the retina of my
eye, though ten feet away in its bed.   Its color and form imprint
themselves, after passing through the canal of the eye, on the
retina.   They touch the optic nerve, and are carried along the
electric wire of the nerve, until they reach their term, and paint
themselves on the sensorium of the brain   They cannot go
further.   That operation of vision, physiologically considered, is
perfected   The object is imprinted on the brain as clearly as my
seal is imprinted on the hot sealing wax.   Yet I do not see that
flower.   I am so absorbed in this conversation with my friend that
I no more perceive that tulip than I see the roses of the Gardens
of Shiraz.

XLIII.

But, suddenly, yes, I see it!   I see its red and yellow colors
and its chalice shape   How?   By what new operation?   The
sensorium of the brain has already been reached, touched, and
affected by the image cast from the rays of light which has
proceeded from the flower.   What new faculty has been brought
into operation?   Clearly nothing cerebral or even physical
Something has suddenly swooped down upon that material
representation, looked at it, studied it, seen it, recognized it
Before that moment of recognition, the image was there as
clearly as after its discovery   But it was unseen, unknown, un-

recognized Who is the mysterious discoverer? Who has seen into the tiny caverns of the brain, and studied just at that point of light at the end of the optic nerve that brightly-colored picture? Another cerebral faculty? Impossible The cells of the brain are imbedded with their mysterious faculties in their own matrices, nor can they move nor be moved, from place to place, by their own automatic power, or by secret energies Each cell has its own energy, its own faculty, its own operation. It cannot come forth from its setting to gaze at pictures, or hear sounds in other places. Clearly, then, the faculty of attention or observation must be an independent faculty, to move hither and thither on its mysterious mission. It must be a swift and subtle faculty to pass from sensorium to sensorium with the rapidity of light It must be an imperious and arbitrary faculty, for there is no disputing its demands, if the instrument is still unbroken Memory must give up its secrets, and unfold its maps of persons, landscapes, sounds, sensations, pleasures, pains,—at its behest. It groups sensations, past, present, and future, together, and forms ideas and principles from their collation. It grasps facts of the external world—takes them from natural history, from human history, from art, from science, and builds up systems, from which in turn it takes principles of guidance,—synthesizing, analyzing, weaving, unweaving across the woof of the brain the webs of fancy or the tapestry of thought; and all this wonderful and miraculous work is the result of that secret and celestial mechanism—the cell? No! the Soul!

XLIV.

But there is something more There is a sister faculty, under that Mother-Soul, whose power is still more surprising Volition is greater than intellect, for intellect may stimulate volition, but volition commands intellect. And if the doctrine of mere sensism cannot account for thought, still less can it account for that mysterious faculty which dominates thought and sense equally. If all movements of thought and will were obedient to sense, what hogs from the sty of Epicurus would we be! What room would there be for all those superhuman deeds that have gilded the

otherwise sombre pages of human history? How would you
explain the nobility of Abraham, as with uplifted knife, and
with all the instincts of nature protesting, he sought to immolate
his son at the command of God? Or the courage of a David
facing the maniac Saul? Or the heroism of a Scaevola, a
Brutus, a Cato, a Germanicus? Or the patriotism of a Hofer or
a Tell? And how would you explain the filling of sandy deserts
with converted voluptuaries from Athens, and Alexandria, and
Rome? Or of a Stylites on his lonely pillar, or the unnumbered
martyrs who gave up their lives as witnesses to the Unseen? If
sense alone created thought, or governed will, how will you
explain this revolt against all its arbitrary dictates? Is it not
more reasonable to accept the existence of a superior faculty, that,
strengthened and enlightened from above, can trample the senses
beneath its feet, and compel to action on far higher and loftier
principles than either sense or reason could suggest?

XLV.

But how pitiful is the soul in its imprisonment! How sad to
see so noble a creation, with all its tremendous aspirations and
possibilities, dependent for its knowledge on the tiny miniatures
of external things cast upon one pin-point of the cerebral substance, and on the other hand, eternally fretted by the rebellion
of those very senses which are its ministers and slaves   Now
and again, in moments of inspiration, it seems to emancipate itself
from these trammels of flesh and to soar out and beyond its prison.
Saints have experienced this in their ecstasies, poets in their
dreams. It comes to some souls in the flush of early morning
with the songs of newly awakened birds, and the smell of wet
woods; and it comes at eventide with the saffron skies, and the
slow death of day. It is at these times that the soul is not so
much lifted up towards God, as driven to drag down heaven and
God to earth. It seems to fling its arms around Infinity and to
embrace it, and be lost in it   The rapture lasts but for one
moment, whilst the soul feels unutterable things. Then once
more it sinks back into its prison, and drags after it the heavy
chain. No wonder that St Paul, raised to the third heaven, and

then lowered to earth, should cry from his exile and banishment:
" Cupio dissolvi et esse cum Christo ! "

XLVI.

How keenly that great saint discovered the workings of the
spirit is evidenced by that one expression. " We know in part;
and we prophesy in part. We now see through a glass in an
obscure manner, but then face to face Now I know in part;
but then I shall know even as I am known " It is like an inter-
pretation of the shadow on the wall in Plato's cave But what a
boundless horizon of knowledge it opens up after death. " Face
to face " No longer through the dusk and shadowy intermediary
of sense; but confronting the reality, seeing all around it, and
through it, and beyond it, discerning the *noumena* beneath the
phenomena of things, and grasping firmly those shadowy and
elusive pictures of substance and form, and space and time and
infinity. What a revelation it will be ! And what an eternity of
happiness, in forever seeking after and finding the eternal and
immutable truths, manifested in the vision of God

XLVII.

But how do we touch the extremes ? " The personal ego," as
Maine de Biran says, " in whom all begins, and the personal God
in whom all ends." Where is the chain that links these vast
extremes of eternity ? Let us see. The main organs of the body
are automatic, but governed by a mysterious something called
Life. The worlds of the universe are automatic, but governed by
a mysterious something called Law But Life is governable by
volition that can conserve or destroy within limitations; and Law
is governed by the Supreme Will that can suspend or direct it at
pleasure. The organic body and the inorganic universe ; Life in
the former, Law in the latter The human volition controlling
Life ; the Divine volition evolving Law—there is a perfect analogy,
so far as the limitations of a Finite and the absoluteness of an
Infinite Being are concerned.

XLVIII.

It is a curious law of our intellectual being—that by which we are perpetually striving to unify all laws, and to seek after a First Principle. In the laboratory the scientist is forever seeking after the one great science which is to harmonize all former discoveries, and make future experiments more easy and more successful by the application of one great principle. Poets, too, have dreamed of this eternal and unique One

The One remains; the many change and pass Philosophers have veiled their dim consciousness of it under the name of the Unconditioned and Absolute. But the higher the scientist, the poet, and the philosopher go in their speculations, the nearer they find themselves to the principle of Unity Yet it is ever elusive and unattainable, vanishing at the moment of touch, then reappearing in the eternal and unquenchable passion of human striving after a unity of law, of principle, of origin, of all things that pass under the names of human cognitions or mental concepts. And, so that One forever remains as an eternal and irrefragable principle of philosophic thought, beyond knowledge, but not beyond reason or belief—accessible to thought as a principle—inaccessible in its attributes and modes, the dread reality of the humble and devout, the persistent and unwelcome visitant, which haunts the brain of the unbelieving and tortures it with its presence, without revealing its identity or the conditions of its being

XLIX.

There is nothing very original in this idea. Poets have sung it; philosophers have analyzed or explained it, saints have traced all truth and love to the single truth—God exists! and the single but sublime oracle—God is Love! The conception of the ideal Good, Beauty, Truth, involves that Unity which is the essence of all Goodness, Beauty and Truth. It is what Carlyle, unable to cast into concrete shape the thoughts that were floating vaguely before his mind, called the Eternal Verities; it is what St. Anselm, centuries before, called the *aliquid unum, quod sive essentia, sive natura, sive substantia, dicitur, optimum et maximum est, et summum omnium quae sunt.* [*Monologium*]

I heard a *Tantum Ergo* this morning in the convent chapel at Benediction Thought floated with the sound, and carried me out and out beyond earth to the choirs of the Seraphic Spirits. Music is the "Lost Chord" that has strayed hither from heaven. If one or two mortals on this grain of sand in the Universe can produce such ravishing melody, what imagination can reach the faintest outer bounds and limits of the harmonies that breathe before the throne of God from the vast choirs of all the Spirits of the Universe!

L.

"Man is the supreme product of Nature," says the evolution-ist. "He is the crown and glory of the universe; the apex to which the vast cycles have tended and terminated." Well, then, why did evolution stop at man? He is by no means a perfect creature. Even his supreme vanity will admit that. But he is now on this planet, in his evolved state, some thirty thousand years since the day he ceased to be simian, or pithecanthropic, and became anthropic in his fulness. It was a slow evolution, for we have no records of him beyond six thousand years; nor have we any proof that he is advancing. Or, if so, whither, and in what way, shall he develop? Will he put on the wings of angels, or sprout the plumes of cherubs? Will he conquer death, and soar, with glorified body, into the empyrean? Or, remaining human, will he exterminate disease, extirpate vice, make life one long summer, and banish disease and misery? Will the vale of tears become a valley of rejoicing to the perfectly-evolved humanity?

LI.

Evolution is no new doctrine. It is only English vanity that imputes its discovery to Darwin It is as old as Democritus, it was understood by St. Augustine; it is embodied in the "endless vortices" of Descartes, it is identical with the monad theory of

Leibniz, it is everywhere taught by Schelling. But all admit
that it is neither a continuous operation, nor a uniform one
Nature leaps a chasm here and there, and creates new species,
which appear to have no connection with those that are left behind But let us suppose that the process of evolution was perfect, that link was knit to link in the great chain; how is it explained that the mighty process was suddenly stopped at man?
He has had plenty of time to have evolved into something
higher The lower forms did not require so much time to
develop into the higher; and there is less difference, therefore
less of a leap of life and progress, between a man and an angel
than between an ape and a man Yet, nature stands still Con-
fucius was as wise as Plato; and Plato greater than Herbert
Spencer. Or, is nature, like the mighty suns, going to take a
leap backward now? Has she ceased to expand, and has the process of recession begun? And, descending the ladder of creation,
is she about to step down from species to species, into the vegetable organism, thence into the molecule, the monad, the atom
again?

LII

Our great mistake is, not in arguing by analogy, but in not
pushing analogy far enough in its widest, most expansive sense.
One argues about the infinity of inhabited worlds, but forgets
that these worlds must be inhabited by beings as different from
us as their suns and planets differ from ours. Our sun is but a
third-rate star; our planet but a minor off-shoot of nebulae. If
all the suns of space have their planets (as we might assume), these
latter must have intelligent, self-conscious inhabitants, but if
these suns are vastly greater than ours and differ in constitution,
density, and brilliancy, so, too, must their satellites differ from
our satellites, and their inhabitants from us, until we can not only
imagine, but reason about beings as vastly superior to us in intellect, as we suppose angelic intelligences to be; and according to
the density of their sphere becoming more and more immaterial,
and therefore less liable to dissolution, until at last we touch on
the subtlety and swiftness, the nobility and spirituality of our

angels; so that we ascend by the strictest analogy of evolution from the dual nature of man to purely spiritual creations, ascending higher and higher in the scale of intellectuality and subtlety, until we touch the fringe of that sea of Spirits that undulates within the precincts of heaven, and there, mount, higher and higher, until we reach the nine orders in all their transcendent beauty and perfection, culminating in the glories of the Archangels, who stand sentinels before the "great white throne"; where, suddenly, we are smitten back to earth by beholding in the innermost sanctuary of the Most High, the Hierarchy of the Incarnation, close by the enveiled Majesty of Him, "whose throne is darkness," and yet " enveloped in light as with a garment."

LIII

But all this only argues the existence of demigods So said Mill about the cosmological argument of the schools. But even on the theories of the evolutionists we cannot stop here. Not only as a fact in *esse*, but as a fiction, yet a logical fiction of pure thought, as an intellectual concept arising from a strict intellectual process, evolution cannot stop except with God. You must either accept the Christian idea of God, as originator of the universe, or God as its ultimate development. He is either Alpha or Omega—the Being from whom all things derive their being; or the Being in whom all things terminate, or, according to the Pauline idea—both. For if matter is eternal, it must have been developing and evolving its energies from eternity; and conceding for a moment that nature can leap the chasm from the inorganic to the organic, we have at last, after countless cycles of years, and endless processes of evolution, this tiny being called Man Man, the lowest type of rational creature we can conceive, is the ultimate development of the eternal processes of the suns But man is only a quite recent triumph of evolution. Yesterday he was an ape, the day before a vegetable, the day before a gas! Then what has Nature been doing from eternity? Is this its highest result? Nay, nay, says the agnostic, there must be higher natures than Man's, if matter, with all its potencies, has had eternity to work in. Then you admit the existence of angels ? Why

not the existence of God?   The very imperfection of man argues
a direct creation in what we call Time.

LIV.

Yes! eternity supposes Infinity.   An eternity of matter in
perpetual repose, inert, inexpansive, unattractive, inoperative, we
may conceive, but we know it to be impossible and non-existent.
But a dead universe might still be regarded as of indefinite dura-
tion and extent.   But a Universe, like ours, in perpetual motion
of dissolution and creation, of repulsion and assimilation, in a state
of perpetual flux and motion, and with the one result of which
we are most immediately cognizant, namely—ourselves, sentient
and rational beings, demands or foreshadows Infinity   But this
time, not the indefinite dead Universe, but an Infinite, if incomprehensible, Mind   For if Mind proceeds from Matter, as Materialists say, it is clear that the operation has not reached its term
of possibilities in human intellect.   That would be a poor result.
But if it can reach higher, why has it not done so?   It has
had all eternity to work in.   Either, then, man is the supreme
achievement of nature, or not.   If he is, Nature, perfect in all its
other operations, has failed here   If not, and if there be some
higher possibilities, then the operations of Nature from all eternity
must have produced Infinite Mind   Man can be explained by
the theory of direct creation.   He is unintelligible by the theory
of evolution, except as a chance accident, flung from the crucible
of being in a moment of lawless and misguided frenzy.   But,
this, too, won't do; for law is paramount, and admits no errancy
or arbitrariness.   Then, you cannot assume the existence of man,
except by direct creation, for if he is the feeble and halting result
of endless processes, working upwards from the womb of eternity,
these endless processes in the infinitude of space would have
developed something far greater and more worthy of such vast
potencies and such illimitable areas of space and time   "Very
well," says the evolutionist, "grant our theory, and we have no
objection to your placing God at the end of the chain of existence"   But this won't answer, because, according to every
axiom of philosophy, the conditioned can never develop into the

Absolute. We are face to face then with this dilemma—Man, the apex of creation, after countless millions of years; and all the energies of nature working in an illimitable field; or man, the handiwork of God, yet the lowest in the scale of rational beings. How absurd the former hypothesis—how simple and reasonable and free from embarrassment the latter. "Who hath wrought and done these things, calling the generations from the beginning? I, the Lord! I am the First and the Last!"[4]

LV.

I think it is in Lewes' *Biographical Dictionary of Philosophy* the words occur: "I can say, *Cogito, ergo sum;* I cannot say, *Cogito, ergo Deus est*"

Lewes had read the philosophers, but he was never admitted into the sacred circle "He hath been to a great feast of thought, and he hath stolen the scraps" All men are agreed that the first proposition has been disastrous to human thought. But where comes in the unreason of the second proposition? If you admit that man exists and thinks, you necessarily postulate the existence of Supreme Thought—that is, God. Descartes and his school would not accept for a moment that theory of modern Materialists —that thought, mind, soul, are purely material operations or functions. To them thought was evolved by will-power, itself immaterial, and its product became immaterial with it. Then you leap at once with the two concepts of Time and Space, as on two vast wings, to Supreme Immaterial and Inorganic Thought—that is, to God. The Finite can never develop into the Infinite, nor the Conditioned evolve into the Absolute But it can prove it—nay, demand it Once admit that thought is immaterial, although requiring an organic substance, in our conditions of being, to evolve it, and you reach, with one sweep of reason—the ultimate, as well as the principle of all thought—God! On the one hand, man's very littleness, as unworthy of the dignity of the universe, foreshadows God; and on the other, the grandeur of his immaterial faculties demands and postulates Supreme Intelligence.

[4] Isaiah 41 : 4

LVI

Yet it is remarkable that the more spiritual or idealistic schools of German philosophy, represented by Hegel and Schelling, are completely at issue with this logical deduction from modern materialism Their programme in the *Critical Journal* asserts that the "great immediate interest of philosophy is to put God again absolutely at the head of the system as the one ground of all, the *principium essendi et cognoscendi*, after He has been for a long time placed, either as one infinitude alongside of other infinitudes, or at the end of them all as a postulate—which necessarily implies the absoluteness of the finite." This reads like a sentence from some mediæval Catholic philosopher, with its Scholastic terminology, until we see further into the Philosophy of Identity— a monistic system which, taking choice between God and the human mind, eliminates the former, or rather amalgamates both under the unmeaning word—Subject-Object Then comes a schism , and Hegel passes out into unknown barren deserts of the "Phenomenology of Spirit," and Schelling follows his spiritual Pantheism until, driven back by inexorable logic, he finds reason is God—the only God; and God is reason—the spectre of itself cast by the retina of the soul on the background of Eternity

Here, too, again we notice one of the striking similarities between the systems and terminology of these stars of the outer darkness and our own great philosophical lights. For here Hegel breaks completely with Schelling, and gives a system of genetic philosophy in which he corresponds, word for word, and idea for idea, with St. Thomas, beginning with the lowest sensuous consciousness and working upwards through reason and experience to the highest speculative thought, and denying that any man has a right to impose his own intuitions, or what he conceives to be his visions, on the acceptance of the world; whilst Schelling reduces all apprehension of truth to each individual's consciousness, or his intuitive perception of all human verities

LVII.

The voice of nature is a voice of loneliness—the voice of one crying in the wilderness The infinite pathos of suffering seems to be everywhere. The autumn winds moaning in the crevices of chimneys, the deep, sad monotone of the sea; the weary plash of rain in the night; the sound of the waterfall from afar; the voice of rivers, deepened from the babble of streams; the moan of the storm in the leafless trees; even the zephyrs amongst the young leaves of spring,—all have an undertone of sadness, as if they too felt the " burden and the weight of all the unintelligible world." And here this evening I start and shudder under the "eldritch light " of an autumn sunset, at the

> Low breathings coming after me, and sounds
> Of undistinguishable motion, steps
> Almost as silent as the turf they trod

It is only the gentle susurrus of the evening breeze, and the zip! zip! of a red leaf falling into its brown grave. I saw it in the springtime, when it gradually unfolded from its cradle; and fulfilling the universal law, expanded its tiny silken gloss to the sunlight. I saw it, again by the universal law, attacked by parasites, which clung to its pale under-side, and left a brown mark of decay after them; I saw it tossed on the storm, wooed by the zephyr, wet with the weeping of the rain and the tears of the dew, shaken by the wanton, careless bird, caressed by the sun, pallid beneath the moon; and now comes its turn, as of all things, to die and fall, and pass into the inorganic kingdom again   But its last sound on earth startled me with its fluttering farewell, and its silent reminder: Thou too shalt pass. It is the law.

LVIII.

We had a terrific magnetic storm last night. Wise people who understand the eternal laws of Nature, and the marvellous interdependence of suns and planets, foresaw it. For there were, all this year, spots in the sun, great rents in the photosphere here and there, into whose horrible jaws you might fling thousands of pebbles, such as this little earth of ours, without the chance of satiating them. So I told my little children in the convent schools here   They received the information with a smile of pitying incredulity   Then there were some magnificent Auroras, up there

in hyperborean regions—great plumes of light cast up from an
unseen cauldron in the blazing heavens, and stretched out in a
great fan of colors, frail and iridescent as a rainbow's   So we said
to ourselves   Something is coming   This is but the stage scenery
When will the performance commence? Sure enough, yesterday
afternoon there were some deep grumblings in that half bronze,
half copper sky, which always holds in its hollows untold terrors.
These were the prelude to the mighty nocturnal oratorio of the
heavens. It commenced, as oratorios do, ever so softly and gently,
a mere susurrus of sound, echoed down along the bases of the
black mountains and fading away to invisible distances   But every
two seconds the sky was a sheet of blue flame, fitful and flickering, and yet broad and deep and permanent enough to show every
outline—leaf, and bough, and trunk, of the belt of forest trees
opposite my window, and every ripple in the river beneath   There
was no sleeping now.   I arose   So did every one in the village
except the little children in their innocence, who slept right
through the storm, and a tramp, who was drunk.   I lighted my
candle, and tried to read.   It was useless   Those broad, blue
flashes, flickering like swallows' wings across my windows, forbade
it   There was nothing for it but to witness in awe and with
strained nerves the explosion in fire and fury of the elements of
heaven.

LIX.

Then it struck me that my stables were in danger   I passed
out into the yard to examine them, and so powerful is the force
of imagination, I distinctly saw fire flickering across the ridges of
some thatched roofs outside my garden walls.   Next day, I was
surprised to find that these cottages were not burned to the ground.
I returned, and sat patiently watching the play of the electric
fluid across the heavens and athwart the landscape   Hitherto, no
rain had fallen; but about two A.M. the flashes became more frequent, as if the whole heavens were a tremendous battery, belch-
ing out blue flame at every moment   And the deep diapason of
the thunder came nearer, and broke in deeper and longer volleys,
reverberating across the valley, and shattered against the black
mountains far away.   The strain became severe, and I prayed

for one drop of rain to certify that nature was melting away in its own terrific anger. But not a drop, only the swift wings of light beating across sky and earth, and the deep growl of the thunder coming nearer and nearer Up to this the town was as still as death,—still with the silence under which all souls are hushed in terror, as if there were no escape, and nothing remained but to wait and pray. About three o'clock, however, as the storm deepened in intensity, a poor half-demented creature rushed wildly into the streets and cried: "The town is on fire! the town is on fire!" It was ghastly, that lonely cry in the stillness and dread

LX.

It was so like the cry of the angels who abandoned Jerusalem in the crisis of its fate: Let us go hence ⎮ Let us go hence! But a more startling sound struck the ears of the trembling people. Two poor jennets, who had been out feeding on the highways in defiance of the law, tore madly across the bridge and into the streets, screaming madly in terror; and their cry resembled so exactly the wail of women, despairing and stricken, that it seemed for a moment as if the whole town had gone mad from fright and rushed like maniacs abroad At last, about four A M, a few drops of rain fell and I said, thank God! But the storm was reaching its climax. The blue flashes, broad and gleaming, gave way before the terrific artillery that now broke right above our heads, and great blood-red and forked javelins of fire stabbed here and there through the inky blackness. It was horrible —those fire missiles flung at us we know not from where, and running zigzag now in the heavens above, now on the earth beneath, and after every flash such a crash of thunder that one could well believe that the end of all things had come; that the fountains of the great deep were broken up; and that Earth and Heaven were rushing together pell-mell into chaos. And the one hope was that the rain was now pouring in a deluge from the skies; and the plash from roof and housetop and gully was almost equal in horror to the weird music in the heavens At last, about 4 30 A M, there was a flash of blinding light, as if hell had opened and shut, then a moment's pause, and then such a snail of sound overhead, such a malignant fiendish growl as of a thousand maddened beasts, that I involuntarily put my fingers in my ears and murmured: Eleison! It was the last bar in the great oratorio of the heavens The sounds rumbled and died far down on the edges of the horizon; the skies cleared; and nought was heard, only the unseen cataracts pouring down their floods from the broken reservoirs of Heaven

A few days later I read, with surprise, that this frightful cataclysm was limited to a narrow belt of atmosphere, not half a mile in depth. Beyond and above, the eternal stars shone peacefully.

LXI.

About six o'clock the evening before the storm, a tramp came into my garden, where I was reading My servant said · A gentleman wanted to see me! So I said: Send him up! We are so polite in Ireland that everyone is a gentleman or a lady, when they are not noblemen I saw at a glance at his boots that he was a tramp Now, I like tramps, just as I like everything planetary and wandering It is because I am such a precisian, that I could not sit down to dinner if a picture was hung awry, or a book misplaced on a shelf, that I love irregularities in others A piece of torn paper on my carpet will give me a fit of epilepsy, but I can tranquilly contemplate the awful chaos of another's study, and even congratulate him on his splendid nerves. So tramps, comets, variable stars, wandering lights of philosophy, stars of the outer darkness, flotsam and jetsam of heaven and earth,—I have a curious sympathy with them all, as fate or fortune blows them about in eccentric orbits This wayfarer told me he was from my native town (which was a lie); that he was a tradesman out of employment (which was another); that he was hungry and thirsty (which was half-and-half). I gave him sixpence, which he instantly transmuted into whiskey Then he lay down under an open archway, and slept all through that terrific storm I have no doubt but that the electric fluid shot through that open arch again and again, during the night, but the Eudæmon, who presides over drunken people, warded off the bolts He woke next morning, stiff, but sound and whole ; and was utterly amazed at the universal consternation.

Section III —LXII.

It has often occurred to me that the revelations of Christianity upon human beliefs had much the same effect as fire upon invisible ink. All the vague, shadowy credences of humanity broadened out and glowed in intense light, the outlines of which no longer faded away into undefined and conjectural speculations ; but became clearly edged and marked, and indelible The Elohim drew together and became God, the Spirit All the ancient trinities—Hindu, Egyptian, or Greek, were defined and determined in the Father, the Son, and the Holy Ghost And that apotheosis of man, and his supreme excellence, which has always haunted human thought with such a suggestion of pride, that it has created gods after its own image,—reversing the process of creation,—was almost realized when the "Word was made Flesh, and dwelt amongst us." And there it remains—this supreme Theogony of Christian revelation. The ever-rebellious mind of man has striven to dissolve it again into the old shadows of verbal abstractions and lofty unrealities. But never again shall the supreme revelation be disturbed It is written in God's handwriting ; and chisel or acid cannot impair its outlines. It is revealed in words that shall not pass, even though the earth, like a worn garment, be cast aside and changed ; and the Heavens, like a reader's scroll of parchment, be folded up and hidden away in the archives of eternity

LXIII.

Hence, human pride is forever revolting against this revelation. The unrestrained intellect is forever beating its wings against this wall of brass, that marks its limitations It would so like to go out, and wander at its own sweet will across the deserts of the Universe, and build its own idols, as the Israelites, even under God's very eye, built their *simulacra* of gold and silver, and said they were their gods. Human folly is never at an end. It only takes different modes and shapes When one thinks of the orgies of the French Revolution, and the apotheosis of Reason under the vilest form conceivable, it seems not too far-fetched to predict that modern civilization may yet revert to the gods of Greece and Rome

LXIV

And, then, when it has wallowed in the sink and sty of uncleanness, its old God-like aspirations, stifled but not extinguished by pride and sensuality, will revive, and it will come back once again to the sweetness and dignity, the celestial graces and eternal hopes of Christianity. There it will find peace, "clothed in its right mind" for a time; until the untamable spirit clamors again for the fierce liberties of untrammelled thought and unlimited license; and leaves its vale of Tempe for the howling desert, and the turbid waters of Marah.

LXV.

What a wonderful camera is the mind! The sensitized plate can only catch the material picture painted by the sunlight The *tabula rasa* of the mind can build or paint its own pictures from the black letters of a book. Here is a little series that crossed the diorama of imagination this afternoon A great bishop, reading his own condemnation from his pulpit, and setting fire with his own hand to a pile of his own books there upon the square of his cathedral at Cambrai; and then constructing out of all his wealth a monstrance of gold, the foot of which was a model of his condemned book, which he thus placed under the feet of Christ, so that every time he gave Benediction, he proclaimed his own humiliation.

LXVI

Number two picture is that of a great preacher of world-wide reputation, going down into the crypts of the *Carmes*, whilst the cathedral was still echoing with the thunders of his eloquence;

and whilst the enthusiastic audience was filing from the doors, and every lip was murmuring: "Marvellous!" "Wonderful," "Unequalled," stripping himself bare and scourging his shoulders with the bitter discipline, until it became clogged with his blood, he murmuring, as each lash fell: "*Miserere mei Deus, secundum magnam misericordiam tuam.*"

LXVII

Number three is that of a lowly village church, hidden away from civilization in a low-lying valley in the south of France. It is crowded, it is always crowded, night and day; and the air is thick with the respiration of hundreds of human beings, who linger and hover about the place, as if they could not tear themselves away. No wonder! There is a saint here. He is the attraction. It is evening. The Angelus has just rung And a pale, withered, shrunken figure emerges from the sacristy and stands at the altar rails. Insignificant, old, ignorant, his feeble voice scarcely reaches the front bench There is seated an attentive listener, drinking in with avidity the words of this old parish priest He is clothed in black and white. He is the mighty preacher of Notre Dame, and he sits, like a child, at the feet of M. Vianney.

LXVIII.

Number four is a lonely chateau, hidden deep in the woods of France, away from civilization. It has an only occupant—a lonely man. He wanders all day from room to room, troubled and ill at ease. His mind is a horrible burden to himself He is a sufferer from a spiritual tetanus. He cannot say: *Peccavi!* nor *Miserere!* He comes to die in the city. Prayers are said for him in every church and convent in France. The Sister of Charity by his bedside presents the last hope—the crucifix. He turns aside from the saving mercy and dies—impenitent. Four months later, after he has been buried, like a beast, without rites, his brother arrives in haste at La Chênaie. The rooms are empty. The dead sleep on The despairing and broken-hearted priest rushes from chamber to chamber, wringing his hands and crying: Oh, mon frère! mon frère!

LXIX

It is said, the brute creation knows not its power If it did, it might sweep man from the earth. The same is said of woman; the same of the Moslem, in reference to European civilization; the same of the Tartar hordes Might we not without disrespect say· The Catholic priesthood knows not its power. If it did, all forms of error should go down before it The concentrated force of so many thousand intellects, the pick and choice of each nation under heaven, the very flower of civilization, emancipated, too, from all domestic cares, and free to pursue in the domains of thought that subject for which each has the greatest aptitude, should bear down with its energy and impetuosity the tottering fabrics of human ingenuity or folly. Here, as in most other places, are hundreds who, freed from the drudgery of great cities, the mechanical grinding of daily and uninspiring work, are at liberty to devote themselves to any or every branch of literature or science. They resemble nothing so much as the sentinels posted on far steppes on the outskirts of civilization, with no urgent duty except to keep watch and ward over tranquil, because unpeopled, wastes, and to answer, now and again from the guard on its rounds, the eternal question: "What of the night, watchman ? Watchman, what of the night ? " " Ay," saith someone, pursuing the simile, " but suppose the guard finds the sentinel with a book, not a musket in his hands, what then ?" Well, then, the student-sentinel is promptly court-martialled and shot!

And it was of these, sentinels of the West, that the very unjust and bigoted Mosheim wrote· " These Irish were lovers of learning, and distinguished themselves in these times of ignorance by the culture of the sciences beyond all the European nations , the first teachers of the scholastic philosophy in Europe, and who, so early as the eighth century, illustrated the doctrines of religion by the principles of philosophy."

LXX

The worst sign of our generation is not that it is stiff-necked, but that it wags the head and is irreverent. The analytical spirit

has got hold of the human mind; and will not leave it until the
usual cycle of synthesis and faith comes back again.   Outside
the Church, I searched for it everywhere—this lost spirit of reverence.   I sought it in the devout Anglican, hiding his face in his
hat, as he knelt in his well-upholstered pew   Alas! He was
killing time in studying the name of *its* maker   I sought it
among the philosophers, and found that from Diogenes down,
they spat at each other from their tubs.   I sought it, rather unwisely, in criticism, and found a good man saying that *The
Saturday Review* temperament was ten thousand times more
damnable than the worst of Swinburne's skits   I sought it, still
more unwisely, in politics, and read that a very great, good
statesman would appoint the Devil over the head of Gabriel, if he
could gain a vote by it   I went amongst my poets, and heard
one call another   "School-Miss Alfied, out-babying Wordsworth and out-glittering Keats;" and the babe replying:

> What—is it you
> The padded man that wears the stays—
>
> Who killed the girls and thrilled the boys
>   With dandy pathos when you wrote?
> A lion, you, that made a noise,
>   And shook a mane, *en papillotes*
>
> What profits now to understand
>   The merits of a spotless shirt—
> A dapper boot—a little hand—
>   If half the little soul is dirt?
>
> A Timon you! Nay, nay, for shame!
>   It looks too arrogant a jest !
> The fierce old man—to take his name,
>   You band-box   Off, and let him rest !

Then I went away. I passed by France, the cradle of irreverence,
and went out from Occidental civilization.   In the East, the land
of the sun, the home of traditional reverences, the place of all
dignity and ceremonial, where you put the shoes off your feet,
and touch your forehead, and place the foot of your master on
your head—here is reverence—the turning to Mecca, the kissing

of the black ruby [b] in its silver sheath in the Kaaba; and the glory
of being an El Hadj, the drinking of the sacred fountain, *Zem-
Zem,* the deep voice of the preacher: *Labbaika! Allahamma!
Labbaika!* I entered a Turkish town in the evening. The natives
had covered their garments under the *ir'ham,* the vestment of
prayer; the muezzins were calling from the minarets   I watched
one—a young Child of the Prophet—as he seemed to swing in
his cradle high up on the yellow minaret, and shouted with a voice
like that of the Angel of Judgment, the invitation to evening
prayer. As he swayed to and fro in that lofty nest, his face seemed
lighted with a kind of ecstatic solemnity, as it shone in the rays
of the declining day.

It was the perfection of prayer and reverence. The setting
sun, the long shadows, the faces to the East, the silence, the
decorum, and the prophetic voice from the clouds   Alas! I saw
a grave father thumping the young prophet on the back when he
descended; and the young prophet winked with an expression:
"Didn't I do it well?" Alas! for the Prophet! Alas! for Allah,
Il-allah! He was calling to a *Yashmak* down there in the street!

LXXI.

On the other hand, I find the summit of reverence touched by
two extremes in Catholicity—the Cistercian, sitting with folded
hands before the oak-bound, brass-hefted Ordinal in the choir;
and the little Irish children in our convent schools at prayer.
The former is the culmination of religious dignity and reverence;
the latter, of Christian simplicity and reverence. And it would be
difficult to say which of the two is more pleasing in Heaven's
sight. But, whether the heavy doors of the Kingdom would
swing open more lightly under the strong and vigorous push of
the Trappist, or the light, soft, timid touch of the child, one thing
is certain, that the Angels might claim kinship with either in that
supreme matter of reverence. And I suppose this is the reason
why, in the two most pathetic instances narrated in Holy Writ,
where the vengeance of God had to be averted from His people,
the priests of the Lord stood weeping in the one case between the

[b] Hajar-el-aswud.

people and the altar; and in the other, the prostrate figures of little children strewed the sanctuary before the face of the Most High.

LXXII.

Once upon a time, in the great city of Cairo, when the markets were full of busy merchants, and the narrow streets were loaded with merchandise, a Dervish came in from the desert, and looking meekly around for a vacant space in the crowded mart, he laid down his square of carpet, and knelt and prayed. He then unfolded his garments, and placed on the carpet a tiny box, but it contained a pearl of great price The passers-by laughed at the poverty of his belongings, and the great merchants, who sold spices and silks and unguents, turned around from time to time, and jeered at the Dervish and his little paper box No one came to buy, nor ask his price; and he remained all day, his head silently bent in prayer. His thoughts were with Allah! Late in the evening, as the asses of the rich merchants passed by, laden with costly goods, they came and sniffed at the little box that held the rich pearl. Then lifting their heads in the air, they brayed loudly: "It is not hay! It is not hay!" And some grew angry, and cried still louder: "Give us hay! It is not hay!" Now the holy man said not a word. But when the sun had set, and nearly all had departed, he took up his box, and hid it away in the folds of his garments, and kneeling, he prayed. Then he gathered up his square of carpet, and passed out into the desert, saying in his heart: Blessed be Allah, Il-allah! And afar on the night-winds he heard the bray of the market-asses. "It is not hay! It is not hay! Give us hay!"

LXXIII.

This is the chief excellence and attraction of philosophy. It is an inexact science. One is always seeking the insoluble—going out into unknown regions after the Inexplicable and Undefined Other sciences hand over to you their coins stamped and minted with the face or sigil of their kings, philosophy is not a *minted coin*, but an inexhaustible mine of all precious thoughts and sub-

lime principles. It deals with abstractions; and to the end of time
it is the abstract that will enchain the powers of that eternal
Inquisitor—the Human Mind. Hence the great philosophers
stand head and shoulders over all others in the vast Acropolis of
human knowledge. Warriors, and statesmen and orators, artists
in words, or marble, or canvas, sit at the feet of the priests of
Pallas; and draw thence their inspiration. Greece is Greece
because of its philosophy. Nay, nay, some one says, Greece is
Greece for its Homer and Æschylus, for Pheidias and Pericles, for
Themistocles and Leonidas! Yes, but where was the fountain-
head of all this inspiration—poetical, patriotic, artistic? Was it
not in that philosophy, imported from India; and which, personi-
fying the best conceptions of the human mind in the form of
deities and demigods, created for dramatist, sculptor and painter,
the noble archetypes of their ideas and works, and gave to her
patriots the inspirement that in defending, or exalting their
country, they earned the favor of the gods, and the guerdon of an
immortality to be shared with them on Olympus or the Elysian
fields.

LXXIV

So Rome is barren of immortals, because Rome was the
school-room of imported sophists, not the cradle or home of
original thought Rome had never a philosophy The spirit of
Greece hovered around her coasts wherever the subtle-minded
children of Attica or Asiatic Greece found a temporary refuge;
and the Roman spirit, accustomed to the direct and violent arbitra-
ment of the sword or mace, never took kindly to the subleties of
dialectics, or the nebular speculations of the aliens. They possessed the earth; and they did not want the sky. They held
the realities of life, and dispensed with the dreams They solved
riddles in their own way. But, as a consequence, whatever of art
they possessed was imported; their great temples were Grecian;
Corinthian columns supported their forums and palaces, their
greatest poem dealt with a Grecian hero, and their greatest orator
derived all his graces of diction and all the subtleties of his eloquence from Grecian models, whose inspiration he never acknowl-
edged, possibly because in the translation into his own speech it

was diluted into the thinnest of rhetoric and the most vapory in suggestion or reflection.

LXXV.

The Greek Fathers, too, unquestionably lord it over the Latins (always excepting St. Augustine, who, if not a Platonist, was decidedly Platonic), at least in two things—sublety of thought and sweetness of expression. Whether it was the genius of the language, which having served to embody the greatest poetry in the world, has now descended to become the handmaid of science, or the effect of climate or ethnical conditions, there is no doubt that the Greek Patristic writings are fuller of rhetorical grace, and suggestive elegances than the Latin. The latter perhaps gain somewhat in strength and precision from this very absence of grace and beauty of expression. But one can well understand how the compilers of Anthologies or Excerpts would select the former as richer in thought and sweeter in expression, and therefore more representative of what the early Church might have been in system and spirit So speculative truth was never alienated from practical wisdom Both combined to form the theogony of the Eastern Church And both, strange to say, rested on Plato and Aristotle combined For, to quote an expression of Coleridge, in wonder (τῷ θαυμάζειν) says Aristotle, does philosophy begin; and in astonishment (τῷ θαμβεῖν), says Plato, does all true philosophy finish And it was in this union of theology and philosophy, indigenous to Greek thought, that the special excellence of the Greek Patristic writings consists

LXXVI

It is very doubtful if there be a single idea in modern philosophy that was not borrowed from the ancients The atomic theory, the theory of monads, archetypal and ectypal ideas, Pantheism in its Protean forms—all were familiar to Pythagoreans and Eleatics, as they are to us For all philosophy resolves itself into belief in one of three theories .—

$\left\{\begin{array}{l}\end{array}\right.$

Monism. {
(a) Mind alone exists—Idealism—the Pantheism of Hegel and Schelling.

(b) Matter alone exists—Materialism—the Pantheism of Spinoza

Dualism. { (c) Mind and Matter exist—Christian Theism.

And, if we study the ancient schools, and at the same time accept St Augustine's bold idea, that Christianity did exist, even though as a penumbra and faintly, before Christ, we shall find that human thought, instead of moving in a straight line towards the insoluble problem of existence, is really turning round and round in concentric circles

LXXVII.

Was not the fall of man known to Empedocles:

τρίς μυριάς ὥρας ἀπὸ μακάρων ἀλαλῆσθαι,

and the absolute necessity for καθάρμοι expiations; and was not the Trinity known to the Platonists:

περὶ τριῶν ἐξ ἑνος ὑποστάντων

and

Τὸ αὐτὸ ῞ΟΝ,
Τὸν δεμιουργόν Λόγον, or Νοῦν, καὶ
Τὴν τοῦ κόσμου Ψυχήν.

And if we have seen before that man's mind tends naturally to the One Supreme Being, or Cause, and One Supreme Law, so, too, the tremendous mystery of the Trinity, before which the Church veils her face with an O, Altitudo! has haunted all philosophical thought from the beginning. But perhaps the most extraordinary manifestation is in the systems of two such cometary lights as Hegel and Schelling. Both of these philosophers seem to trace a trinity of action and interaction in all nature, working upwards from incipient consciousness to the great mystery, which, alas! they leave in abeyance. We place these trinities of thought side by side, to show how fantastically the greatest minds can operate on theoretic assumptions; and also to show what strange dementia has passed into the history of what is called Philosophy.

HEGELIAN.

The Idea.—Three elements:

 1.—In Itself.
 2.—In opposition to contrary idea.
 3.—In union with it.

or

 1.—The Idea in itself.
 2.—Out of itself.
 3.—Into, or for itself

The Faculties ·—

 1.—The Perception of the Senses.
 2.—The Understanding that divides perception.
 3.—The Reason that unites.

The Sciences :—

 1.—Logic.
 2.—The Philosophy of Nature.
 3.—The Philosophy of Mind.

The Religions —

 1.—The Oriental Religion
 2.—The Greek Religion.
 3.—The Christian Religion

Union of Philosophy and Religion.—

 1.—In the Christian community at its beginning.
 2.—In the Organized Church.
 3.—In the State.

SCHELLING

The Potencies :

 1.—(Potenz der Reflexion) Reflective Movement.
 2.—(Potenz der Subsumption) Subsumptive Movement.
 3.—(Potenz der Vernunft) Reasoning Movement.

These potencies are exercised thus :

On Matter :—

 1.—Expansion
 2.—Attraction
 3.—Gravity.

In Dynamics ·

    1.—Magnetism.
    2.—Electricity.
    3.—Galvanism.

On Organisms :—

    1 —Reproduction
    2 —Irritability.
    3 —Sensibility

The same three potencies are exercised

On Mind—In Knowledge :

    1.—Sensation.
    2.—Reflection.
    3.—Freedom.

      In Action :

    1.—The Individual.
    2 —The State.
    3 —History

Finally the two philosophers agree on three great cardinal prin-ciples ·

    1.—The identity of Thought and Being
    2.—The identity of Contradictories.
    3 —The *processus* of things, making the human mind the
        ultimate term.

No wonder that a French writer, after the study of these "weird speculations," should say :—

"I must frankly confess that my first sentiment as I leave these strange speculations of modern Germany is one of astonish-ment, that in the country of Leibnitz they should have been able to enthrall men's minds so long."

LXXVIII.

But, with all that incongruity and utter unreasonableness, it is certain that what are called Hegelians of the Right would find their conclusions lead infallibly into the dogmatism of the Catholic

Church, just as the "identity of contradictories" seems to be
found in the highest ethics of Christian faith, and Schelling's
Pantheism, crude and blasphemous, is but the truncated and un-
developed form of Christian mysticism.   So that all philosophy,
after passing through the tortuous mazes of human speculative
thought, emerges in the Gospel; just as the wildest theories of
existence, and thought and being, terminate in the Eternal, Self-
Existent Cause!

LXXIX.

I was pulling up some withered asters to-day.   A robin came
over in a friendly way and looked on.   I was grateful for the
pretty companionship.   It was familiar, and I hate stand-off and
stuck-up people.   I knew he admired my industry, if not my
skill   He looked very pretty with his deep-brown back, and
scarlet breast-plate, and his round wondering eyes watching mine.
Alas, no! he was watching something else   A rich, red, fat
worm wriggled from the roots of the dead flowers.   Robin
instantly seized him, flung him down, bit him in halves, then in
quarters, then gobbled up each luscious and living morsel, and
looked quite innocent and unconcerned after the feat   He had
swallowed as much raw meat as a grown man who would dine
off three or four pounds of beafsteak, and he was his own butcher.
And this is the wretch that poets rave about!

LXXX.

But hark! that ripple, that cascade of silver sound, as if from
the throat of an angel!   Not the shrill continuous anthem of the
lark, as he shivers with the tremulous raptures of all the music in
him; nor the deep bell-tones of the blackbird, as on a May
morning he makes all the young forest leaves vibrate with the
strong, swift waves of his melody, but a little peal of silver bells
on a frosty morning   Who is it?   What is it?   An Oread from
the mountains, who has lost her way hither; or a Hamadryad from
yonder forest who is drawing out her wet tresses after her level in

the silver cascade! No, but that butcher, that cannibal—that glutton! I'll begin soon to believe that prima-donnas drink; and that poets eat like mortals.

LXXXI.

No, no! In spite of this horrible disillusion I will not, I cannot believe that Keats, Keats of the "Hyperion," Keats of "The Ode to the Nightingale," Keats of the immortal sonnet, did actually and verily get drunk for six weeks together Can you even conjecture it, that the Greek dreamer who saw such wonders in the Grecian urn, and who looked through the

> Magic casements opening on the foam
> Of perilous seas in fairy lands forlorn,

did actually scorch his palate with cayenne pepper in order to enjoy all the more the cool deliciousness of claret? And yet it is not incredible. His letters about Fanny Brawne, and to her, reveal a strong sensuous soul, a fitting counterpart to his Charmian, —a Roman, not a Greek,—epicurean, Pagan, unrestrained, incontinent; and all in the frailest body that was ever hung together by the subtlest threads of an immortal spirit. There, my robin has flown with his worm!

LXXXII.

And "mad Shelley!" The first of English lyrists. Nay, nay, I cannot retract, if it is a literary heresy a hundred times over. I place him high up there on the shelf, side by side, nay, even above Shakespeare "There is a good deal of lying about Shakespeare," says a certain distinguished American So there is! Goethe commenced it in that very silly and salacious book, "Wilhelm Meister's Apprenticeship." Some day men will assure themselves on irrefragable evidence that Francis Bacon and William Shakespeare were one and the same person; and that Francis Bacon was not a great philosopher, nor an original thinker (that is conceded already); and that William Shakespeare, the greatest of dramatists, is not the greatest of poets. The great interpreter of the human, the poorest interpreter of the divine, was Shakespeare. But Shelley! Like his own skylark, he never leaves the skies. At least he never sings on earth. He is a denizen of the empyrean. He lives in clouds and lightning, and walks on their upper floors. He has his feet on the shoulders of the winds, and is the pilgrim of darkness and solitude He has not thought one weak thought, nor written one dull line His soul is "girt by the deserts of the universe"; and he seems to ascend, in the flesh, to the soul of some planet, that

> "Swings silent in unascended majesty"

He is the poet of high thought, the prophet of abstractions, the magician, who impersonates on canvas the impersonal and abstract; and fills his pages and the universe with all kinds of spiritual and transcendent creations. And yet, there is his apology for free love and atheism, and there is that hideous blasphemy, which should make every line he wrote worthy to be burnt by a public hangman, and their incinerated relics cast into the common sewer, and yes! there is the body of Harriet Westbrook dragged from the slime of the Serpentine, and he with Mary Godwin and Claire Clairmont over there in the Capri of the Villa d'Allegri Alas! there is the robin and the worm again!

LXXXIII.

Nevertheless, turn away your imagination for a moment from the "mad Shelley" of Eton and "Queen Mab"; of Harriet Westbrook and Claire Clairmont, and try and see only the Shelley who took the epileptic woman in his arms to the friend's house, the Shelley who never touched meat nor wine, who lay for hours with his head near the blazing fire, or on the burning roofs of Pisa; who chased the flying Allegra through the convent cloisters, and saw her rising from the sea; who gave away every fraction of money he possessed, who went down to his sea-death, and seemed to his friends to hover above the furnace or crematory on the Italian sands, then recall the music as of Ariel in his incomparable lyrics, the choral anthems in his great dramas; his odes to the Skylark and the West Wind, and you reluctantly declare that he was the ἐσσάμενος πυριπύρ, if ever there was one

Well, well, how easy it is to forget the mangled worm in the song and plumage of the bird!

LXXXIV

Is there an explanation of this most singular blending in one soul of such ethereal purity and such infernal and sordid malignity? How did the mind that followed the skylark into the immaculate recesses of clouds and sunsets, fling up the volcanic and destructive scoriae of the *Revolt of Islam* and *Queen Mab?* He tells us in his pathetic letters to his alarmed publishers: " I write for the συνετοί ! You might as well go to a ginshop for a leg of mutton as expect anything human or earthly from me " And then " I do not think that twenty will read my ' Prometheus !' " What gave such a spirit this bias towards anarchy and every kind of moral and social and spiritual lawlessness? One can conceive Shelley, trained otherwise, becoming the poet of all sweet and elevated and aspiring souls. Alas! now we have to anthologize him carefully, and look closely between the purple and golden leaves of the culled and fragrant flowers to see that no deadly, though beautiful, serpent lies coiled there His is the too common and terrible creation—a fair spirit in a woman's form, trailing away into the scaly coils of a snake!

LXXXV

Some fine people, or, at least some people who affect fine tastes, despise the dahlia. Not so I It is a faithful hardy servitor, remaining with us, through the universal abandonment, to the last. Long ago the geraniums have disappeared in cuttings, the red and yellow bells of the begonias have strewn the brown beds, the chrysanthemums with their fragile, cut-paper leaves, are hiding away in the greenhouse The dahlia, quite independent of autumnal winds, hangs its rich carmine and purple head, full of oval chalices, or flaunts its great star-disks of scarlet flowers in the rich wilderness of leaves And down comes leaf after leaf into its wintry grave, sometimes falling gently as a consumptive patient passes away, sometimes blown to death by the:

"Wild West Wind, the breath of Autumn's being."

Yes, indeed! my horizon is belted rather closer and nearer than I like by the mighty foliage of woods and plantations This cuts away all view of the blue mountains I should like to see. And in the deep sleep of summer peace, it is rather choking in its profusion and proximity Nevertheless, it has its advantages— not the least, that it faces, like a strong phalanx, the swift march of the West Wind, and out of the collision and the struggle come sounds of battle that are inspiring, the clash of host upon host, the shout of the advancing battalions, the defiance of the resisting legions. But down they fall in myriads, the slain of the autumnal fight, and the forests will be stripped naked and sub- dued, and the winter storms with all their ferocity will sweep soundless through the naked and quivering branches. But that wild West Wind, rainless and deepening the shadows of the already closing night,—how it suggests spirits and the dead who live! At least these sombre October evenings I become almost painfully aware of the immediate presence of the dead Strange I never feel the proximity of father or mother, but my sisters— one in particular, the only dark-haired in the family—has haunted me through life. I no more doubt of her presence and her light touch on the issues of my life than I doubt of the breath of the wind that flutters the tassel of my biretta in my hand. Yet what is strange is not her nearness, but her fairness. I should not be in the least surprised if I saw her face shining swiftly from the darkness, or saw her form outlined against the twilight sky. But why I cannot speak to her, or touch her, there is the problem and the vexation.

LXXXVI

And yet, when one comes to think of it, it is seen that such a revelation would destroy all the zest of life by solving too easily the ever-interesting enigma. God's wiser ways demand our faith, were it only for our own sake If all were revealed, all would be commonplace. It is better to believe and hope than to see. If that sister's face did flash suddenly out of the unknown and become so real that I could recognize its spiritual features, would it increase my faith or better my life? Alas, no! After the shock of surprise, I might treat it as a delusion of sense. Wisely has the Evangelist put his finger on the lips of Lazarus. If we had been told what he experienced in eternity—would the world believe? No; the world would laugh and go its way.

LXXXVII.

So, too, with that mercy from on high that veils our future in impenetrable mists. Physical science has done a great deal; the occult sciences are now moving forward to take their place. The weather can be forecast. Meteorologists can wire from place to place the depression that foretells a hurricane. But no man can tell me what will occur to me within an hour, a day, a year. And would I seek to know it, if the possibility of such a revelation were at my disposal? No! I would drag the veil faster down on the arcana of the future, and walk forward boldly, holding the hand of God. I will not tempt the future, for I see what a miserable life would have been mine, could I have foreseen the vicissitudes of the past. Nor will I fret, or be anxious about what may never be. The worst evils are those which never occur. And where would be our faith in Providence—the Far-seer—if our weak eyes could penetrate the dusk of the way we shall yet have to walk?

LXXXVIII.

My flowers have lingered patiently all along the dull autumn days, keeping their colors bright under the gray skies and sombre surroundings. The gladioli put out of their sheaths their superb blossoms, like convoluted vases of the richest Venetian glass, the asters held up their faces to their sister stars, the great rich dahlias filled their purple honeycombs with rain and dew; but all seemed anxious to adorn the mother earth from which they sprang, and loth to leave the soft autumnal air, and the sweet caresses of wind and soft, pure rain. Last night, however, came a frost, a bitter frost, and all now is wilted and withered unto death.

Nothing has escaped. The leaves are black in their decay, the flowers hang their stricken heads All is over The pomp of summer and the glory of autumn are at an end. The *hortus conclusus* is now a *hortus siccus,* until the time of the snow-drop and the crocus comes again !

LXXXIX.

This year has died, like a lusty old man who drops off suddenly, retaining his vigor to the last, and putting off decay to the silent metamorphosis of the tomb The trees had refused to change color until the final days of October; but then with a suddenness which made the change more vivid, they put on all the varied colors of smouldering fires, carmine and umber and ochre. It was not the burial, but the cremation of Nature. It was intensely beautiful ; and there was a look of silent patience in these smouldering forests, that made their dissolution intensely pathetic. And low skies, barred with deep gray banks of clouds, between whose parallel ridges not the sun, but a dim sunlight shone, leaned down over the dying landscape, until evening, when the gray melancholy lifted a little, only to show the greater sadness of death, lighted by that lingering sunset Then, one day, a fierce autumnal hurricane sped out of the red regions of the west, and at night, the *mise-en-scène* of Nature was over, all the purple trappings with which she had clothed herself for her final valediction and stage-farewell, were flung aside, and there remained only the skeleton framework of stage and wings, where she had acted so pompous and so picturesque a part.

XC

To-day a child in its mother's arms came into my garden. I looked at it, and saw at the same time the necessity of the Incarnation. God could not resist taking that loveliest form—the highest to which material things have reached. The yellow curls, thick and close and fine as silk floss, falling down upon his neck, the clear, limpid eyes, beaming with pure delight; the white teeth, and its ineffable joy, as it played at hide-and-seek behind its mother's neck, and then becoming suddenly serious, stroked his mother's cheek, and stared at her with eyes of wonder—no! If God has chosen to unite Himself to His creation, He could not have chosen a lowlier, nor a lovelier form. How beautifully these mediæval painters interpreted this mystery of the Human and Divine! And with what theological exactitude, yet with what artistic and withal sympathetic instincts they drew from the deep wells of imagination and devotion their Madonna and Child. Was it Tennyson that found fault with the serious look in the Child's eyes in that eighth wonder of the world—the Sistine Madonna? Look more closely, O poet, and you will find that Raffaelle was right.

XCI.

I cannot agree with the theologians who say that God united Himself to man as His highest rational creature. Man is the lowest in the scale of rational beings. You cannot conceive lower without drifting into the regions of monsters It was because man was the lowest reason in the scale of creation that God chose to join extremes—to knit Himself, the highest link with the lowest. "He emptied Himself, taking the form of a slave"

XCII.

But mark the swift and sudden transformation of the creature! "Remember that thou art but dust, and unto dust thou shalt return!" What a gulf between the ruthless sentence and this— "Know you not that your bodies are the temples of the Holy Ghost?" What wrought the change in the inspired pages?
The Incarnation!

XCIII.

I never could understand that mediæval idea of the worthlessness and contemptibility of the body It was easy to understand it under the Old Law, or by the light of reason alone But, by the light of Revelation, and in view of the stupendous fact that God chose it as the dwelling-place of His Son on earth, and His eternal, if glorified and transcendent Tabernacle in Heaven, it seems almost a denial of that ineffable mystery to speak of the body as a "sewer of filth," "a tabernacle of corruption," etc. Viewed in itself it is true that its marvellous and miraculous construction—the adaptability of each organ to its wants, the subtle and complex mechanism, awake enthusiasm in the scientist. The eye alone is a concentrated omniscience, so small in compass, so vast in comprehensiveness and power. But all is mortal and frail. It is but the solidifying of a few gases, that are dissolved in the putrefaction of death. What then? Science says it is a miracle, an eternal and inexhaustible wonder. But science also says it is but a passing whim of restless, constructive Nature—a delusion, a dream, a vapor, a myth. The ancient Scriptures seem to declare the same, but hark! here is a new Revelation, that apotheosizes this figment of clay, and clothes corruption with incorruption. What is the key of the new dogma? *Et Verbum Caro factum est!*

PART II

WINTER

WINTER

Section I.—I.

I notice these early evenings of winter a curious light in my garden; and across the river there is a faint twilight amongst the trees, so faint it is like the shadow of moonlight, or a terrestrial reflection of the Milky Way. I have read in some old book that it is the phosphorescence of decay. Everyone has seen the strange, pale light that accompanies the effluvia from decayed fish, and the beautiful phosphor-tinted waves which mariners gaze at, and poets rave about, in the incandescent tropical seas, are but the clean ocean waters heaving restlessly under a horrible burden of decomposition. This is realism with a vengeance! And, as I am a sworn foe to realism, and refuse to see aught but what I can idealize, I behold in the pale blue light that hangs above the dead forest-leaves, or the unctuous meteors from the leprous scum of the ocean, some idea of a soul, some promise of immortality. It is the poet's soul of nature, framed from primeval fires and reverting, under paler conditions, to its original state; and taking with it, out of the decaying matter which once it vivified, the one element that ensures its own immortality.

II.

Death—the great mystery! You remember how Tolstoi forces it on Levin's vision in that dread *Anna Karénina*. It is so inevitable, so repulsive, that one yearns to find in it some hidden charm, some mercy, that will show even beneath its hideous features the eternal and unchangeable beauty, that is, the goodness of God. And now it is all around. Nature is dead. Bare trees, grassless fields, empty gardens, flowerless beds, gloomy skies, sunless days —ay, all is dead, dead! And, as you trample under foot, these wet days in the early winter, great, soft masses of red leaves, rotting chestnuts, fallen acorns; and think of all the glories and generous promise of Spring, and all the luxuriant splendor of

(73)

Autumn, the question involuntarily arises: Ut quid perditio haec? Wherefore this waste? Why all this prodigality of Nature for nothing? Where is the law of parsimony: *Entia non sunt multiplicanda sine necessitate!* Until you lift your eyes on high and see that this, too, is a law of nature   Wherefore the eternal destruction and evolution of nature—the construction and destruction of suns and planets? Wherefore the waste of light in the universe, if only an infinitesimal portion of our sun's light reaches his planets? And sound? And the never-ending vibrations of electricity? Is all this lost, and "cast as rubbish to the void"? It cannot be. There is some explanation of the mystery

III

Ay, says the scientist, so there is   There is nothing lost, or mislaid in the universe. Matter is indestructible, so is force eternal! The perpetual interplay goes on, without haste, without rest—the never-ceasing weaving in the looms of Time of the garments of the Eternal! How do the verses go?

> In the currents of life, in the tempests of motion,
> In the fervor of act, in the fire, in the storm,
>> Hither and thither,
>> Over and under
>> Wend I and wander.
>> Birth and the grave,
>> Limitless ocean,
>> Where the restless wave
>> Undulates ever
>> Under and over.
>> Their seething strife,
>> Heaving and weaving
>> The changes of life
> At the whirling loom of Time unawed
> I work the living mantle of God

Ay, but that mantle is woven out of mists and shadows, out of clouds and rain, as well as out of suns and lightnings; and it is studded and hung around with humble bells and pomegranates, as well as with the pearls of stars, or the fleeces of comets. And nothing is too mean to be rejected as contributory to the whole fabric and tissue of beauty. The widow's mite was acceptable in the temple; the grass grows greenest above the grave. There is a beauty in decay; there is a kind of glory in destruction, as of honor in creation. There is nothing lost   All is fair and beautiful in the end   Only, there must be an object—otherwise all is waste power, as of a gristless mill that grinds itself away   And that object clearly is the garment of the Eternal, the sacerdotal vestments in which God is ever arrayed for the sacrifice that is never consummated.

IV.

And, as in matter, so too in mind.   In its eternal reproduction nothing is lost   It is impossible not to sympathize with what the world calls its failures   For every failure has in it the germ of a great success   Shakespere was unknown for one hundred and fifty years after his death   And many a titled booby whose horse he held outside that London theatre probably despised him as a potboy, and flung him a *pourboire* with contempt   Shelly was defunct for fifty years after his death , and Wordsworth for fifty years during his life.   Dante lay dead for centuries · then he rose to immortality.   All the celebrities of these centuries, contemporaries of these immortals, and overshadowing them with their borrowed splendors, have long ago passed out unto the unknown   The failures have risen up to perfect and permanent success   So, too, even now.   The great men of our age are unknown   They will be heard of in a century or two perhaps   A fashionable beauty at a watering-place will attract more attention than the young girl who has just won her gold medal in Greek or Science. Any skilful golfist is of more account than the Senior Wrangler. The loud-voiced, many-gestured demagogue occupies more space in public attention, and in the public press, than the silent student, who at midnight is building up great fabrics of thought for the future, or discovering some subtle solution for the political enigmata of the present.   But in a different sense from that intended by the poet :

The One remains, the Many change and pass

Thought is permanent, words evaporate You cannot kill ideas, nor imprison them. Nay, you cannot oppose them, or contradict them, if they are built on the foundations of unalterable truth. And as the most forlorn and rejected things are taken up and woven in Nature's laboratory into all beautiful and glowing forms, so the silent thoughts of the unknown are woven into action by those who never heard the author's name, but who have been thrilled into doing under the spell of a voiceless inspiration.

V.

Hence, too, it would seem that the pen is greater than the voice. It lasts longer and reaches further The *littérateur* is a greater power than the politician He inspires the latter; and outlasts him. Rousseau precipitated the French Revolution; and survived it He created Marat and Robespierre; they did not extinguish him He will live when they are forgotten. So much the worse; but we are only noticing facts. Of the two great men who held the mind of England for the last half of the nineteenth century, the literary man will outlive the statesman. Newman will be an active and perennial force when Gladstone is but a name. The one left behind him thoughts, the other deeds But thoughts are longer lived than deeds. So, too, moral teaching lasts longer than pure intellectualism, and is far more fertile of good Supreme intelligence does not win humanity. There never was such a silly comparison, even in the chaotic writings of unbelievers, than that which was instituted between Socrates and Christ—the one, a hard, cold, reasoning sophist, the other, the incarnation of tenderness and love We soon get tired of that infinite wrapping and unwrapping of words in the dialogues of the former. We never weary of the tender pathos of the latter Compare the Banquet where Socrates drank all the young men under the table, and went out to argue in his barren, disputative way in the streets; and the Last Supper, where Christ gave Himself to His Disciples; and, having sung a hymn, went forth to His Agony ! Contrast the hard, mechanic, pettifogging question· Didst thou not say, Cuto ? with the "soft wailings of infinite pity"—"Filioli mei"; "Jerusalem, Jerusalem, how often would I have gathered thy children "; " Our friend, Lazarus, sleepeth ", " Little children, love one another ", " Simon Peter, lovest thou me ? " " Eloi, Eloi, lamma sabacthani ? "

VI

Timanthes, unable to express the grief of Agamemnon at the death of Iphigenia, painted the father with head covered and face enveiled. And the sun, unable to bear the horror of the death of Nature, veils his face from us these short days of winter Ay, indeed, they are dark days! Just a kind of mournful twilight between the night and the night And what is worse, it is a weeping twilight We have no cold until January and February; but drip! drip! drip! comes the rain all day long, flooding rivers, filling swamps, creating lakelets everywhere; and all night long it is the same soft swish of rain, rain, rain upon the roof, flooding the shoots beneath the eaves, dripping from the bare trees; and you can hear the channels running flooded to the river, and see the swollen river sweeping noiselessly to the sea. Oh, but it is dreary, dreary, like the moated grange, and the " rusted nail, that held the pear to the garden wall " Yet these days, too, have their enjoyments. I confess I like a real, downright wet day. Not one that is rainy by fits and starts, so that you must go out, and get muddy boots and dripping mackintosh; but a day when the conduits of the sky are turned on fully, and the great sheets come down steadily, steadily, or beat in fitful gusts against your windows, and wash them clean, and the most hopeful weather-prophet, scanning every quarter of the sky, cannot see the faintest break of white cloud to warrant him in presaging that, sooner or later, it will clear We have plenty of these " cataract " days in Ireland, and they are simply delightful!

VII.

Delightful? Yes, to be sure And first, you have the intense joy of unbroken solitude. You are alone—absolutely alone for a whole day! The knocker is muffled, the bell is silent No foolish people who want to waste an hour on you, will venture forth to-day. Those who have real business to transact, will defer it. Then your conscience is at rest. If you do stir up the fragrant wood-fire, and watch the merry blazes dance up the deep chimney, and wheel over your armchair, and take up your latest purchase, crisp and clean from the publisher, or musty and stained from the second-hand "catalogue," there are no qualms about luxurious idleness; no thought of that country-school to be visited, or that horrid scandal to be uncarthed, or that grimy lane to be patrolled. You cannot go out—that is all about it! There, listen! Swish go the cataracts; patter, patter go the bullets of rain on your windows! The whole landscape is blotted out in a mist of smoke, gray sheets of water are steered across the fields and trees by the jealous wind; little jets of brown liquid are thrown up from the puddles in the streets where the rain-drops strike them. The channels are choked with the eager running of the streamlets from the streets; the brown river sweeps majestically along. There is no use in trying. You *cannot* go out. Wheel your chair closer, watch for a moment, for the greater enjoyment, the desolation and death without. Then glance at the ruddy flame, and, finally, bury yourself deep, deep in your book. No fear of interruption, one, two, three hours pass by in that glorious interchange of ideas. Life has nothing better to offer you. Enjoy it while you may!

VIII.

How you would hate the miserable optimist, who, intruding on such sacred seclusion, would say with a knowing look: "'Tis clearing away in the west! There is a break down there behind the trees! we'll have a fine afternoon!" Imagine, a sickly, pallid winter sun looking down on such a wet, bedraggled landscape; and, in unholy alliance with your conscience, ordering you away from that cheerful, neighborly fire! And how you would bless the cheerful croaker, who, looking north, south, east, and west, would shake his head sadly, and say: "No stirring abroad to-day! You wouldn't drive a dog from your door in such weather! We shall have forty-eight hours' continuous rain!" Forty-eight hours! Think of it! Think of it! How we will poke in long-forgotten drawers, and look up old accounts, and see how extravagant we were in our heyday, and examine old diaries, and re-read century-old letters There, you took them up by chance, and now, entranced, you sit on the edge of a chair, or on an open trunk, and read, read, till your eyes grow dim with fatigue, or— tears. Ah! indeed, the letter, frayed and yellow, is almost falling to pieces in your hands You hold it together with an effort Letter by letter, the old familiar handwriting begins to dawn on you, and you read. It is all "dear," or "dearest," and "Surely you must have known that I never intended to hurt," and "Are you not over-sensitive, dear, and too prone to take offence?" and "Come over informally this evening, and let us forget." You poise the letter in your fingers and try to remember. Yes! you wrote a dignified and very cutting letter in reply; and a great sea evermore rolled between you and the friend, whose face these many years has been upturned to the stars Or it is a letter from a child at school, largely printed and ill-spelled, asking you for a little favor. You refused it, as a duty, of course, as if there were any duty to one another in this world but love. Or, it is from a poor friend, who has gone down in the struggle, and is in sore distress, and begs "for auld lang syne" to help him You could have spared that twenty or fifty dollars easily; but you were prudent. You argued. He is extravagant, 'tis his own fault. It will be a lesson to refuse him. Alas! you wouldn't have liked to see his face as he read your letter. He has long since sunk beneath the current, and his children are begging their bread. Well, fold it up, but don't burn it It is a voice from the grave

IX.

I do not think there is any circumstance in the even life of Immanuel Kant, that is more painful to his admirers than his cold refusal of a few ducats to poor Fichte, to help the latter back to his native province. And I think there is hardly on record a more touching and dignified letter than this appeal of Fichte's, wrung from him only by the direst distress. "By a residence in my native province, I could most easily obtain, as a village pastor, the perfect literary quiet which I desire until my faculties are matured.

My best course thus seems to be to return home,—but I am
deprived of the means; I have only two ducats, and even these
are not my own, for I have yet to pay for my lodgings   There
appears then to be no rescue for me from this situation, unless I
can find some one who, in reliance on my honor, will advance me
the necessary sum for the expenses of my journey, until the time
when I can calculate with certainty on being able to make repay-
ment   I know no one to whom I could offer this security without fear
of being laughed at to my face, except you   .   .   .   I am so con-
vinced of a certain sacrifice of honor in thus placing it in pledge,
that the very necessity of giving you this assurance seems to
deprive me of a part of it myself, and the deep shame which thus
falls upon me is the reason why I cannot make an application of
this kind verbally, for I must have no witness of that shame.
My honor seems to me really doubtful until that engagement is
fulfilled, because it is always possible for the other party to suppose that I may never fulfil it."

He never added, poor fellow, that in the background, behind
the imagined vicarage, was the form of his betrothed, Johanna
Rahn, who was only waiting for these reluctant ducats to become
the faithful wife that she proved herself to be in all the after-
years.

X.

Now it is quite certain that no one can read that letter without
sharing the sense of shame, that must have suffused the face of
the writer, and tingled in his fingers as he wrote it   And no one
can read of Kant's refusal—gentleman, scholar, and philosopher,
as he was—without feeling equal shame.   And yet how different
are the sentiments.   The one is the shame of great pity, the other,
the shame of disappointment.   We are sorry for Fichte, because
he is reduced to so pitiable a condition even of honorable mendicancy; we are sorry for Kant, because of his "lost opportuni-
ties."   But we would retain for ever the letter of the former, as a
relic of honorable shame; we would gladly forget the refusal of
the latter, as a stain on a great reputation.

XI.

Ah me! those accounts—Dr and Cr. and L.S.D.! What desperate plungers and wastrels we all were in our heyday! What a stoical contempt we had for money! That picture which we fancied, and which the dealer assured us was a real Van Dyck; that vast encyclopedia, twelve guineas for that Tissot's Life of Christ, which we instantly gave away, because of its horrid French realism, that summer vacation—how that hotel bill did mount up! We shake our heads mournfully over ourselves—ourselves, mind, of the past, not ourselves of the present—there we are always devout idolaters! But those items—Charity 2s. 6d., charity 5s., charity 15s., charity 20s.; are these, too, regrettable? Happily, no! We cast our bread upon the running waters; and, after many days, it was returned.

XII.

And these diaries! Dear me! How brief your life's history! Into how small a space have you concentrated the thoughts, ideas, desires, emotions, passions, that swayed you for so many years! That day, so full of hope, or shame, or sorrow, or ambition, or anxiety—how swiftly you have dismissed it in one line! You remember you thought it would never end. You thought that suspense intolerable, that affront unbearable, that injury irreparable. You took a despondent view of life, a despairful view of men. You said in your anger: *Omnis homo mendax!* How little it all looks now. What a speck in the vistas of years! How childish now seem your anger, your impatience, your fretfulness! How keenly you realize that the worst evils are those which never occur! You worked yourself into a fever of passion over possibilities. You saw ahead but rapids, and shallows, and rocks. Lo! your life has glided smoothly over all, and you smile at the perils that encompassed you. And that bitter disappointment—that misunderstanding which threatened such dire ruin to your prospects, lo! it has gone by harmlessly, and you are ashamed of your vindictiveness and hate and childish apprehensions. The great wave that came on threatening to engulf you, you have

buoyantly surmounted, and you are out on the great high seas,
whilst it has passed onward, and broken harmlessly on the shore.

We look before and after, and pine for what is not   Foolish
enough! Live in the present, and pull down a thick veil over
the future, leaving it in God's hands. Live, live, in the present,
sucking out of the hours of life all the honey they will yield.

Mors aurem vellens, "Vivite," ait, "Venio."

XIII.

But there is a somewhat different lesson to be gathered from
these same old, frayed, and yellow records of the past. I have
purposely omitted the first line of the quotation, which runs thus:

> Pone merum talosque , pereant qui crastina curant ,
> Mors aurem vellens, "Vivite," ait, "Venio."

I rather like that picture of grim Death, flicking the ear of his victim, and whispering "Make the most of it, old fellow, I'm
coming for you soon."   But the "pone merum talosque" sounds
very like old Omar; and after all, this voluptuous life won't do.
All men are agreed upon that, except that most miserable class
of men of whom perhaps Des Esseintes in Huysman's novel is a
type; and who closes his worthless, pleasure-seeking life by a fate
that seems sufficient retribution: *Sur le chemin, dégrisé, seul,
abominablement lassé.*   Neither will it do to seek that milder
Epicurean paradise in which without labor, or suffering, and
merely by mental training and mind-abstraction, there is perfect
and profound peace. I do not say that men should not practise
mind discipline so perfectly that they can shake off easily the
minor worries of life   This is very desirable   Nay, it should be
a part of all education, to teach that the will is paramount, that
the minor faculties must obey it, and that a memory that loves to
go back upon remorse, or an imagination that is prone to dwell
on a perilous future, must be curbed by the superior power, and
learn to abide in the present. But this is a long distance away
from the religious peace connoted by the famous lines of St.
Teresa:

Nada te turbe !	Let nothing trouble thee !
Nada te espante !	Let nothing frighten thee !
Todo se passa.	All things pass away.
Dios no se muda !	God alone is immutable !
La pacienza	Patience obtains everything.
Todo lo alcanza	
Nada te falta :	He who possesses God wants nothing :
Solo Dios basta !	God alone suffices.

XIV.

Philosophy has aimed at the former. Religion has secured the latter. That perfect peace—the Nirvana of the Asiatics—has never been attained by mortal; cannot indeed be obtained until after the soul has migrated from being to being, and has become so attenuated that it has lost self-consciousness. To attempt this in ordinary life is to fail. It seems easy to say: Abstract your mind from all earthly things; let men be as shadows beneath you, live in the higher atmosphere of thought, and dwell alone with your own soul, let neither love, nor vanity, nor ambition, nor any earthly desire have place in your heart. and you will know what is meant by perfect peace. Alas! we have struck our roots too deeply into the earth to root them thus up remorselessly without pain and the more we seek such peace the farther will it fly from us What then? Is there something better? Something higher? No! there is nothing higher than perfect peace; but it must be peace through holiness In other words, there is no use in abstracting ourselves from earth, if we cling to self. After all, it is self that torments us; and if we could wean ourselves from all things else, so long as self remains, there is no perfect peace.

XV

I was rather struck with this thought on reading Hutton's monograph on Cardinal Newman. It is not very interesting reading, because it is too philosophical, in the sense that it is too synthetic We all like analysis of character—the drawing asunder and unravelling of the various threads that make up human life.

But when an author begins to draw big conclusions on things in general from these threads, it is apt to weary But, it is wholesome to learn that the great Cardinal did, in early life, grasp the principle that "Holiness is better than peace!" It seems a paradox, under one aspect, because we generally understand that peace is the concomitant, or result, of holiness. But the meaning clearly is that the soul that seeks peace without holiness will never find it; that life, an imperfect thing, is inseparable from trial, that difficulties are to be overcome, not to be avoided, that the soul that shrinks into itself behind the ramparts of philosophic thought, will be discovered, and that cares will creep over the wall, and that, finally, it is only by self-abandonment, and the annihilation of our own wills that we can foreshadow in life the peace of eternity This is what the Lord meant when He said: "*My* peace I leave unto you, *my* peace I give unto you! Not as the world gives, do I give unto you!"

XVI.

Nevertheless, whilst all this is true, there are secondary helps in reflection which are not to be despised. And one of these comes from retrospection Remorse for failures or mistakes is foolish. They are part and parcel of our imperfection. The past should not be allowed to cast a shadow of gloom on the present, nor to project itself across our future But it has its lessons—the supreme one, that anxiety is not only want of faith, but foolish in the extreme; and the other, a lesson of supreme gratitude to the merciful Providence who has ordered our lives so peacefully. The little souls that fume and fret under the little worries and vexations of life, should often take up their diaries and read them. There they will see how trifling were the things that poisoned their daily happiness, how insignificant the grains of dust that made the discord of their lives. A little courage would have brushed that dust aside and restored the soul to harmony and happiness. But no! we preferred the luxury of knowing that we were unhappy, and grudged ourselves the little labor that would have restored concord and peace Nay, most people nurse their miseries, and help them to grow, as if they believed that the monotony of peace were undesirable; and that a life varied by vexations were preferable to a calm and equable existence free from worry, and mapped without the red or black lines that connote disaster or suffering

XVII.

Then, I would make such little souls walk the hospitals at least once a year Nothing reconciles the unhappy to their lot, but to see others suffer more, and to see what they themselves have escaped The philosopher who suffers from *taedium vitae*, the fine lady who is *ennuyée*, the querulous, the discontented, should see the possibilities of suffering that are, alas! the inheritance of our race Here, within earshot of the busy hum of city life, is a staid building No pretence to architecture without, within, everything sacrificed to cleanliness and neatness. A few yards away, on the pavements of the great city, the votaries of Vanity are sweeping by, their little frames filled out and decorated with all the appliances that Art and Fashion can invent. They walk with the proud gait, the stately movements of young gods and goddesses. The earth is theirs; and theirs is the heritage of the sky and sea. Here, ranged in long rows, are the couches of their suffering sisters Very low and humble they are, as their breasts heave with the convulsions of difficult breathing, for that tiny occult mechanism has built him a resting-place in their lungs, and is living by exhausting their life. Round, lustrous eyes, hectic cheeks, dry, hot hands, wet hair, are their signs and symbols of disease, and creosote, formaldehyde, carbolic, have taken the place of the White Rose, or Heliotrope, which they shook from their raiment only a little while hence, as they spurned the very pavement beneath their feet

XVIII

Here again is another Temple of Hygeia, or rather of Death, for in these cancerous and tubercular cases the fair goddess is ruthlessly expelled by the skeleton god Tossing on couches of pain, their entrails gnawed by the fell disease, or visibly rotting away from the disease in cheek, or tongue, or teeth, or breast, the poor victims linger on through a hell of agony, and invoke the King of Terrors in vain. And here is another Temple where some two thousand are lodged,—beings once rational, but now with reason dethroned,—helpless, animals, ships without a rudder, tossed hither and thither through the stormy seas of their imaginings, with no power of guiding and directing themselves through the fierce impulses of animal instincts and desires. It is a cage for wild beasts Witness the iron-barred windows, the padded cell, the various instruments of restraint, the strong men and women to cope with the paroxysms of insanity. And this is a Temple of Justice, wherein the elements dangerous to society are incarcerated A thousand cells radiate from a central hall. In each is an outcast Seated on a plank bed, staring at white-washed walls, fed like a beast through an aperture, each wretched soul ponders on his misery, eats his heart with remorse, or curses that society which, for its own safety and well-being, thinks it necessary to separate him from the rest of his fellow-mortals thus

XIX.

And so, side by side, the gay and the sorrowful, Fortune's darlings and Destiny's victims, move, in a kind of Holbein picture, toward the inevitable. Now, who hath cast the dice, and appointed the lots of each? It is not merit, for in most cases my Lady of pain on her couch of suffering is a very much superior being to my Lady of pleasure on the pavement But that is not the question now The question now is, how can you repine at trifles, and fret yourself to death over imaginary troubles, like Molière's *Le Malade,* when you have escaped the coffin, the hospital, the gaol, the Bedlam, and all their terrible concomitants? And if you have come to middle age, or have mounted the mid-hill and crest of life, and are passing peacefully into the valley, how can you repine, when you have left so much misery behind you, and the fair vista of an honored old age stretches before you. Oh, but that disappointment ! That success of my neighbor's ! That prosperous marriage ! That successful speculation ! He taken and I left ! He with ten thousand a

year, and I with only five! And he, with ten letters after his
honored name, and I with only six! Avaunt, thou ingrate! Thou
who hast never proven—

> How salt a savor hath
> The bread of others, and how hard a path
> To climb and to descend the stranger's stairs.

XX.

I would put side by side, in parallel columns with the Table
of Sins in every Catholic prayer-book, an examination of escaped
horrors thus ·—

Hast thou ever been under the surgeon's knife? Hast thou
ever seen the doctors in their white waterproofs, or bloodproofs,
gaily chatting in the operation-room, and testing the edges of
their knives, and thou on the table? Hast thou seen the sponges
and the lint, and the splinters, and the hot-water, and the nurses
standing by the table, watching thee? Hast thou ever known
the sickening odor of the anæsthetic, which is to send thee into
the unknown bourn, from which thou mayest never return? Hast
thou ever had sentence of death passed on thee by thy physician?
That cough is phthisis, that little nodule of flesh is incipient can-
cer, that flush and chill is typhus; that sudden pain in thy left
arm is cardiac trouble; that inability to grasp thy pen is incipient
paralysis, that strange hesitation about thy words is brain disease. Hast thou ever dreaded the slow approach of insanity?
Hast thou, like a certain great Cardinal, lived all thy life beneath
its horrible shadow? Hast thou fallen into the grip of the law,
and carried with thee the indelible stain of the prison? Nay, do
not frown down the question as impertinent Did not Philip Neri
say to Philip, as he saw a criminal haled to execution · There
thou goest, Philip, but for the grace of God! And if thou hast
escaped all these things, and the many more too numerous to
mention, go down on thy knees, and thank thy God for His
mercies!

XXI

Thank God for the greatest mercy of all—that He has drawn
down an impenetrable veil over thy future, and lifts the curtains

of thy destiny, only fold by fold, and day by day. What would it be if the same Hand had unrolled for thee the map of thy life, and shown thee in thy adolescence all the terrors of thy future years? How thou wouldst have glided over the pleasures of thy existence with indifference, and fastened the eyes of thy imagination on the dangers and the pitfalls, the sorrows and the shames, that are marked so clearly on the diagram of thy existence! How thou wouldst extenuate and make little of life's pleasures; and exaggerate its pains! And with what terrible foreboding wouldst thou approach crisis after crisis in thy life; and forget the chance of victory in the dread of defeat! Verily, God is merciful! It is only to His great martyrs, most of all to the Queen of Martyrs, that He reveals the far-off Mount of Suffering; and allows the shadow of the three crosses cast by the setting sun of Olivet to darken the pathway of an entire life!

XXII.

I wonder, is there a human being who would willingly take the ordering of his destiny out of the hands of Divine Providence, and cast the horoscope of his own life? Would he accept the proposal if made to him thus

"Now you can frame and form your future according to your own desires   You can have all that the human heart may desire —wealth, position, honors, influence, old age   But you must accept with them their concomitants; and the burden of your own imperfections   You can frame your future destiny; but you must bear it on your own shoulders; and look for no assistance from above"

No Christian believer would accept such a proposal; and it is doubtful even if a pure Agnostic would not shrink from the responsibility   We might elect to have the framing of our own futures, bit by bit, but to round our whole lives in the circle of our fantasies and wishes is a something we would shrink from   And then there is always the possibility of disappointment and defeat with the self-reproach that would accompany both, if we made our own election. *Now*, if we fail, the failing is not of our own choosing.   We can place it at the door of Destiny: or, with higher faith and meekness we can say it is the Will of God. But the sense of responsibility and remorse is absent, which would not be the case if disaster and defeat followed close in the wake of the voyage we had mapped for ourselves along the high seas of life. There! What a meditation I have made over an open trunk! !

XXIII.

Swish, swish, comes still the rain; but now it is night. The short day has wept itself out; and its narrow twilight has yielded to great, black night All the greater security for you, my home-loving friend. It is dark at four o'clock, and here are five long hours of uninterrupted, unbroken peace with your books and pen. How the former glint and wink in the firelight and lamp-light! All day they were dull and silent. They seem to feel that their time has now come, and they display all the finery of bookbinding to attract attention I can almost imagine them say-ing, like the little children : "Take me ! Take me ! " and pouting, if left behind. Which shall I take ? Well, tastes vary Sometimes, I take a violent fancy for biographies—the inner histories of remarkable men. I like to see them turned inside out, and all their greatnesses and all their weaknesses revealed How im-perative a thing was genius! How it compelled work even to the starveling, and compelled admiration even to the unwilling! But, what an unhappy possession ! If happiness were the end and aim of existence, better be a hind than a poet, "a fool i' the forest " than a " swan of Avon." But this is the unvarying equi-librium of life :

To learn in sorrow what they teach in song

XXIV

Sometimes, too, I put aside human lives, and wander abroad on the wings of travellers, away to the South, to the isles of the Mediterranean, bearing still on scarp and cliff the ruins of the great Romans. Further still, to the "Isles of Greece," haunted by all the melody of the ancient language, and by the ghosts of all the singers and heroes that are immortalized in verse, or statue,

or drama.   Further still, to the silent monasteries of the Levant, or
the still more sequestered and archaic convents there above the
Ægean Sea.   Further still, to the shores of Palestine—the sacred
land—the home at Nazareth, where I should like to live forever
—the cave at Bethlehem—the Sea, where Christ walked upon the
waters, and to whose voluptuous cities, now crumbling ruins, He
preached   Further still, to Egypt with all its mystic religions
buried beneath its sands, and only the Eternal Sphinx looking
out with its pathetic eyes for the reincarnation of its deities.
Further still, to the lands of the Kaaba, and the Fire-worship-
pers, where the air is warm with hot scents above, and fetid with
the germs of disease beneath near the surface.   Further still, to
the cradle of civilization, India, whence Aristotle drew his wisdom—the land of the Vishnu, and Siva, and Siddartha; of strange
mysterious rites, where the natural fades away into the supernatural, and the visible calls to the unseen , the edge of the mysterious Orient, whence all faiths have come, to broaden out into
mysticism and superstition, or to be concentrated into the vital
and life-giving doctrines and ethics of Christianity.

XXV.

But I have two constant, never varying loves—my philosophers and my poets.   I cannot conceive a greater mental pleasure
or stimulant than the study of mental philosophy.   It is, after all,
the *great* study.   It is so clear, so defined, so perfect in definition
and principle and axiom, that you feel quite safe and walking on
level ground, until suddenly the great gulf yawns under your
feet, and beneath you is roaring the unplummeted sea.   You look
down, down.   It is crystal-clear, but no soundings.   Here Plato
gazed, and Aristotle pondered!   Here Kant watched during his
ninety years, only to turn away sadly in the end.   Here, too, our
child-philosophers of this unthinking age, fling their little lines
weighted with modern discoveries   Alas! they will not even sink
beneath the surface.   And the great deeps are still unfathomed,
and the great gulf unspanned   And yet the quest is not unfruit-
ful.   If it only taught humility, it would be a great gain.   But
it does more   It is like the vision of the Holy Grail that :

> Drove them from all vainglories, rivalries,
> And earthly heats that spring and sparkle out
> Among us in the jousts, while women watch
> Who wins, who falls ; and waste the spiritual strength
> Within us, better offered up to Heaven

At least, we know of no dishonored Knight of Philosophy. Votaries of other sciences may be impure. And alas! for our poets—the sacred fire does not always burn up carnal concupiscence. But Philosophy seems always to have kept her clients clean from grosser appetites and fleshly desires, and if they erred, it was through the spirit, and not through the flesh.

XXVI.

There is no author so worshipped by youth, so contemned by experience, as Lord Macaulay I remember turning over and over like a delightful sweetmeat in the mouth those words of his:

"It was a scene which Salvator would have loved to paint , and around which Claude Lorraine would have thrown all the glowing effulgence of the setting sun."

I had another melodious caramel from Telemaque .

Il me mena jusqu'au vaisseau ; il demeura sur le rivage

These were the happy days when we did not trouble much about sense, so long as we had sound. But in more mature years, the impertinent logic of common sense interferes, and tells us that there is color-poison in that sweetmeat In a word, that it is not true And every Macaulayite must suffer disillusion Nay, it seems really surprising that such an omnivorous reader should have committed himself to so many utterly untenable positions, Words came to him too easily, and he wrote too rapidly to be accurate. And then,—well, then, the public forgives a good deal to its favorites , and this he knew But I think the most extravagant statement he made is that in his feeble essay on Lord Bacon, where he says· "The ancient philosophy was a treadmill, not a path It was a contrivance for having much exertion and no progress Every trace of intellectual cultivation was there, except

a harvest.   There had been plenty of ploughing, harrowing, reap-
ing, thrashing.   But the garners contained only smut and stub-
ble"   Macaulay does not conceal his sympathies with that purely
utilitarian philosophy which places a shoemaker before a sage
or a poet, and thinks the discovery of the powers of steam of
far more importance than the institution of Christianity.

XXVII

But is it not strange that, although the Baconian philosophy
is justly credited with all these mechanical and material improvements that go to make what is called progress in our day,
the world, which utilizes these improvements, persists in placing
the leaders of purely metaphysical thought in kingly supremacy
over all the race?   Bacon himself descends to the rank of a
second-rate philosopher, when placed side by side with a Hegel
or a Fichte.   No one would think of mentioning Stephenson in
the same breath with Reid or Hamilton, or, in our own days, of
placing an Edison or Marconi on the same level with Herbert
Spencer or Lotze.   Man's mind will ascend, in spite of material
conveniences, far above purely physical and transitory things, and
will busy itself for ever in seeking to measure space and infinity.
And it is not on the crutches of the inventions of natural philosophy, but on the wings of speculative thought, it will ever seek
to penetrate the unknown   All that human ingenuity can ever
devise will never reach beyond the wings of Icarus.   Its desires,
passions, ambitions, reach higher   Mechanical inventions or discoveries, however ingenious and useful, can never become aught
but toys in the hands of a Child of the Infinite.   One thing alone
lifts him into the empyrean, the elevation of pure thought, subli-
mated by faith, and raised by its power to regions otherwise
impossible and inaccessible.

XXVIII.

All great writers have had their visions.   "In sleep, in a
vision of the night," revelations come.   The Hebrew prophets
stand out conspicuous by the multitude, the sublimity, or the

horror of their dreams   Lucian seemed to have followed them, or imitated them   St Augustine had his beautiful vision of Chastity, which left him in the agony of self-reproach, the prelude to his conversion   Every one knows the sublime picture of Philosophy drawn by the imagination of Boëthius:

"While I was pondering this in silence, and using my pen to set down so tearful a complaint, there appeared standing over my head a woman's form, whose countenance was full of majesty, whose eyes shone as with fire, *and in powers of insight surpassed the eyes of men*, whose color was full of life, whose strength was yet intact, though she was so full of years that none would ever think she was subject to such age as ours   One could but doubt her varying stature, for at one moment she repressed it to *the common measure of a man, at another she seemed to touch with her crown the very heavens ;* and when she had raised higher her head, *it pierced even the sky*, and baffled the sight of those who would look upon it.   Her clothing was wrought of the finest thread by subtle workmanship brought to an indivisible piece. This had she woven with her own hands, as I afterwards did learn by her own shewing.   Their beauty was somewhat dimmed by the dulness of long neglect, as is seen in the smoke-grimed masks of our ancestors.   On the border *below* was inwoven the symbol Π,[1] on *that above* was to be read a Θ.[2]   And between the two letters there could be marked degrees, by which, as by the rungs of a ladder, ascent might be made from the *lower* principle to the *higher*.   Yet the hands of rough men had torn this garment, and snatched such morsels as they could therefrom   In her right hand she carried books, in her left was a sceptre brandished "

Macaulay can hardly have seen this description, especially the lines we have ventured to italicize.   But it is easy to understand how the Reformers esteemed as a compliment, as he tells us in that same essay on Lord Bacon, the reproach that was so fiercely levelled at them : " Nullo apud Lutheranos philosophiam esse in pretio "

---

[1] Πρακτική
[2] Θεωρητική.

XXIX.

Macaulay, too, had his vision, as he tells us in the least-known, yet, perhaps, the best of his poems. This, too, was in woman's form

> Oh, glorious lady, with the eyes of light,
>   And laurels clustering round thy lofty brow,
> Who by the cradle's side didst watch that night,
>   Warbling a sweet strange music, who wast thou?

The answer appears ambiguous, for no one seems able to decide whether it was philosophy or literature But, evidence inclines somewhat to the former; and still more evidently to the former under any but a utilitarian aspect:

> Without one envious sigh, one anxious scheme,
>   The nether sphere, the fleeting hour resign ;
> Mine is the world of thought, the world of dream,
>   Mine all the past ; and all the future mine.
>
> Fortune that lays in sport the mighty low,
>   Age, that to penance turns the joys of youth,
> Shall leave untouched the gifts that I bestow,—
>   The sense of beauty, and the thirst of truth.
>
> Of the fair brotherhood who share my grace,
>   I, from thy natal day, pronounce thee free ;
> And if for some I keep a nobler place,
>   I keep for none a happier than for thee

This would seem to point to Literature as personified by the Vision; for Macaulay did not lay claim to be considered a philosopher Yet, when she recalls her work, and her protection of her votaries, one is insensibly reminded of the figure that appeared to Boethius.

> In the dark hour of shame I deigned to stand
>   Amid the frowning peers at Bacon's side ;
> On a far shore I smoothed with tender hand
>   Through months of pain the sleepless bed of Hyde.

> I brought the wise and great of ancient days
> To cheer the cell where Raleigh pined alone;
> I lighted Milton's darkness with the blaze
> Of the bright ranks that guard the eternal throne.

Still more shall we give our vote for Philosophy, when she makes her promises of protection and strength to her client

> When friends turn pale, when envious traitors fly,
> When hard beset, thy spirit justly proud,
> For truth, peace, freedom, mercy, dares defy
> A sullen faction, and a raving crowd

> Amid the din of all things, fell and vile,
> Hate's yell, and envy's hiss, and folly's bray,
> Remember me, and with an unforced smile,
> See riches, baubles, flatterers, pass away.

XXX

So it would seem that Lord Macaulay, the most successful man of letters of his generation, did experience that fine tonic of strong minds—the envy and jealousy of his contemporaries   It is strange that this curious and venomous antagonism does not seem to enter the sacred precincts of Art, nor yet the domain of Science   The reason is evident   Only experts who had passed through a professional training will venture to criticise a picture, or offer an opinion on a new discovery in Science.   But in literature, everyone is qualified to judge; and to reject or accept, condemn or magnify a new appearance.   Philosophy, however, has her atonements and consolations.   All will pass !   It is the book-mark of St. Teresa over again—honor, dishonor; the smile, the sneer; the glory, the gibe, the laurel, the thorn, all will pass.

> Yes, they will pass away; nor deem it strange;
> They come and go, as comes and goes the sea;
> And let them come and go, thou, through all change
> Fix thy firm gaze on Virtue and on me !

XXXI.

Some day, when science has made such advance that human labor will be required no longer, men will sleep by day, and watch the stars by night. For, of the two revelations of Nature which strike the senses, unquestionably that of darkness is the more magnificent. We see but one sun by day, and that a star of the second or third magnitude ; we see countless suns by night of every color and brilliancy. And scattered amongst them, here and there, vast nebulæ, the seeds or laboratories of other universes; and we know that creation and destruction, the weaving of gases into suns, and the dissolution of suns into gases ; and the evolution of planets around every sun ; and the creation and conservation of vast intelligences on each planet—that all these processes are eternally going on, there in the workshops of the Eternal Mind, that stretches in its vast immensity through space, and is ubiquitous in its operations as well as infinite by its presence. What is the little work of our planet, lighted by one pale star, to this ? What the birth of mere plants and flowers, the revolution of momentary seasons, the petty history of men, with their little wars and conquests, compared to the vast operations of the universe ? You see littleness by day, greatness by night, limitations in the sunlight, infinity in the dark ; man's little work by day, God's stupendous operations by night   And so, when we come to read more familiarly the book of the heavens, and astronomy becomes a popular, from being an occult science, men will watch the stars all night ; and derive from the evergrowing wonder and mystery of the Universe deeper veneration and greater love for the Mighty Spirit that rules and operates through all

XXXII.

Hence in the olden times when men thought much, and spoke little, they deemed the darkness divine   'Ω τὸ θεῖον σκότος, "O divine darkness!" said the Areopagite   "Who hath made the darkness his hiding-place," said that great thinker St. Paul, and there " dwelleth in light inaccessible." "If you pierce this darkness," said Nazianzen, "who will flash forth ?" Yes! darkness filleth space. Darkness is the ocean; the suns are but the lamps

that float hither and thither on its surface   Consider only that
immense field of utter and impenetrable darkness that stretches
from the remotest orb of our solar system to the nearest fixed
star !   With the tremendous velocity of light—186,000 miles in a
second—it takes four hours to traverse our solar system, and
reach its outer world, Neptune, or to bring back one ray to
us from that remote and solitary world   But what is that to the
awful chasm of darkness that lies beyond ?   For, from Neptune,
a soul winged with the velocity of light would take not four minutes, but four years to reach the next sun and system !   What a
black yawning immensity ! What a universe of darkness ! Looking back even from its threshold, our sun is but a glinting and
flickering star , the planets are invisible.   Very soon the sun
itself dies out in the darkness, and all is night, night !   Once and
again in a century, perhaps, a mighty comet comes dashing out
of space, as an express train would flash out of a tunnel, and
swishes away with its long streamers of light into the darkness
again.   At intervals, there is a rumble or crash of the debris of
worlds that broke up centuries ago   All else is midnight or
gravelike blackness, until we break into the light of *Alpha Cen-
tauri*, and behold the sister-suns, for ever gravitating towards each
other, and for ever kept apart by the Invisible Hand , and wheel-
ing in circles of light around their resplendence, vast planets,
drinking in life and beauty, and sweetness, from these glorious
lamps in the streets of the Eternal City !   And, away once more
through another ocean of darkness to the light of a more transcendent sun !

XXXIII.

It struck me, one of these cold frosty nights in late Decem-
ber, as I walked to and fro in my garden, and saw the surpassing
splendors of the Winter constellations,—what a cataclysm there
would be, if that Infinite Hand were lifted for a moment from
His Creation   No one, even the most sceptical, denies that Law,
Supreme, Inexorable Law, guides and governs our Universe   But
Law is merely another word for Will   So surely as the mariner's
hand is on the helm of his ship, or the finger of the engineer is
on the throttle of his express engine, so surely is the Hand of

God upon the mighty mechanism of His universe. Of course, worlds break up with their tremendous concussions, and scatter their fragments through space, to be resolved again into their original gases. Suns, too, are quenched, and their corresponding planets starved out of life, and frozen into lunar deserts. But this is only part and parcel of the Divine Economy, that builds out of ruin, and breaks only to reconstruct on a larger and greater plan. But let us suppose that a sun, like our own, could break from its moorings in space, and, taking the whole system with it, should plunge across the deserts of the universe, and carry its tremendous and liberated forces into the orbits of other suns and systems; and let us suppose that these, in turn, struck by this terrific and lawless energy, should be driven from their orbits, and carry their weight and velocities into the heart of other systems, until all were driven from their centres, where they had swung in perfect equilibrium,—what a fearful cataclysm it would be! What ruin upon ruin, destruction upon destruction would ensue! What conflagrations would light up the black deserts of interstellar spaces, and what glowing and incandescent gases, liberated by such gigantic convulsions, would stream across the universe! What awful thunders would shake the foundations of earth and rock the thrones of Heaven! And how all would finally settle down into primeval chaos, and darkness would fold its wings over a universe once more dissolved into atoms!

XXXIV.

What a grotesque, beautiful, ridiculous, sublime, little being is Man! Hanging on for a brief moment by the slender foothold he has on that little bubble in space, the Earth,—he looks out from its darkened side into the Immensities that wheel above him; and he wants to understand them all, nay, to grasp them in his tiny fingers, and with his little mind. An insect, looking out with wide, wondering eyes from an oak leaf in a forest, and feeling his way timorously with his antennæ, is not more insignificant. And yet, this man is in reality *the* mystery of the universe. For the latter is intelligible enough, and to larger comprehension, even simple in its greatness. And it also demands God.

He, too, is intelligible, because He is all greatness and sublimity. There is no need for reconcilements and adjustments there All is simple ; and all is great. But Man— " Gentlemen," said Fichte, in his introductory lecture on " The Destination of Man," in the University of Jena, " collect yourselves—go into yourselves—for we have here nothing to do with things without, but simply with the inner self." They drew themselves together " Gentlemen," he continued, " think the wall (*Denken Sie die Wand*) " They thought the wall " Now, gentlemen, think him who thought the wall " Not so easy There was evident embarrassment They shuffled in their seats. Some rose up. The wall was easy enough. They themselves were the mystery !

XXXV.

Yes, say what we will, Man is the Mystery of Creation. God is no mystery to Himself, nor perhaps to the colossal intelligences that He has created. Nay, our own poor reason reaches to His existence at least. We see immensities and worlds swimming in space ; but see also order, law, everywhere And we know there must be an Ordainer and a Legislator And then we mount, step by step, to His ineffable attributes It is only when we turn our eyes inward on ourselves, that we are smitten with astonishment. For, whereas all without us is cosmical, uniform, perfect, all within us is chaotic and contradictory We are a miracle and a mystery to our own comprehension. We know, but cannot tell why we know. Our senses are the sources or rather the conduits of knowledge, yet they deceive us. Our passions degrade us, or elevate us To-day we grovel in the sty of Epicurus ; to-morrow, our desires waft us into the empyrean Our fellowmen are infinitely lovable, and infinitely hateful. Brute and angel, like the Woman Beast that stares across the Egyptian sands, we watch for the reading of the riddle ; but, unlike her, we cannot wait

Section II.—XXXVI.

One of the most repulsive things I ever read is de Quincey's description of the nebula of Orion. You will find it in his article on "The System of the Heavens," in Volume III of his works It is a fantasy, but an extremely morbid one. He sees in what is now recognized as one of the most beautiful objects in the heavens "the horror of a regal phantasma which it has perfected to eyes of flesh" "All power being given to the awful enemy, he is beautiful where he pleases, in order to point and envenom his ghostly ugliness." "Brutalities unspeakable sit upon the upper lip, which is confluent with a snout; for separate nostrils there are none." "But the lower lip, which is drawn inwards with the curve of a marine shell—oh, what a convolute of cruelty and revenge is there! Cruelty!—to whom? Revenge!—for what? Pause not to ask, but look upwards to other mysteries!" Probably, one of the greatest of these mysteries is, how the human mind could draw on the deep background of the infinities such a picture of horror and ugliness. It is the dream of one in delirium —the horrid spectre of a mind distorted by drugs, and weaving on the mirrors of infinite space the revolting pictures that are drawn on its own warped and twisted and shapeless faculties. True! it lasted only for a moment The imagination gradually resolved itself into gentle and harmonious lines drawn by reason; and he says: "He is now a vision to dream of, not to tell; he is ready for the worship of those that are tormented in sleep; and the stages of his solemn uncovering by astronomy are like the reversing of some heavenly doom, like the raising of one after another of the seals that had been sealed by the angel in the Revelation"

XXXVII.

What a contrast with the Greek mythology, pictured in the constellations! How these great artists, in the dawn of civilization, drew on the map of Night their own healthy dreams! If, on their stages, they represented horror after horror, tragedy after tragedy, it was a kind of religious symbolism, marking the doctrine of Fate, and the steady Nemesis that follows upon and dogs the footsteps of crime; but, when they ascended on high, and drew on the heavens their symbols of immortality—the apotheoses of their heroes and their gods—they drew nothing revolting or inhuman or sanguinary; but wove the eternal stars into their legends of heroism and duty, and cast around the burning constellations a drapery of music, and painting, and sculpture,—put Cassiopeia on her throne, sent Perseus to rescue Andromeda, joined the Hunt-ing Dogs in "their leash of sidereal fire," drew the imaginary chords of light across the framework of Lyra, put a sword into the hunter's hands, and swung another at his jewelled belt, and fretted the long filaments of light into the hair of the queen who sacrificed hers in the temple of Venus to ensure the return of her husband

XXXVIII

There is no doubt that Greek thought was healthy thought And health brought beauty; and beauty has brought immortality How much of modern thought, especially of modern poetry, may be traced to the influences of opium, would be a nice question to determine. It seems that with many writers the brain will not work at its highest capacity, unless under the influence of the drug. Most of our modern writers have come under its spell. We owe some of the most spiritual and imaginative poetry to its inspi-rations. Some poets could never have touched the high altitudes they reached but for its help. Yet, the highest is not the healthiest, at least in common estimation The human Shakspere is placed above the divine Dante, because he is human. There is something in the subject, as well as in its treatment The sober Dante, in-toxicated only by genius, ascended into the highest empyrean of human thought, the equally sober Shakspere touched ordinary humanity to transfigure it. But Coleridge could not have written the "Ancient Mariner," nor Shelley his marvellous "Prometheus," were not their imaginations excited by laudanum. Then, who shall say that the divine dreams come by inspiration, or who shall say the reverse? Or who shall mark the healthy from the morbid elements that go to compose that curious amalgam called Literature?

XXXIX.

What a contrast between that morbid conception of a monster, cruel and merciless, into which the imagination of de Quincey turned the nebula of Orion, and the concluding passage from Richter, in the same essay. It is the voyage of a human being into the infinite.

" Suddenly, as thus they rode from infinite to infinite, suddenly, as thus they tilted over abyssmal worlds, a mighty cry arose—that systems more mysterious, worlds more billowy—other heights, and other depths—were dawning, were nearing, were at hand. Then the man sighed, stopped, shuddered, and wept His over-laden heart uttered itself in tears, and he said 'Angel, I will go no further. For the spirit of man aches under this infinity Insufferable is the glory of God's house. Let me lie down in the grave, that I may find rest from the persecutions of the Infinite , for end, I see, there is none ' And from all the listening stais that shone around issued one choral chant—' Even so it is, angel, thou knowest that it is , end there is none, that ever yet we heard of.' ' End is there none ? ' the angel solemnly demanded. 'And is this the sorrow that kills you ? ' But no voice answered, that he might answer himself. Then the angel threw up his glorious hands to the heaven of heavens, saying : ' End is there none to the universe of God ? Lo ! also there is no beginning.' "

There is a deep and solemn truth in that line : " The spirit of man aches under infinity ! " He is not equal to it. Its vastness weighs upon him like a thick atmosphere on feeble lungs. Like one, lost in a desert, the solitude appals him, and he cries aloud for help, for companionship

XL.

Yet, what a wayward being he is ! All his aspirations are towards the infinite that oppresses him He loathes his prison—the earth ; he despises his fellow-prisoners. Humanity is beneath him , the earth is too small to bear him. Looking through the bars of his prison-house, across the levels of twilight seas, he yearns to go out and be lost in the sun-mists that gather away on the horizon ; and if a faint sail shimmers on the line of the sky and sea, it is to him the burden, and the jealous burden of a soul, that, emancipated, is pursuing its happy way to the Infinite So, too, does he dream in mountain solitudes, looking up from vale to peak, and from peak to cloud, happy in the thought that some day he may go thither, unhappy in the reflection that "his sojourning is prolonged." Yet, give him this infinity whilst still in the flesh, and lo! he "aches under it." He tires of stars and systems. His wonder ceases when his imagination is satiated. Knowledge destroys the magic and the mystery of the Universe. The wilderness of galaxies becomes an unpeopled solitude. He is perishing amidst the splendors of space. He cries aloud in his agony. He wants the earth, and men!

XLI.

Yes! till disembodied, earth is his home—the little theatre of his sufferings and joys. Here he is placed by the Omnipotent; and here he has to accomplish his destiny. He is finite and must take his limitations. His wings will not bear him far towards the Infinite. They grow weary and droop, and he falls Yes! here on this little planet are his destinies environed by time and space. Here shall he find the little loves, the little cares, the little worries, the little joys, that make up his daily experience However high he soars in the empyrean, a line draws him back to earth. He is an imprisoned immortal He is created for the Infinite, but not permitted to seek his place as yet. That will come Meanwhile, let him dream and aspire, for that is good, and reminds him that here he hath no lasting habitation. But he must not despise the little part he has to play on this planet, nor must he segregate himself too much from sympathies with his own feeble and much-complaining race. And there are two watchwords to inspire him—one, the password of the night-watch—Duty! and one, the password of the relief at dawn, and that is—Destiny!

XLII.

And yet, what an insolent and insatiable little parasite he is! Knowledge begets wonder; and wonder gives way to contempt. Tell him all the fairy tales of science; and his open, round eyes stare at you, first in incredulity, and then in surprise. Tell him

that the Demon-star, Algol, is twice as large as our sun, that its
dark satellite, moving only 3,000,000 miles apart, is the same size
as our sun, with a density one-fourth as great, that this satellite
extinguishes its own luminary for us for a space of twenty minutes
every two days and ten hours,—he stands still in surprise, stares
at the celestial prodigy, weighs it in his own mind, until this
latter growing under the exercise, first equals, then surpasses
the limits of the wonderful; and then growing far beyond it,
looks on it with a certain contempt. Or, tell him the two component stars of Mizar are forty times as great as the mass of our
sun, 150,000,000 miles apart from each other, and moving with a
velocity of fifty miles a second, his little mind strives to battle
with these stupendous figures, then seizes them and holds them;
then in its marvellous elasticity surrounds them and encompasses
them in the net of his own imagination, finally, goes so far beyond
them that it regards them as infinitesimal accidents in space.
Nay, you cannot tire it, nor exhaust it. The circumference of
human thought is conterminous with the horizon of space!

XLIII.

What then does Richter mean, when he speaks of the soul
"aching" under the Infinite? Clearly, he means the Infinite
Void—the Material Infinite! It is the hollow eye of Infinity,
bare of God, that glares on him and terrifies him The sense of
infinite solitude becomes unbearable—such solitude as oppresses
the mind when one stands beneath the crater of Vesuvius, knee-
deep in hot ashes, and sees above him a canopy of fire, and all
around the horrors of utter desolation. Viewed thus, creation
becomes simply a universe of volcanic forces, pitched and heaved,
hither and thither in endless chaos, the little planetary worlds
with their tiny and solitary sweetness, insignificant oases in the
deserts of infinity. It was such a vision as the fiend' saw, when
Sin opened the eternal gates —

> Before their eyes in sudden view appear
> The secrets of the hoary deep, a dark
> Illimitable ocean, without bound,
> Without dimension, where length, breadth and height,

And time and place are lost , where oldest Night
And Chaos, ancestors of Nature, hold
Eternal anarchy amidst the noise
Of endless wars and by confusion stand.

In this " vast vacuity," this " womb of Nature, and perhaps her grave," man's spirit faints away. The senses of sight and hearing are smitten with the tumult and din of worlds hustling through unlighted space. He sinks down, and cries: " Father, where art Thou ! "

XLIV.

Why then is the little being so impatient of his lot , so eager for the Infinite? Because it is not the infinity of emptiness, but the immensity of God he is unconsciously seeking. It is not the universe he wants; but the God of the Universe The end and term of his existence found, he seeks no more. He no longer aches under infinity , but basks in its immensities. He no longer dreads the hollow eye of Nature ; because he knows the eye of the Father is upon him ; he no longer dreads the awful mechanism around him, because he knows he is in the workshop of his Friend. And the vast deserts of the Universe are closed to his sight by the

      . . . empyrean Heaven, extended wide,
In circuit, undetermined square or round,
With opal towers and battlements adorned,
Of living sapphire, once his native seat :

and

      . . . the Almighty Father from above
From the pure empyrean where He sits,
High throned above all height, bends down His eye
His own works and their works at once to view.
About Him all the sanctities of heaven
Stand thick as stars, and from His sight receive
Beatitude past utterance.

XLV.

I dare say this idea of the limitation of human action and feeling, and the eternal craving after the infinite and illimitable in the human mind can be seen exemplified in most human lives. Especially is it observable in men of thought or fine sensibilities But I have seen it confessed clearly only in two lives, that of St. Augustine, as revealed in his *Confessions;* and that of Maine de Biran, as revealed in his *Thoughts.* This latter was one of those unhappy immortals, who to their own sorrow, but the everlasting benefit of mankind, have been tortured by nerves. He was so finely constructed that his emotions swayed to the slightest touch, swinging low down in the deepest depression at a word or look or a reverse or a dyspepsia; and again thrown high into the empyrean of exalted reflection by equally minute and trifling causes. These *Pensées* would be pitiful reading were they not relieved here and there by gleams of inspiration—great lightning-flashes of thought athwart the low thunder clouds of despondency. His life was an alternation of desires for solitude when in society, and impatience of self when in solitude. " La commerce des hommes," he writes, "m'a gâté et me gâte tous les jours", but he was forever craving for their companionship amongst the woods and waters of Grateloup. " I walk like a somnambulist in the world of affairs." But when it came to the point to choose, he refused to say the word, and turned back to politics. He is a stranger amidst the pomps and ceremonies of the French Court; he hates himself for his presence there, and his nervous unsuitableness; but he cannot remain away. He clamors for the infinity of thought in solitude; but craves for the limitations of action in society.

XLVI.

Very early in life, and long before he became a Christian in thought and feeling, he recognized the dual nature in man, and writes strongly against Voltaire and Condillac, and all the tribe of writers of the sensist or materialist school. He will not admit the sovereignty of sense, he demands the supremacy of the soul. Granted But does he find peace, the peace for which he is forever clamoring? He admits it is the *summum bonum*, nay, the only good here below. He confesses his contempt for the things which the world prizes He has seen them, and tested their hollowness He flies from them and buries himself in the desert of his own soul. The philosophy of the Porch is now his religion. He will be self-sufficing. He will subdue all riotous feeling of passion and even sensation; and, under the arbitrary rule of the soul, he will find peace. He will desire nothing, and therefore want nothing. All shall be harmony of nicely adjusted thoughts and sentiments, of passions subdued and reined by a strong hand; Nature shall yield its manifold treasures of peaceful bliss; and an imagination, rightly controlled, will serve to lift the soul beyond time and death, and project another existence on the canvas of eternity. But the oaks and streams heard still but the agony of a disappointed and despairing soul. Yes! all was satisfied, but the insatiable—*La Soif de Dieu!*

XLVII.

He liked, as all such souls like, every line that speaks of the beauty and happiness of a solitary life. And all literature, Divine and human, is replete with those threnodies of the heart— the desire to be away, and at rest. "Would that I had the wings of a dove", "O for a lodge in some vast wilderness!" Was the author of the "Imitation," merely parodying the words of St. Augustine in all the many curious ways he had of uttering the same thought: "*Noli foras abire; in teipsum redi; in interiore homine habitat veritas!*" And I suppose most people (always excepting the artists themselves) must have felt a little *attendrissement du cœur* at the closing lines of that favorite duet in *Trovatore* "There shall be rest! there shall be rest!" Certain it is that Maine de Biran was forever craving rest, rest, rest—from the fever of fashion, from the turmoil of politics, from the stings of wasps, the hollowness and insincerity of the world; and he was for ever dreaming, dreaming in the Court of Versailles or at the Tuileries of his woods and walks, of the rustling leaves, the singing of birds, the purling of streams, the peace of the mountains, the solitude of the valleys. Then came the reality. Lo! here is all

this sylvan beauty, and here is solitude deep enough for a Bruno!
And here is peace, and deep profound thought, and the absorption
of the soul in the reveries of metaphysics. Alas, no! or not
altogether A cloudy sky, an indiscretion at table, a look, a
word; and lo! the paradise is broken up So dependent is the
soul on the caprices of the body! There are two principles in
man—*et primum quod est animale!*

XLVIII.

"Bene qui latuit, bene vixit!" It was a favorite maxim of Descartes who had also another favorite doctrine, which I recommend
earnestly, namely, the sanitary value to mind and body, of long
fits of idleness. Maine de Biran would not, and did not, accept
the latter. He could not. He was made otherwise, a thing com-
pacted out of nerves, and fed by a planet and a star—by Mercury
and Phosphor. He knew well the glorious blessing of such a
constitution, and—its curse! He admits that the dull, practical,
geometrical reasoner has less joy out of youth, but more security
in age. And that if the nervous dreamer and thinker has visions
of the gods in his heyday, he must suffer by diabolic apparitions
in the evening of his days It is the eternal equilibrium of things
—the just apportionment of fate to mortals. The most careful
chemist does not sift and mix on his glass measure the drugs that
make for life or death so carefully as the Fates dole out their destinies to mortals. Or, rather, not *destinies*, but the factors of destinies—the powers of action or suffering, of reason and imagination, of mental or physical constituents, that go to construct the
sum total of those transient dreams or experiences which we call
Life.

XLIX.

But the maxim of Descartes· "Bene qui latuit, bene vixit,"
he loved it, but did not accept it Or rather, accepted it only in
theory. It is the motto of those who are surfeited by fame, or
notoriety; not of those who have never tasted either. Men can
despise riches when they possess them; fame, when the fickle

goddess woos them   But all men would like to drink from the
cup of Tantalus, and grasp the skirts of the phantom, Fame.
Yet, Maine de Biran, let it be said, had even a nobler ambition.
He deplores the necessity of his taking part in political and social
matters to the exclusion of intellectual pursuits, for which he believed he possessed a certain aptitude.   And life was passing by;
and nothing done   All this external nation which he detested, but
which arrested every movement towards the life of solitude and
retreat which he coveted, induced at least a condition of intellectual atrophy from want of exercise, and he saw himself far advanced into middle age, without the prospect or hope of realizing
his one ambition—" avoir laissé quelque monument honorable de
son passage sur la terre." A victim of circumstances, a prey to
ill-health, with all the power and the desire of becoming the foremost thinker of his age, he remained to the end—*un philosophe
manqué.*

L.

It is quite clear that thought and existence are not identical;
and that each must have its own rules, aspirations, conditions.
For example, the illimitable sea at sunset, with just one solitary
sail on its way to infinity, fills us with the strangest emotions.
We can gaze and gaze at it for ever.   It is a soul, emancipated,
and passing out on its voyage to the unknown eternities.   But, lo!
some one says.   Beneath that line is the coast of France, and that
schooner is bound for Cherbourg!   The spell is broken!   Why? Because the abstract, the illimitable, is suddenly bounded by the concrete and determined; and the soul beats itself against that rude and
imperious barrier.   Or we watch the heavy rain-clouds, these winter
evenings, driven up and on by the southwest wind   Their gloomy
battalions file over our heads, black and threatening, like the
remnants of a conquered army, driven on before the exultant conquerors.   We can see them, with some pleasure, drifting, drifting
towards the unseen northeast.   It is an undefined, an abstract
destination.   But, let some one say: The clouds are drifting over
such or such a mountain, they are now above such a town, now
over such a village.   Again, the spell is broken!   We don't care

to watch them any longer. They are no longer creatures of the
infinite. We see them swoop down, and draw their wet skirts
across the mountain heather; or the roofs of houses, and then
vanish in mere rain and storm.

LI.

What is the fittest form of worship in the temple of the Eternal,
under that awful dome of blackness that leans on the horizons of
infinity? If we consider for a moment the total want of proportion between our weak praise and the immensity of God, we are
tempted to take refuge with the mystics, and say, *Silentium sit
laus !* St. Augustine seems to have felt most intensely this utter
inadequacy of man to sing worthily the praises of God. " When
the Psalmist cried out, '*Magnus Dominus et laudabilis nimis,
quoniam magnitudinis ejus non est finis*,' he wanted to show," says
St. Augustine, " how great He is   But how can this be done?
Though he repeated, *great, great*, the whole day, it would have
been to no purpose, because he must have ended at last, for the
day must be ended   But His greatness was before the beginning
of days, and will reach beyond the end of time." So, too, says that
wonderful old poet-saint, Synesius, of whom we know but too
little :

> Ὑμνῶ σέ, Μάκαρ,
> Καὶ διά φωνᾶς.
> Ὑμνῶ σέ, Μάκαρ,
> Καὶ διά σιγᾶς.
> Ὅσα γὰρ φωνᾶς
> Τόσα καὶ σιγᾶς
> Αἴεις νοερᾶς
> Πάτερ ἄγνωστε,
> Πάτερ ἄρρητε.

Whilst all this is true, it is also true that we need a language
of praise. Does not the Evangelist place the very words in the
mouths of the Seraphim, by which they may glorify God?

LII

And what more worthy language ever was, or could be, invented for this sacred purpose than the Psalms of David ? I have an idea that our piety, as Catholics, would be more robust, and that we would be brought more close to God, if the inspired words, the language of the Holy Spirit, formed a larger portion of our daily prayers We have many and excellent books of devotion, but after all they are compiled by men, and breathe but a human language But the words of Scripture are the words of the Holy Spirit; and they are winged with the fiery tongues of the Paraclete. Could there be, for example, a more sublime act of charity than the seventeenth Psalm, *Diligam te, Domine,* with the sublime poetry of the verses 8–17 ; or a more piteous appeal for mercy than Psalm 21, *Deus, Deus meus, respice in me,* with all its pathetic foreshadowing of the Passion ; or a more glorious bit of nature-painting than Psalm 103, *Benedic, anima mea, Dominum ;* or, lastly, a more tender and childlike profession of faith and obedience than Psalm 118, which is so familiar to us in the daily Office, and which I had marked twenty golden years ago in my Douay Bible as *Pascal's Psalm ?*

LIII.

That is a fine expression of Plato's, *Lux est umbra Dei* Light is the shadow of God. *Et Deus est Lumen Luminis.* And God is the Light of Light How closely his language approaches the words of the Nicene Creed! Could they have been adapted from him by those Oriental Fathers ? The idea runs through the whole of the inspired writings. " He dwelleth in light inaccessible." " Erat lux vera " And the " Lamb was the lamp thereof." Yet we read that He is surrounded by darkness. " He bound the heavens and came down ; and darkness was under His feet And He made darkness His covert ; His pavilion round about Him, dark waters in the clouds of the air." This, and other figurative language would seem to convey the idea that God, the Light, is hidden away in His creation, not like a far sun localized in a defined space of darkness, but permeating as a hidden force all space and all darkness, as lightning is concealed in the dark folds of a cloud   And, as lightning is hardly seen in light, but illumines a whole world in the darkness of the night; so it is at night, God's illumination breaks upon the soul of man, and He feels all around him the presence of the Divinity.

LIV.

For, it was really a happy thought of that mediæval writer, who wrote so little but so well, that it is darkness that reveals to us the universe.   If there were no night, but perpetual day, man could never have reached a conception of the immensity and grandeur of the heavens   We should see the blue vault of heaven without knowing it was a sea of darkness in which the lightships of God floated.   We should know our sun, and have a dim idea of the moon as a bright silver cloud, but no more   Lo! darkness envelopes the earth, and reveals the heavens.   Here, from his little watchtower, the eye of the little creature takes in all the vastness and sublimity that lie around him; he sees himself on the lonely deck of a little ship in space.   He knows his insignificance and God's greatness and he is humble.   Lo! once more come the dawn and the light.   The curtains of the night are drawn, immensity vanishes, the little ark of humanity swells to a vast world where he is king and master.   And all the vast deceptions of life, which had faded before infinity, throng around him once more to cheat his senses and flatter his pride.   The ghosts do not vanish at dawn, they are the creatures, not of darkness, but of light

LV.

Hence, I suppose, that saying of Euripides. βαθύτεραι γὰρ νυκτὸς φρένες   Night-thoughts are deepest   The sense of immensity, the darkness, shutting out all those myriad sensible objects that fret and distract the mind, the silence, always unbroken except by soothing sounds of winds or waterfalls— all these help to cast back the mind upon itself, and by concentrating its faculties, to intensify thought and subdue emotion.

Could this be the reason, apart from the leisure it afforded, why the Son of God found strength and respite by spending the night in prayer in the solitude of mountains? This was foreshadowed, as the Psalmist foreshadowed the Divine Being Himself, by the midnight prayer of David. *Media nocte surgebam ad confitendum tibi.* And all the saints have loved the night-prayer There is no hour so dear to them as the Matin-hour, which is in deepest darkness, as it precedes the dawn And is it not proverbial that scholars love the time of night-thoughts; and that "burning the midnight oil" has passed into a metaphor for lonely studies at the deepest part of the night? Yes, we want solitude to think deeply, and "night uttereth knowledge to night" in other senses than the Psalmist meant.

LVI.

If all knowledge comes through the senses, that knowledge must be necessarily limited, for our senses are very weak The lower animals possess senses far more acute than ours, as their anticipations of atmospheric changes clearly demonstrate. Nay, even, they seem to be able to forecast great cataclysms on earth, as they manifest signs of perturbation and fear before earthquakes or volcanic eruptions, where man sees no cause for alarm The sense of hearing with us seems the dullest of the senses We feel the heat of the sun, and rejoice in his light But what of the tremendous reverberations and thunders that are forever flung into space from the convulsions of that mighty furnace? Not a sound reaches us. Here, to all outward seeming, is a meek sun, shedding beneficent heat and light on his satellites, and silently performing his allotted duty in the universe. But reason will not tolerate this assumption It argues that if a tiny black cloud, perched half a mile above the earth, can vomit flame and thunder, so as to drown the loudest noises on earth, what an unimaginable tumult of sound breaks from that fiery furnace, which flings out its waves of flame a quarter of a million of miles beyond its surface Now, wherefore this waste? The heat and light of the sun are not scattered objectless through space Why should sound? Or, has it a purpose in Nature, which, though it never reaches us, is nevertheless accomplished?

LVII.

It is really difficult for us to get rid of the idea that this little planet of ours is the centre of the universe, that all space revolves around it as on a pivot, and that all things in heaven and on earth were made for man. Our pride is always striving to disprove what reason and science assert. Yet we shall never understand things until we get outside ourselves, nor shall we ever grasp the secret of the universe until we begin to acknowledge the weakness of our understanding. "My thoughts are not as your thoughts," said the Lord; "nor My ways as your ways" All that science, with its Argus eyes, has hitherto testified is this: Space is a universe of darkness, and the murk of midnight, and cold, pierced here and there by suns, which, though to our imaginations they are colossal and gigantic, are nevertheless pinpoints of light in the vast deserts around them These lamps in the midnight are surrounded by tiny moths of planets, that are forever seeking to destroy themselves in the flame, but are kept apart by an unseen hand And that is all Yes, all to the limited faculties and purblind sight of this little parasite called man. But what if that desert of darkness were transcendent light to other eyes than ours; and what if outside our limited cognizance, the vast regions of space were all light and no darkness; and what if the irregular patches of constellations stretched themselves, in obedience to the eternal law of cosmical symmetry and beauty, into a great line of light, sentinelling the outer darkness of our space, and forming a mighty cordon around the white central throne; and what if, after all, "the music of the spheres" and "stars quiring to the young-eyed Cherubim" were more than poetic fancies, and that, in fact, the whole universe is eternally resonant with praise; and that the tumultuous thunders of countless suns and worlds are toned down into the organ accompaniment of the Hosannas that echo forever, and forever and ever, around the great Throne of God! Clearly, there is nothing for us, little ephemeræ as we are, but to sit still, and see the salvation of God!

LVIII.

But there is one thought that continually obtrudes itself on our waking senses at night—*God is a Spirit.* It is an idea that is too seldom before us as a subject for meditation It is one of those sublime truths that, with all their meaning, flash suddenly upon our intellects, and bewilder them. The fact is, we seldom see truths in their entirety. Each has as many facets as a crystal; and now we see one , now, another. There are some truths whose farthest side we never see, as we never see the far face of the moon But we are so dazed and bewildered by sensible objects that, daily and momentarily, strike our senses, that the idea of God as a Spiritual Essence or Being is unfamiliar to us We always represent Him to the imagination as a human being—old, venerable, kind—yet a man, and therefore limited and imperfect. Now, this is not an adequate conception of God. But can we form an adequate conception ? No But we may form a worthy conception, worthy of us, if not of Him ; and this we cannot do, unless we strive to understand those words of our Lord: God is a Spirit !

LIX.

But how can we form an idea of a spirit ? Is not this impossible in our condition of being ? It is not. We cannot paint a spirit, nor describe it, except in human terms But we may conceive it, or at least those abstract qualities which we associate with it. The thought, for example, that we are surrounded by God, as a fish by the sea, as a bird by the air, that He is closer to us than breathing, nearer than hands or feet, conveys an idea of His omnipresence, which we could never understand if He were represented under a merely human form. Then the idea that He is a Spirit, endowed with subtlety, immensity, penetration, leads us to understand His omnipotence far better than a representation of hands and feet , and, lastly, when we combine with that idea the final perfection of goodness and love, we come to feel that in us, around us, above us, is that mysterious Entity, invisible, intangible, in whose embraces we float, in whose arms we rest, secure in the double conviction that here are the two faculties which assure our safety, here and hereafter—merciful omnipotence and all-powerful love.

LX

I do not find fault with painters and artists who strive to draw on canvas their conceptions of Deity. They cannot do better. They must rise above mere symbolic representations. The Eye in a Triangle, the Circle with wings of light, are very feeble embodiments of God. Nothing then is left but the representation of God as the *Pater Aeternus, Creator coeli et terrae.* But this corporeal representation excludes the idea of spirit, although otherwise meant. And they, who never lift their eyes beyond that symbol of paternity, and never try to see the spirituality of God, fail to surround their imaginations with the loftiest conceptions of that transcendent Being, who, in using human language to express His manifold perfections, could only say, I AM WHO AM. But it seems that there was at least some special significance in that saying of our Lord's: *Deus est spiritus;* for the word spirit in Hebrew, Greek, and other languages signifies a gentle gale of wind; and as this surrounds us, wraps us all around, penetrates us, soothes us, compels us, refreshes us, though we neither see it, nor know whence it has come, or whither goeth, so with that ineffable Being, in whom "we live, and move, and are."

LXI.

The sense of the presence of a guardian-Angel—a dear, familiar spirit, dividing with his care for us the blisses of Heaven, to be the companion of our mortal pilgrimage, is very soothing and strengthening. One comes to love that unseen being, ever at our side, watchful, zealous, merciful, loving, protecting. But it is its very unseenness that makes us love it, and also the sense of our dependence. For if the sense of protection is the secret of maternal and other perfect, unselfish love, on the other hand the feeling of weakness and dependence constitutes filial affection. But, let us expand even to infinity the attributes of our Angel, let us see him as a speck in a sea of light, let us know that he, too, is dependent on the Supreme, and then, let us add up, in the feeble arithmetic of reason, all that we know of fine spiritualities, their unearthliness, their purity, their unselfishness, their power, their love, and then multiply this sum of all conceivable excellence by the vast ciphers of infinity, and we shall have an idea of that transcendent Being, who filleth the deserts of the universe, and lightens their loneliness with His Infinite Beauty, and in whose embraces we, the least ones of His intelligent creation, repose in security and peace, whilst He veils His splendors from us.

'Ος πάντα πληροῖ, καὶ ἄνω παντὸς μένει
'Ος νοῦν σοφίζει, καὶ νόου φεύγει βολάς

Who filleth all things, yet abideth above all ,
Who giveth wisdom to the mind, yet fleeth all scrutiny

LXII.

And yet this will not do for all persons, at all times The soul faints in contemplating God as a Spirit It needs the visible, the tangible Hence the Incarnation, if it were not necessary, would be inevitable.   Hence, too, the absolute necessity of the Real Presence, if faith and love were to be preserved amongst men. The Israelites of old needed the perpetual monitions of God to keep alive their feeble, intermittent faith. Nay, with all the terrible reminders of His presence, how frequently and how foully they fell! Under the very shadow of the clouded mountain, and with its thunders pealing above their heads, they fell into the basest idolatry. We cannot boast that we are of stronger fibre than they. How then could God substitute a Book for His Presence ? The New Law was to perfect the Old If so, God must have come nearer to His people. The cloud vanished; the pillar of fire disappeared, the ark was destroyed But where was God ? Nearer in His personal presence Certainly This was inevitable If Jehovah vanished, it was to leave a closer and nearer substitute of His presence But how ? As a Spirit? No ! This would have been as far from the craving sense of men as the God of the Deluge, or Sinai How then could He come nearer to men, nearer to their senses, as well as to their faith ? Only in one way. *Verbum Caro factum est , et vidimus gloriam ejus, gloriam quasi Unigeniti a Patre, plenum gratiae et veritatis.*

LXIII.

The New Law would be more imperfect than the Old, if God did not come closer to His people. But this could only be accomplished by His visible presence But there could be no visible presence of God, but as Man God should therefore become Man to reveal Himself fully to the world This He did in His Incarnation But again it was quite clear He could not remain forever visibly amongst us On the other hand, a merely historical Christ would have left the work of union and revelation imperfect. A Book is no substitute for a Being, especially when that Being is God To complete the whole scheme of Divine economy, therefore, the presence of God should be maintained. Otherwise, the Christian would have been of less consequence than the Israelite, to whom Jehovah spoke and manifested His presence But how could the presence of God become a lasting memorial of His love, and yet be veiled in such shadows and accidents that man should have perfect faith, yet be not "overwhelmed with glory"? Only in one way—the only possible way consistent with the dignity of the Most-High—the way His Divine ingenuity discovered for the most stupendous mystery He has wrought— namely, the entombment of the ever living and eternal under the lowliest and most perishable of elements in the ineffable Sacrament of the Altar.

LXIV.

Carlyle, in his extreme old age, and when every vestige of faith or religious credence had left him, admitted to his biographer, Froude, that the Mass was the only relic of religious faith now left in the world. It was a curious and even valuable admission. He had no love for Catholicity. The old spirit of Calvinism, in which he had been reared, survived under the dark gloomy philosophy he had tried to place in its stead ; and there is no heresy so antagonistic to the brightness and beauty of Catholic Doctrine as Calvinism But the old sage had read and thought and seen much ; and even in the pale light of history, he had observed the great fact, that the sacrifice of the Upper-Room in

Jerusalem, and of Calvary, the sacrifice of the Catacombs and the Deserts, was perpetuated through all the succeeding ages of the Church's history, and was now, what it always has been, the great fact in the ever varying history of mankind. And so, too, if ever the day should come when civil holidays will completely usurp the place of Saints' holidays, the world will hesitate, again and again, before it removes the great festival of "Christ's Mass" from the calendars of men.

LXV.

It comes as a sudden sun in the darkness of mid-winter Its illumination, as of hope, stretches far back into the gloom of November, and far forward, as a memory, into the cold and storms of January Weary men look to it as a time of armistice or truce, when they may forget they are enemies, and believe they are friends and brothers. For, alas! that it should be true, all men accept the verdict of the stricken Job, and believe that life is a warfare, and most men think themselves Ishmaelites, with the hands of the rest of mankind against them. They do not like it—this struggle for the survival of the fittest It is hard, scientific, brutal But so they are taught; and so they learn all too aptly. They would fain unlace their helmets, and unbuckle their armor, and unloose their greaves; and lie down by the common stream to drink and repose, before taking up their weapons again Well, Christmas is just such a time The little Child suddenly appears; and contention is hushed Humanity asserts itself in Him who assumed it, and all the belligerents bow down Courtesies are interchanged, the finer feelings come uppermost, men grasp one another's hands in friendship They think of the fallen—the dead They touch the fingers of those who are far off They allow a tear to gather and fall. It is well! Soon must they take up the weapons and go forth; and steel their hearts against the finer thoughts, that still remain to humanize them.

LXVI

If I mistake not, some such instance of sudden pause and human awakening occurred in the Civil War. Two detachments of Union

and Confederate troops had been watching each other for days
seeking the hour for the successful destruction of the enemy
At last they came into touch with each other   The scouts announced their proximity   There was a river with a bridge between
them , and the great objective on either side was the capture and
retention of that bridge   Both pushed forward, reconnoitered,
charged   Just as they gained the entrance on either side, the
foremost troopers checked their horses, and pressed back their
comrades to a sudden halt   For right in their track, on the
roadway, was a child of two summers   It was playing with
flowers, with all the delightful innocence and unconsciousness of
childhood. It knew nothing of its peril   " It feared no danger,
for it knew no sin "   Then it saw the advancing troopers, who had
slowed down to a walk   Its eye caught their splendid uniforms,
and the trappings of their horses, and it smiled.   The foremost dra-
goon leaned down, and picking up the waif, placed it on the pom-
mel of his saddle.   Friends and enemies gathered around, and
sought its smiles.   It was a pause of pity in the game of destruction   Men wondered at one another, and grew ashamed, and
smiled   Gloved hands met, and scabbard made music with scabbard   Then they parted, and went their several ways once more.
It was Christmas, and the Christ !

LXVII.

Where do the words occur: *La vie est un combat ; pas un
hymne*   Yes !   but is this the design of the Creator, or rather the
result of man's own perversity ?   But, admitting that life must be
a warfare, why should not a hymn mingle with the clash of arms,
and even drown it ?   Not a hymn over the fallen—a hymn of
triumph over defeat and death , but a hymn of praise to the Lord
of Battles for the peace His wisdom hath imparted to ourselves.
And is not this duty of praise, this obligation of worship, and
stealing the " Sanctus " from the lips of Archangels, the one duty
which we, through false humility, or selfishness, neglect ?   We pour
out our painful *Misereres* in the ear of Heaven   Why should not
an exultant *Magnificat* occasionally rise above them, if it were
only to prove to Heaven that we are not altogether mendicants,

but mindful of our eternal destiny to take our places on the thrones
vacated by the spirits who forgot their obligations of praise in the
paroxysms of pride ? What is the hymnology of the Church for,
if it be not to put the canticles of joy and praise upon our lips?
Let us have our days of weeping and our places of mourning, if
you like, as the Jews down there in the Valley of Hinnom, with
their faces against the foundations of the temple that shall never
be rebuilt.   But let us also remember that we are Christians;
that the Alleluias of Resurrection are ours ; and that the wisest
of Christian philosphers has bidden us . *Gaudete, gaudete semper,
iterum dico, gaudete !* And that a greater than St. Paul hath said :
" Can the children of the bridegroom mourn as long as the Bridegroom is with them ? "   And He is with us, so long as the eternal Sacrifice shall be offered—our Emmanuel, God with us, for
ever !

LXVIII.

We had a frost, a killing frost, last night. It came to beautify,
and to destroy. It was a dread Apollyon under a virginal and
beautiful disguise A light snow sifted down from the gray sky
in the late twilight; and the frost came and hardened it on the
trees, until the leafless branches took on a perfect white plumage,
and a great silence wrapped all the earth   The evergreens were
more heavily coated than the trees whose foliage was deciduous,
but these latter, where the snow fell thinner, and whose branches
were thickly interlaced, looked very beautiful, although one felt
that the loveliness was delicate and frail.   One particular spot in
my garden was a perfect marvel of beauty, so faint and fragile
was the exquisite tracery on branches and tiny leaves   The sun
came out, gave a new radiance to the landscape, and then dissolved the whole picture into weeping and wintry death again.
And I marvelled at the magic of the frost, and all that it could
do with that simple element of water, until my foot struck a dead
thrush lying on the gravelled path   I took it up   It was frozen
hard as a stone—all its spring-music hushed for ever and destroyed.   The same secret force that had created beauty, had
annihilated it.   I went into my greenhouse   All the plants that

we had housed carefully for the May-time, were wilted and withered   The magician of the frost and snow was the Apollyon of flower and bird.

LXIX.

What a singular coincidence it was that Johnson should have engraved on the dial-plate of his watch, and Sir Walter Scott on the sun-dial in his garden the self-same words νύξ γάρ ἔρχεται! For the night cometh ! The former was constitutionally indolent; but his conscience was forever protesting against it   The latter was seized with a passion for work, especially in the latter part of his life, within which he concentrated as much labor as was possible without straining the mind to the breaking-point   But this idea of work, as identical with life, seems to have seized on all great thinkers   It is their solution of the problem of the universe —the one way of disentangling the threads of the mighty problem. *J'y suis !* And whatever my hands find to do, I shall do it with all my might. " The night cometh ! "   So said the great Divine Teacher. Let me hasten, then. It is no time for idle dreaming. Swiftly the little circle rounds to its close. To-day is mine ; to-morrow is doubtful. Very soon I shall no longer be above the earth, but beneath it. Here, then, hand, eye, brain, lend your help ! I need to leave behind me some record of my being. *Non omnis moriar !* There is a double sense in the words   I shall pass to a new existence, but shall remain on earth immortalized by my work. Its beneficent influences shall pass down the long valleys of the years, make sweet the bitter and fertile the barren, until men whose faces I shall never see shall bless the dead hand that grasps theirs from the grave! So think these great masters of thought. It is a noble ambition !

LXX.

Yes, work and worship. These be the watchwords of that night which we call day. They are certainties, not merely possibilities—the certainties of that great monitor and task-master, Duty   Speculations are only useful inasmuch as they lead on to work and worship   Mere conjectures about the mystery of being would be fruitless and profitless, if they ended with themselves in a ceaseless, unending round of difficulties propounded, only to be postponed. But the highest speculations resolve themselves, sooner or later, into the conclusion that, out of all uncertainties and possibilities, one thing alone remains positive and well-defined, and that is that our primal obligations whilst we remain on this planet are worship of the Invisible and Uncreated, and work of some kind in the elements that go to make up life. For we, too, have a kind of creative or conserving force within us. And we have to evolve order and beauty out of our surroundings —the brown earth, the barren sea, the souls of men; or we have to help in keeping intact such work as the progressive centuries have wrought for mankind, and to keep earth, and sea, and human lives from reverting to primitive chaos.

LXXI

That great line of Hesiod's.

Ἔργα νεῶν, βουλαί τε μέσων, εὐχαί τε γερόντων,

is generally translated

> In the morning of life, work;
> In the meridian of life, give counsel;
> In the evening of life, pray

Not bad for a pagan   Yet would it not be better to say, pray in youth; work in middle life; give counsel in old age. For, surely, youth needs prayer for enlightenment and strength, and distrust of self, and holy fear   And it is in manhood, we work best, physically and intellectually; for our energies do not reach their perfection till then, the wheels of life moving faster as we go down the hill of time towards eternity   And it is the tradition of mankind, that wisdom comes with age; for if the cunning of Ulysses is lost, the experience of Nestor supervenes, and grey-beard wisdom has a mellowness that no ability, or study, or talent can give   The oil that flows down the beard of Aaron is holy,—holy with the balsam of experience, and consecrated by the years that have brought in their train the consecration of the Most High

LXXII.

When one has come to relish the sweetness and the strength of every word spoken by our Divine Lord to His disciples or the multitude, there is a holy impatience with the Evangelists for not having given the world more of that Divine wisdom I have said when one has come to realize the sweetness and strength of the language of the Divine Teacher, because it needs experience, and thought, and comparison, to understand how true was that expression of the wondering crowd · " Never man spake like to this man ! " I should say, not. All human teaching in Dialogue, Enchiridia, Discourses, Pensées, Maxims, etc , sinks into ragged and beggarly insignificance before the wisdom of the Word. There can be nothing more foolish and banal, not to say, blasphemous, than to compare the teaching of any philosopher with the teaching of Christ. And hence, there is no verse in all the Holy Scriptures so tantalizing to the followers of Christ as that last verse of the Gospel of St. John : " But there are also many other things which Jesus did, which, if they were written every one, the world itself, I think, would not be able to contain the books that should be written." The Apostle might have added, " did and said ", for we know we have not a tithe of the sweet and beautiful discourses of our Lord The recorded words are fragments, analecta, of long sermons in the Temple, by the sacred sea, on the mountains, by the wayside. Take the Sermon on the Mount Do we not know that our Lord must have spoken long and earnestly before He summed up all in the deathless Beatitudes ? And the discourse at the Last Supper—well, no ! it would be hard to add anything to that ! But, it is certain that all that our Lord said in Nazareth and Judæa has not come down to us Silence has fallen for ever on these sacred conferences, and no man now can reveal them !

LXXIII

Yet what would we not give for just a little more ? What did He say when Lazarus went back to his sisters at Bethany, and all the wealth of love in that humble home was poured at His feet ?

What were the unspeakable confidences to His Mother at Nazareth, before He went out on His mighty mission? In what language did He pray to His Eternal Father from the solitude of the
mountains and under the eternal stars? Would we not give up
all the Socratic disputations for a tithe of these things that are
now hidden from us? And Marcus Aurelius? And Seneca?
Yes, and more! We would sacrifice Shakspere and Milton and
Dante; and in these all merely human wisdom is enshrined—nay,
we would make a holocaust of all the national literatures of the
world, if the lips of the Evangelists could be unsealed, and if we
could get ever so little of a deeper insight into the unspeakable
and, alas! unrevealed depths of the Soul of Christ!

LXXIV.

George Eliot, in the first fervor of her apostasy from the
Christian faith, wrote thus to a friend.

I have many thoughts, especially on a subject I should like to work
out The superiority of the consolations of philosophy to those of
(so-called) religion. Do you stare?

She did not carry out her pious design. She was young then,
only thirty. Perhaps as the years went by, and experience took
the spurs from enthusiasm, she thought better of it. Or perhaps,
wider reading than Strauss, or larger views than she found in the
kiln-dried ethics of Spinoza, may have modified her views of philosophy as an active factor in life. Or, perhaps, under trial, she
may have found philosophy a broken reed Like so many more,
who in the intensity of human pride believe in Stoicism, she may
have found it wanting "Sufficis tibi," sounds well; but music
will not heal the wounds of the soul. "Sufficit tibi gratia mea,"
sounds equally well, and is the sovereign salve for broken or
despairing humanity.

Section III —LXXV.

There is a large, and ever-increasing class of people in these
querulous and inquisitive times, who are forever demanding
perfection everywhere, except in themselves One of these came

into my garden yesterday. I take a little pride in my spring-
flowers, and I expected to hear several notes of admiration No.
He was in the interrogatory mood "Why haven't you freesias?
A garden is nothing without them. And the new American
fuchsia is lovely. I hate these crocuses. They are vulgar things.
How are your vines coming on? None! Do you mean to say
you have no vines? Everyone now has vines 'Tis a great mistake to pay four shillings a pound for grapes, when you can grow
them yourself so easily" "Well," I replied, "I admit there is
room for improvement. And a man should be grateful for such
gratuitous advice as he gets from time to time None of us is
perfect. We are only aiming at perfection In the near future,
perhaps, when people will buy books, instead of borrowing them;
and when this universal mendicancy into which our country has
fallen (for if I am to judge by my daily post, we are in a state of
hopeless insolvency and bankruptcy), has yielded to more hopeful or perhaps more honest conditions, I may be able to realize
your ideals And then I shall extend the field of my operations;
and ask your permission to cultivate that half-acre of yours which
now is growing a luxurious crop of dockweed and thistles"

LXXVI

I would not mention in these philosophic pages such a trifling
passage of arms, but for that remark about my crocuses Now, I
rather like that little crocus. It comes to you, just after the
snowdrops, when all other more gaudy things are hiding beneath
the hard earth; and they put up, and flaunt the little bit of color
which God has given them, and just at the time when we want it
most sadly I cannot help feeling grateful to them, but after
that remark of my friend's, I must confess, I began to look
askance at them. Vulgar? Well, I suppose they are And
then came a curious association of ideas That word of contempt
took me back in one flash of memory to a scene I had once wit-
nessed, more than a quarter of a century before, in Dartmoor
prison. I was in the prison sacristy, vested for Mass The bell
had rung, and the convicts were defiling past the sacristy door
into their places in the chapel. All had assembled; and my con-

vict acolyte had opened the door of the sacristy, when the clank
of chains smote upon me, and twelve or thirteen prisoners,
chained wrist to ankle, passed rapidly by the door. They were
clad in yellow, a bright but dirty yellow. They were the dangerous prisoners, who had attempted escape, or committed some
fresh crime in prison.

LXXVII

There was something inexpressibly hideous about that yellow
convict garb. I had seen prisoners clad in parti-colored yellow
and brown, carefully mixed, half and half It was only ludicrous.
This complete yellow garb was frightful. Then and there I conceived a violent aversion to that color. I discovered that it was
also the emblem of disease The quarantine flag is yellow. I
discovered other abominations in connection with it. I wrote it
down as the outcast amongst colors, the symbol of all physical
and moral degeneracy. I found then that it was the Imperial
color in China. This only increased my aversion. Then one day
a friend (such a friend is never long wanting) reminded me that
yellow was also the " Turner " color; and furthermore, that it
was the national color of the Irish, taken from their sunburst.
Nay, that up to a very recent period in their history, the Irish
invariably dyed their outer garment, a short, winged cloak, in
saffron! My discomfiture was complete I tried to bluff him. I
maintained that green was our national color, and, in Pagan
times, dark blue. He reminded me that within a stone's throw of
this village is Saffron Hill, and that old men still remember the
acres of yellow crocuses grown there to dye the cloaks of our
ancestors.

LXXVIII.

I began to believe then that yellow was unquestionably
respectable, when that sudden, contemptuous remark sent me
back to Dartmoor again; and the old, sickening feeling of fear
and repulsion rose spectre-wise from the vault of memory What
creatures we are; and what slaves of our senses! I never knew
a man who could picture to his imagination the whole of a ship

at sea. In the dry dock it is easy enough You see the entire
hull, even to where it tapers away at the bottom, you see the
sharp edge, which, like the coulter of a plough, cuts the resisting
waters, you see the great, fin-like screw at the stern But you
see none of these things at sea You see but the stately half-hull
resting on the waves; and no more And you cannot even
imagine the rest Try! And your fancy comes back at once to
what your senses testify, and no more So, in dealing with Nature.
We shudder with horror at the sensation of some harmless little
thing creeping on our neck, or hand. We ruthlessly destroy it
We say it is hideous Our sense of sight testifies that that beetle,
or earwig, is a monster of ugliness, and we instantly destroy it
What is all this? The knowledge of the senses? No! The
ignorance, crass and stupid of the senses Look closer! Here,
take this glass, and behold what a miracle of Omniscience you
have trampled out of existence.

LXXIX

"Now, now, now," I hear some one say, "this is absurd.
Everyone knows you are credulous enough to believe a circus-
poster, and sentimental enough to find poetry in an earth-worm."
I admit the soft impeachment I do not believe that under the
bell-tent of the circus you or I shall see all that appeared on the
gaudy poster; but is it an exaggeration to the wondering eyes of
childhood? Do not the children believe it all; and think the
poster a wretched presentment of all the glories and Arabian
Nights' splendors beneath the canvas? If I do not believe, so
much the worse for me. I have become critical and analytical—
the worst mental condition into which a human being can fall But
who will declare the poster to be exaggerated and untrue, when
the children believe it all, even after their experience of the reality.
It only proves the relativity of knowledge But about that earth-
worm! And poetry? How can you combine them? Well,
genius can do everything Did not Tennyson make poetry out
of a veal-pasty in "The Princess"? And if I disinter a now-
forgotten poem from a forgotten poet, who once was so famous
that his enthusiastic fellow-countrymen buried his masterpiece

with him, I shall not be blamed; and there is one great picture where the despised earth-worm caps the climax of intensity.

LXXX.

I hear some witling say, " Buried his masterpiece with him." A rather doubtful compliment, *n'est-ce pas ?* No ! It was a genuine compliment, such as his countrymen invariably pay to their immortals. The masterpiece was " The Messiah ", the poet was Klopstock, the race was German; the lines ran thus:

> Earth grew still at the sinking twilight ; the twilight Gloomier , stiller the earth Broad ghastly shadows, with pale gleams Streaked more dimly and more, flowed troublous over the mountains. Dumb withdrew the fowls of heaven to the depths of the forest ; Beasts of the field stole fearful to hide in the loneliest caverns. *Even the worm slunk down* In the air reigned deathlike silence.

I may be wrong, but I think that is a stroke of genius. Our generation has gone into ecstasies over Tennyson's minute observation of Nature and natural objects. The color of the ashbuds in the month of March, the slanting way in which a lark sinks down on his nest, the lone heron on the windy mere, the creeping of a wave along the halls of a sea-cave—all have been noticed, and all have been admired. But that line about the earth-worm hiding itself in the convulsions of Nature under the horrors of the Crucifixion has haunted me from the day I read it, many years ago, in Taylor's " Survey of German Poetry "

LXXXI.

Klopstock, I believe, has long since gone out of fashion even in his native Germany. And Carlyle, for us, has long since dethroned him , and enthroned his own godkin, Goethe, in his place. I confess I cannot whip my mind into a ferment of enthusiasm about Goethe ; just as I cannot bend the knee to Burns, or other Philistine deity I have conscientiously tried, and failed I have read through " Elective Affinities," and " Wilhelm Meister's Apprenticeship," and the rest. It was weary work, lightened only

by the Ariel-presence and ever-to-be-remembered song of Mig-
non   The world will ever be grateful to Goethe for that   It is a
breath of spring air amid mephitic vapors—the carol of a bird,
suddenly heard on an artificial, gas-lighted, meretricious stage   In
deed, Goethe's masterpieces are his lyrics   The Mason-song, made
familiar by Carlyle's translation ; and the song of the Parcæ in
Iphigenia are likely to endure.   But I have a shrewd suspicion
that the good court-ladies who crowned him with laurel-wreaths
in his old age, and after the performance of that same drama, had
in mind his wonderful masculine beauty, as well as the splendors
of his genius   And I also think " Faust " has captivated the world
not for its philosophy, which is jejune enough, nor for its morality,
which is invisible ; nor for its art, which is weak in the opening
scenes of the First Part, and in every scene of the Second , but
for its tender tale of human love and sorrow.

LXXXII.

For just the opposite reason, Schiller never reached the popularity of his friend and rival.   What deceptive things portraits,
especially photographs, are !   For more than a quarter of a century, I have had a photograph of Schiller in my album , and I
had formed the idea of a poetic face and form, more than Byronic
in its beauty.   The firm set of the features, clear-cut and Grecian
in their outline, the long hair streaming in ringlets on the
shoulders, the bold, flashing eye, and the proud, curved lip, gave
one the idea of a self-reliant, world-despising intellectual giant.
Alas ! life is all a disillusion !   I read in later life the following,
and was most reluctantly undeceived

"In his bedroom we saw his skull for the first time, and were
amazed at the smallness of the intellectual region   There is an intensely interesting sketch of Schiller lying dead, which I saw for the
first time in the study , but all pleasure in thinking of Schiller's portraits and bust is now destroyed to me by the conviction of their
untruthfulness   Rauch told us he had a *miserabele Stirne*   Waagen
says that Tieck, the sculptor, told him there was something in Schiller's
whole person that reminded him of a *camel.*"[3]

[3] Life of George Eliot

No enthusiasm, certainly no feminine enthusiasm, would be proof against this! And when you add to this, that he had a *Gansehals* (goose-neck), the disillusion is complete.

LXXXIII.

It is strange how great minds invariably turn, by some instinct or attraction, towards this eternal miracle—the Church   Carlyle admits in his extreme old age that the Mass is the most genuine relic of religious belief left in the world   Goethe was for ever introducing the Church into his conversations, coupling it with the idea of power, massive strength, and ubiquitous influence. Byron would insist that his daughter, Allegra, should be educated in a convent, and brought up a Catholic, and nothing else   And Ruskin, although he did say some bitter things about us, tells us what a strong leaning he has towards monks and monasteries, how he pensively shivered with Augustinians at St. Bernard, happily made hay with Franciscans at Fiesole; sat silent with the Carthusians in their little gardens south of Florence, and mourned through many a day-dream at Bolton and Melrose   Then he closes his little litany of sympathy with the quaintly Protestant conclusion : But the wonder is always to me, not how much, but how little, the monks have on the whole done, with all that leisure, and all that goodwill.

LXXXIV

He cannot understand! That is all. But why? Because he cannot search the archives of Heaven.   He knows nothing of the supernatural—of the invisible work of prayer—of work that is worship   He has never seen the ten thousand thousand words of praise that have ascended to the Most High ; and the soft dews of graces innumerable that have come down from Heaven in answer to prayer. He has painted, as no one else, except perhaps Carlyle could, the abominations of modern life ; and he has flung all the strength of his righteous anger against them   He has never asked himself why God is so patient, whilst John Ruskin rages; or why fire and brimstone are not showered from Heaven, as whilom on the Cities of the Plain. He had read his Bible, year

by year, hard words, Levitical laws, comminatory Psalms, from
ἐν ἀρχῇ to Amen; and, what is more rare, he believed in it. Yet
he never tried to fathom the mystery of the unequal dealings of
God with mankind. He never saw the anger of the Most
High soothed, and His Hand stayed by the midnight prayer and
scourge of the Trappist and the Carthusian. Dante could never
have written the *Paradiso*, if he had not heard Cistercians chant-
ing at midnight!

LXXXV.

So, too, he failed to understand how a mountain-monk would
positively refuse to go into raptures about crags and peaks, and
fix his thoughts on eternity "I didn't come here to look at
mountains," was the abrupt answer of the stern monk to the
nineteenth century æsthete. What then? You must think of
something, my shaven friend, or go mad "I thought of the
ancient days, I had in mind the eternal years," was the reply
Very profitless employment, certainly, to the eyes of modern
wisdom, which believes that "work is worship"; but that worship is not work How can it be, when you see no visible results
—no piling up of shekels, nor hoisting of sky-scrapers, no hog-
gish slaughter-houses, nor swinish troughs, only psalms that die
out in the midnight darkness, and silent prayer from lonely cell
away on that snow-clad mountain summit?

LXXXVI.

I notice that this is the one feature in Catholicity which the
Protestant mind can never understand. It appreciates cordially
the Catholic work of rescue—the rescue of the waif from the
street, of the Magdalen from the gaol or river, of the drunkard
from the bottle, of the gambler from the table, of the orphan
from destitution and vice. And so it will tolerate, but only
tolerate, educational or charitable institutions or communities—
what we call the Active Orders But the Contemplative Orders
it cannot understand. Why a number of monks and nuns should
be shut up in cloistered seclusion, cut away from all sympathy

with human life and endeavor, apparently unproductive and useless factors in the great giant march of progress, is unintelligible.
Of course, it is! Because God is unintelligible, or rather ignored.
Because all modern religion, outside the Church, develops itself
into humanitarianism—that is, positivism—that is, atheism in its
crudest and most naked aspect.

LXXXVII.

In fact, all controversy between the Church and the world is
rapidly resolving itself into this. Is God to be placed in the fore-
ground of His universe, or is man? The Church strenuously
affirms the former; the world, the latter The Church says, God
is everything, man, nothing, except in God. God, the centre to
which all things tend, and from which all things radiate; man,
not the apex of creation by any means, only a unit in creation,
made sublime by his aspirations, his hopes, his sufferings, and his
destiny. A generation that has lost all faith in Thirty-nine Ar-
ticles or other formulary, seeks vainly for something that will
take the place of vanished beliefs The next thing to hand is
humanity—man, the little god of this planet. *Agnoscimus!* we
know no more! And the Eternal Church keeps tolling its bell
through the world; and the burden of its persistent calling is the
monotone of Time, echoed from Eternity. God, and God, and
God!

LXXXVIII.

George Eliot, too, that fine mind, darkened, alas! so early to
all that was really sublime, had a curious sympathy with Catholic
faith and worship She bitterly laments the fact that Nurnberg
has become Protestant, and that it had but one Catholic church,
where one could go in and out as one would. She goes into the
Protestant St. Sebald's, where a clergyman was reading in a cold,
formal way under the grand, Gothic arches. Then she enters
the Catholic Frauen-Kirche, where the organ and voices were
pealing forth a glorious Mass. "How I loved the good people
around me, as we stood with a feeling of brotherhood amongst

the standing congregation till the last notes of the organ had died out" And at her first glance at the Sistine Madonna, as she sat on the sofa, opposite that miracle of art, a "sort of awe, as if I were suddenly in the living presence of some glorious being, made my heart swell too much for me to remain comfortably, and we hurried out of the room" Probably, the finest testimony ever given by a subtle and refined temperament to the magic of art! One could forgive a good deal to that spontaneous act of veneration

LXXXIX.

By the way, what a singular chapter in the history of literature is her life and works and destiny. Even during her lifetime she had as many commentators as Shakspere   Her peculiarly masculine intellect, which took up and discussed with ease, begotten of conscious mastery of the subject, problems in human life which might have puzzled Plato, had apparently fascinated modern thought, and made her the idol of a generation which prides itself upon being, above all things, intellectual.   It would be a marvel, indeed, if in all the hero-worship of which she was the object, there were not a fair amount of extravagance.   It is easy enough to exaggerate the merits of a writer, who has excited our wonder by powers of observation—shall we say, creation ?—that were unique. And there was a very strong temptation to see ever beyond the vision of the writer, and to conjecture deep suggestion and lofty wisdom beneath apparently simple elements.   Goethe's " Faust " is supposed to be a revelation of mysteries, hitherto unguessed, and which the initiated only can read.   I have heard it styled " The Bible of Freemasonry " Tennyson's Idylls are supposed to be essentially allegorical, the meaning of the allegory being sealed, notwithstanding his own revelations, until some generation shall arise, more mature in its wisdom than ours. And George Eliot is supposed to have given us not only a system of philosophy, but even a religion in her writings, the key of which lies with the future ; and then—the millennium !

XC

The truth appears to be that she was a woman of singular natural gifts, and with a taste for subjects and studies which belong traditionally to the masculine mind.   In fact, she stands alone among her sex for her brilliant enterprises in the highest sphere of philosophic thought, her marvellous knowledge of the human heart and its workings, and a power of analyzing human thoughts and feelings, which is unique in modern literature.   In the golden age of French literature, many brilliant women thronged the *salons* of Paris,—great wits, great conversationalists, and amateurs in the sceptical philosophy, which was just then becoming fashionable. But none of them essayed to be what George Eliot has become. She towers above the de Staels and Sévignés, as Shakspere above a troubadour.

XCI

Altogether, she is, perhaps, the most remarkable figure in modern literature   Her life was very tranquil; yet she paints very passionate scenes.   She passed through few of the vicissitudes which make life tragic for the sufferer, yet she realizes them as clearly as Jane Welsh Carlyle.   The world has long been wondering how Charlotte Brontë, a simple country girl, brought up in the seclusion of a Yorkshire parsonage, could have even conceived such a character as Rochester.   But much more surprising is the fact that Marian Evans, reared in the quiet monotony of a country life, could by sheer powers of fancy, and without having seen a single type of her creations among men and women (if we except her clerical characters) could create such opposite characters as Silas Marner and Tito, or such types of religious enthusiasm as Savonarola and Dinah Morris.

XCII.

And she writes without apparently one bit of sympathy with her creations.   There is a tone through all her works as of one who looks upon the eccentricities of humanity with the pitying contempt of a being far removed above them. It is as if Pallas had come down to earth, and framed out of her wisdom these strange puppets of humanity, and paraded them before us, and said: "Behold! These be types of women and men; mark how they speak and act! I will tell you every motion that stirs them; every passion that excites them; I will lay bare their minds and hearts; and perhaps you will see some things which you yourself have experienced."

XCIII

It is absolutety certain, however, that this rare genius did retain to the end of life all her religious instincts and sympathy, although, alas! she broke away from all religious beliefs. She loathed her task of translating the *Leben Jesu* of Strauss; and loathed still more the asperity and bitterness of the author. Could anything be more significant and pathetic than her confession, that she could only find strength and resolution to write the story of the Crucifixion by gazing on a figure of the Crucified that surmounted her desk? Could anything be more admonitory than her old-age admission that the basis of all happiness consists in possessing definite religious beliefs? Could anything be more reassuring than her attachment to the Bible (although Lewes repudiated it with scorn) to the end; and the fact that the Imitation of Christ lay upon her bed when she was dying? and that these two books, the inspired and the semi-inspired, with that *Commedia* that all men have agreed to call divine, were the constant companions of her senility and illness? Could anything be more terrible to the votaries of humanitarianism than her confession to her friend, as they passed up and down Addison's walk at Oxford: "I see no hope for humanity, but one grand, simultaneous act of suicide"?

XCIV.

It is strange, too, how the old Greek idea of Fate, under the form of a Nemesis, or Retribution, not to be propitiated or averted, became a leading dogma of her life. It is the leading idea in Spinoza's Ethics, Strauss accepted it. Emerson formulated it thus:

"The specific stripes may follow late upon the offence , but they follow, because they accompany it   Crime and punishment grow out of one stem   We cannot do wrong, without suffering wrong "

This doctrine might be controverted.   It might be accepted as a kind of halting Christianity , it might even do good to be so accepted and preached, always with the scholium—that crime is not unpardonable with God, if it is unforgivable by Nature and Society   But the curious thing is, that the most violent opponents of dogma are obliged to fall back upon dogma in the end , and that Naturalism would find it difficult to explain the secret power that makes for Retribution, whilst it denies the Higher Intelligence that can punish or pardon according to Its own supreme decrees

XCV.

Probably, this was the reason why George Eliot adopted as a practical maxim of life that Comtist doctrine: *Notre vraie destinée se compose de resignation et d'activité*   Work, work, work.   Work blindly, but unceasingly.   You will blunder ; nay, you will criminate yourself.   And behind you is Nemesis with her whip of scorpions   You cannot escape the lash   You are the galley-slave, with the cannon-ball tied to your ankle, and the warder over you with whip or musket, and the oar in your bleeding hands.   What then ?   Well, then, you must be resigned.   There is no mending matters.   It is Fate   There is one hope—the grave.   Tears and prayers and penance are unavailing   The Fates are inexorable. They cannot be moved aside   There is no repentance ; only Retribution.   So says Nature in her every tone.   And we are Nature's children.   We cannot say *Our Father*, for we have none Let us take up our work, then, and go silently forward   And if the lash falls, let us yield to it, and swallow our tears with our bread.   This is Life, and there is none other

XCVI.

Did she suffer, I wonder, from the retribution she preached ? She violated the universal law in her pretended marriage with

George Henry Lewes. What was the penalty? A certain biographer puts it—"the estrangement of friends, the loss of liberty of speech, the foremost rank amongst the women of her country, and a tomb in Westminster Abbey." Did she feel all this? Or was the pleasure of perfect domestic felicity and a happy fireside a compensation? We cannot think so A note of depression runs through all the records of her married life. She seems to be always deprecating criticism, always watching the faces of her visitors. How poor a thing is philosophy, or logic, in face of a violated law! How disgusting the very apologies that men make for the emancipation of passion from law! Her great author, Feuerbach, asserted that enjoyment is a duty; and that it was the merest affectation to turn away from immodest or indecent scenes. Strauss sneered at the text which laid down the law of Christian chastity. Rousseau praised Sophie for her sin. Are not these grave and reverend personages, whose authority is all-sufficing? Alas, no! Society is inexorable, Nature is arbitrary, and conscience imperative There is no escaping the Nemesis of Sin, except by Repentance.

XCVII.

The existence of evil in the world is a stumbling-block to many philosophers who cannot understand how inevitable in their own theories it is in a world of limitations and finite beings The existence of pain is a still greater mystery to those who refuse to believe that it has its own wonderful secrets, which might well be purchased at even a dearer price. Pain, that purifies the victim, preaches to the strong, and evolves in victims and helpers virtues of which they were not even cognizant For if it be true what a certain French cynic has said, that there is something in our worst misfortunes which does not altogether displease our nearest friends, let this be understood not in the sense that they rejoice in our misery, but in the sense of relief that they themselves have been spared so much pain. But for those who are closer and dearer, that seemingly selfish satisfaction does not obtain Nay, they would gladly change places with us on our beds of pain, from which we preach to them the charity which they practise to us, and give even to the selfish the pleasure of immunity from the evils that afflict ourselves.

XCVIII.

George Elliot did not escape the common lot. She suffered; but her suffering made her neither strong, nor interesting. It was the suffering of a well-to-do dyspeptic. One cannot sympathize well with this lady, whose drawing-room was turned into a cave of the Sybil, where she sat at the left-hand side of the fireplace, and awed visitors trod lightly on the soft carpet, as they were ushered into her presence, with a kind of admonitory reverence by her second husband and biographer And if they thought at the same time of the enormous cheques that lay in her bureau from her publishers—£10,000 for one novel, £5,000 for another, and so on—somehow it must have mitigated their apprehensions, diluted her philosophy, and dulled their heroine-worship And yet, perhaps, this is wrong Nothing succeeds like success, and there is no success, to some minds, if the final chaplet does not fall from the hands of Mammon. But this easy though busy life, unbroken by alternations of struggle and stress, is not what one expects from literary giants, it is too epicurean and intellectual to be interesting. One misses the plaint:

> Ah ! who can tell how hard it is to climb
> The steep where Fame's proud temple shines afar?

XCIX.

I confess I am more interested in that painful, uphill struggle, which most literary men have to face, and of which Richter most probably speaks (for it was his own experience) when he says :

" But often wilt thou shed thine own blood, that thou mayst the more firmly step down the path that leads to old age, even as chamois-hunters support themselves by the blood of their own heels "

This suffering and struggle give strength and enlightenment. You cannot really understand life until you have tasted the sense of *camaraderie* that comes from drinking out of the same bottle and sharing the same crust,—I was near saying, and occupying the same branch, like that Bohemian who gave his town address as

"Avenue de St Cloud, third tree to the left after leaving the Bois de Boulogne, and fifth branch"

Isn't that delightful? And imagine those starving geniuses,— Balzac, Chénier, Murger, Karol, or some such like, bending over the ashes of their manuscripts which they had ignited to keep up a little heat, when the snow lay thick on Nôtre-Dame, and the mercury was some hundreds of degrees below zero!

C.

All successful writers are unanimous in warning off young aspirants from the thorny path of literature. Grant Allen would give them a broom, and bid them take to crossing-sweeping; Gibbon, de Quincey, Scott, Southey, Lamb, Thackeray,—all showed the weals and lashes of the hard taskmaster; amongst moderns, Daudet warns that brain-work is the most exacting of all species of labor, and must eventuate, sooner or later, in a bad break-down, Mr. Zangwill says, somewhat grandiosely. "Whoso with blood and tears would dig art out of his soul, may lavish his golden prime in pursuit of emptiness; or striking treasure, find only fairy gold, so that when his eye is purged of the spell of morning, he sees his hand is full of withered leaves" And dear old Sam Johnson, who certainly passed through his Inferno and Purgatorio before he settled down in the comfortable paradise at Streatham, epitomizes his hardships as author in the well-known line:

Toil, envy, want, the patron, and the gaol.

CI

Nor can all these aspirants claim the steady nerve and calm philosophy of Jean Paul, who can see in poverty but "the pain of piercing a maiden's ears, that you may hang precious jewels in the wound " It is a bitter thing, a severe initiation into mysteries otherwise unintelligible; and hence it is, I suppose, that with the eternal hope of youth, the ambitious see but the goal and the prize; and like Alpine climbers, undismayed by the fate of others, and utterly oblivious of danger, they refuse to see crevasse or avalanche, or sliding glacier They only see the peaks far away, shining like amber in the morning sun; and they promise themselves that, at evening, they shall stand on that summit where no foot of mortal had ever trodden before It is somewhat melancholy, and yet it is the one thing that gives to the biographical part of literature that interest, amounting to sympathy, that is the right of the strong, who have fought their way through difficulties to success.

CII.

It would be well, however, that this sympathy took a practical turn, especially where genius is concerned, and I know no more touching instance of this inspiring hopefulness than the letters of his sister Laura to Balzac. She stood by him and encouraged him, when his parents turned him from the door as a fool, because he gave up the comfortable profession of notary, and took to the dry crusts and rags of literature; she sympathized with all his struggles, rejoiced in all his triumphs, she advised him, controlled him, encouraged him; and she stood by his bedside on that fatal day, August 18, 1850, when, after thirty hours of fearful agony, he died in the city that refused to recognize his talents till after death. A lurid, tempestuous, passionate life—misdirected and misapplied! His biographer told the truth when he said that Paris was a hell, but a hell, the only place worth living in, and of this he vowed to be a Dante. He succeeded but too well; and it would have been better for him and the world if he had left the secrets unrevealed. But, at least, Laura was his Beatrice.

CIII.

Poor Henry Murger, too! All that one can remember of him is his mother's intense devotion; his horrible disease, *pur-*

pura, which he laughingly declared he wore with the dignity of a Roman Emperor; his chivalric devotion to the Sister of Charity who nursed him in hospital—"A good Sister you were, the Beatrice of that hell   Your soothing consolations were so sweet, that we all complained whenever we had the chance, so as only to be consoled by you;"—his anticipation of O. W. Holmes' poem, "The Voiceless"·

> Nous avons cru pouvoir—nous l'avons cru souvent
> Formuler notre rêve, et le rendre vivant
>   Par la palette ou par la lyre,
> Mais le souffle manquait, et personne n'a pu
> Deviner quel était le poeme inconnu
>   Que nous ne savions pas traduire

Then, his childish warning off the priests: "Tell them I have read Voltaire"   Finally his cry: "Take me to the Church, God can do more than any physician"   His final happy death, after receiving the last Sacraments   Poor fellows! with their sad motto. The Academy, the Asylum, or the Morgue!   How the heart of a Vincent de Paul, or a Philip Neri, would have yearned over your helplessness and your genius, and wept for your follies and your sins!   And how lesser folk would have liked to burst into your attic, and tear your valuable papers from the fire, and send ruddy blazes out of more ready material dancing up the chimney, and pelted you with sandwiches till you cried, Hold! and then sat down with you on a soap-box or on your dingy bed; and filled out in long ruby glasses the Margaux or Lafitte you had not tasted for many a day, and finally settled down to a calm, long, soporific smoke, and listened to the song, the anecdote, the *bon mot*, that would turn the gloom of Phlegethon into an Attic night, and the lentils of a Daniel into a supper of the gods!

CIV.

Pascal, too, found a rare helper and sympathizer in his sister, —the Madame Perrier, who wrote his life so briefly, but significantly.   Not, indeed, that he needed any spiritual strength or support from any external power, for he was a self-contained spirit, and thought little of human help. And his genius was colossal Like Aristotle he seems to have thought out a whole scheme of creation, unaided. It is rather a singular instance of human folly that he should have been considered a sceptic. There is no stopping the tongues of men. The same chaige was levelled against Dr Newman Mozeley attributes the great popularity of the Oratorian in England to that. Perhaps there were never two men who believed more intensely and unreservedly. But the Frenchman lacked serenity. He lost his nobility by engaging, not so much in a lost cause, as a bad cause He descended to cynicism and sarcasm—the expression of a form of lower mental condition. And this, too, affected his greatest, if most imperfect work. When the *Provincial Letters* are forgotten or neglected as splenetic sarcasm, and have passed away like the Junius and Drapier Letters, and have become but the study of the connoisseur, his " Pensées " will remain, broken fragments of an incomplete, but immortal work.

CV.

What judgment will posterity pass on them? It would be difficult to say. But if we may gauge the future by the present, we would say that the verdict of a more enlightened age than ours will be, that Pascal was no sceptic, though a bold inquirer; that his marvellous mental keenness and vigor were only equalled by his rigid asceticism, that Nature had made him pious, and circumstances made him proud; that these "Thoughts" which reveal to us his inner life are beautiful and deep beyond words, that they would have even the color of that inspiration which comes from Nature and Grace united, were it not for a dark shadow which stretches itself over all, making the philosophy of them less clear, the truth of them less apparent, the study of them a task of anxiety and suspicion, instead of being one of edification and delight.

CVI

In fact, I know but of one case where a sister's influence was hurtful ; and that was the case of Ernest Renan. It is impossible to explain how a woman, and a Bretonne, could have lent the aid of her sisterly influence to wean him away from the sanctuary, and then from the Church itself.   There is something inexpressibly revolting about it, because I think, of all human loves, that of a sister is the most abiding and unselfish   In a mother's love there is a kind of identification with her child, his triumphs, his defeats, which, by the reflection on herself, takes away the absolute disinterestedness   Conjugal love is more intense, but for that reason more intermittent   But there's not a trace of self in that earnest wistful gaze which a beloved sister casts after the poor young fellow who has just gone out from the sanctity of home-life into the world's arena ; nor a thought of self in the way the silent heart broods over shattered hopes, and takes back to its sanctuary the broken relics of the idol, once worshipped, now, alas! only protected from the gaze of a scornful world.

CVII.

Post tenebras lux !   The motto, of all places on earth, of the city of Geneva!   Well, no matter   Here is light now in early spring, or rather in expiring winter, and it is very welcome.   For much as I love my fire and lamp, there is a certain regeneration in body and soul and spirits, in these days which are lengthening out, bit by bit, as the sun ascends higher in the heavens, and the dawn breaks earlier, and the twilight lingers even in the steel-blue sky.   Winter is still here.   The sirocco-breath of the east wind withers all vegetation, and seems to dry the very blood in the veins of men   Delicate people crouch all day by their fires , and look out despairingly at the gray, mournful skies, and the earth parched and hardened by the wind.   And yet there is hope; for the days are drawing out, and the nights are shortening ; and there is light, light , and we feel we are rushing on to the time when the summer twilight will fade away only to break out into the resurrection of a roseate summer dawn.

CVIII.

I could not help feeling this evening, as the great red shield of the moon rose solemnly above the trees, and Jupiter hung like a dewdrop in the purpled sky, that it should be a great consolation for us to know, that whatever may befall us, little creatures of God, —death, life, sorrow, joy,—the great wheel of existence swings in its beautiful and perfect equilibrium before the face of God; and that even when we shall have departed hence, and our place shall know us no more, there never shall be rift nor break in that cosmical perfection of sun, and star, and season, that seems to know its own beauty, and to exult in it before the face of its Maker "When the morning stars sang together," may be more than a figure of speech; and it is something to know that, above this little globe of sorrow, which we so strangely call "the valley of tears," the great universe is swinging softly and majestically; and that neither Time, nor Death, the two great solvents, can wither the beauty, or tarnish the lustre of all those other creatures of Omnipotence that are so far beyond the reach of our powers to comprehend; but not beyond the scope of reason to imagine, or interpret.

CIX.

Then I began to consider, why did that thought strike me just then, and not at any other time? I had seen burning noons and glorious sunsets without number; I had watched the faint sickle of the new moon in the West, and thanked her for her benevolence, when, gibbous and hunchbacked and unbeautiful, she made all things beneath her beautiful But this idea of the symmetry and perfection and harmony of Creation had not struck me so forcibly before Then I remembered that it was but imperfect moons and declining suns I had seen. The former excluded all idea of rounded and perfected beauty; the latter, with all their splendors, were the funereal accompaniments of the death of day. But this great, red moon, burning through the latticed trees, and then paling away as it mounted higher and higher in heaven, was a symbol of the perfect beauty to which all things tend; and it rose in the night-dawn, young and beautiful, and with all the promise of uninterrupted empire all through the silent but eloquent watches of the night, until the white dawn came, and it would fade away, silent as a ghost, down the long avenues of paling stars, towards its grave in the West

CX.

You see then, to be an optimist you must have two associations—youth and the idea of ultimate perfection   Hence every child is an optimist, believing that all things are fair and beautiful, and absolutely idealizing the ugliest things until they put on the wings and outlines of perfect and immaculate loveliness   It is the glorious exaggeration of imagination without experience to clip its wings and bring it down to earth   It is only when the wheels of life begin to move more slowly, as they get clogged and debilitated, that we begin to take analytical views of life , and as our shadows lengthen in the sunset, we allow the past to project its gloom athwart our life-path, until it ends in the near perspective of the tomb   Then, we begin to reason, and shake our heads mournfully, and speculate, and haply become merely resigned. But the full tide of life creeps slowly through our veins ; and we begin to pity our far-off selves, who in the imprudence and inexperience of youth, we remember to have been intoxicated with the delirium of life, and to have said aloud, or to our own hearts: All is fair and beautiful ; and all is well !

CXI.

Then, too, we must have the idea, so uncommon, so slippery, so often confuted, and as often revived, that all things round to final perfection.   It needs a healthy brain, or well-defined religious principles, to comprehend it.   The whole of literature seems to be a wail of protest against it.   Now and again, a great optimist, bravely cheers us onward with an expression of faith, like the song of Pippa ; or the lines :

There shall never be one lost good !   What was shall live as before ,
   The evil is null—is naught—is silence implying sound ,

What was good, shall be good, with, for evil, so much good more ,
  On the earth, the broken arcs ; in the heaven, a perfect round.

But this is rare ! Even when Tennyson seeks to lift his verse on the wings of hope, he finds they are broken, and he falls to earth and sorrow again. And yet, there is no word so detested by men as that word "pessimism"; nor is there any verdict so dreaded by those teachers called philosophers and poets, as the sentence that their teaching is pessimistic. How is this ? With so strong a tendency towards the evil thing, how is it that men so much dread the evil reputation ? Yet, when you come to consider it, you will find that these writers, one and all, fall into that dreadful category of St Paul: "Without God, and with no hope in this world."

CXII.

On the other hand, you will find that the teachers who point with hope to this final perfection, even though they do not belong to the household of the faith, seem to be carried, almost in spite of themselves, along the current of pure, intellectual thought, towards it. All the terrible contradictions of life seem to merge in one great unification; and that is, that the great positives of life,—virtue, holiness, happiness, health,—are the realities that abide, and continue with a perpetual and seemingly unconscious bias, or rather destiny, towards final perfection; and that the negatives,—sin, vice, disease, death,—although obstructions, can never pass beyond their negative form; and finally fade away, or are merged in their positives, until Evil disappears; and there only remain the Beautiful and the Good These thinkers, whom some call *Ensemblists*, or those who view Life and the Universe as a whole, come very close to the poet who sings :

  for somehow good
  Shall be the final goal of ill ,

and very near the Apostle of the *Gaudetes*, who assures us "that the sorrows of this life are not to be compared with the glory to come that shall be revealed in us."

CXIII.

But this dream of final perfection and loveliness, after all, is it a forecast of what shall be in the final evolution of our species; or rather is it not the noble and cherished tradition of a race that once possessed it, and lost it?   It would be difficult for the Hegelian school to construct a scheme where all things would round to perfection, considering that they place their theories on the finite and limited nature of things, which therefore are necessarily imperfect; and from whose very essence arise the concomitants of imperfection—sin, disease, death.   Hegel denies the immortality of the soul, except in the restricted and unsatisfactory sense of an absorption in the Universal of the individual   But how we are to pass the bounds of imperfection, that is limitation, and reach to the Unlimited, the Perfect, he cannot say.   And with the more modern evolutionist theory, the idea is still more intangible and difficult to seize   The slow processes of the suns have not brought us far on the road to final perfection   There is evil— disease, vice, death.   Has the horizon of human hope a gleam of a better land beyond it; or do not rather the shadows darken as we approach, without the lamp of faith, that bourn of all human sufferings and joys, where the shadows of death encompass us, and the perils of hell may find us?

CXIV.

On the other hand, how noble is the tradition, that we did possess that perfection to which all things tend, but fell from it; that, therefore, final perfection is not the lurid dream of insensate beasts, so much as the far foreshadowing of what must be, because it once was; that, therefore, being fallen, we have the power of rising again to the heights whence we were precipitated; and, above all, we are not a race, moving on to the goal, and sifting itself of all its weaker elements, so that in the survival of the fittest, its dreams of ambition may be attained   But the majesty of the individual soul shines out conspicuous in the lofty scheme of rehabilitation and resurrection, and race-abstractions, race-destinations, etc, give place to the supreme importance that attaches to each single creation of the Almighty in His scheme of universal redemption. When we speak, therefore, of the tendency of all things to final perfection, we mean the recovery of lost rights and happenings, lost dignities and glory; and these not incommensurate with our state; but our righteous privileges and prerogatives, which the sin of our ancestors forfeited; but which we may, through the sacrifice of our Elder Brother, gloriously win back again.

PART III
SPRING

SPRING

My garden looks well just now, although the cold lingers, and now and again a shower of hail, flung from some refrigerator high up in the heavens, threatens to break the fragile stems of my tulips, and to scatter the white, milky blossoms on my apple-trees The crocuses, frail, little things, although too delicate for winter that "lingers even in the lap of May," have long since disappeared, leaving only the long green leaves from which the yellow and purple blossoms have vanished. The beautiful hyacinths too, with their wax-like bells, in white and purple and crimson, have fallen to earth and languish there. Their superb blossoms, full of that subtle perfume that haunts us from our childhood, were too proud for the long smooth stalks that bore them , and, under the heavy April showers that filled their sweet bells, they were borne downward to earth; and, like so many other fallen things, are unable to rise again. But the hardy daffodils and narcissi spread their broad discs or their saffron trumpets to the sun ; and, despising the legendary origin of their name, the latter refuse to droop or languish over lake or grass or brown bed; but flaunt their chaste splendors to sun or breeze, and look down upon the more highly decorated denizens beneath them, as a pure soul might look upon the meretricious splendors of fashion, and rest happy in its own simplicities.

II

But the tulips, transplanted from their marshy beds in Holland, appear to have absorbed all the coloring from earth and sky and transmuted it into their own emphatic and pronounced splendors They are extremely beautiful I can imagine a St. Francis or some minor poet saying ·—

"Who made you, little ones, and who made you so lovely and so frail?"

Was it on the broad disc of the resplendent sun, whence light, with its component tints, for ever issues, that the Artist spread His colors, and was it with its soft, lambent pencils He drew on those glistening and curled leaves such flames of beauty and harmony? Did He watch the gentle dawn to catch the pink blush that He has limned just here, and the reluctant evening for the red flush of impatience, or the saffron of sorrow, that He has wrought into your soft and shining depths? And was it from the corona and photosphere of His mighty palette that He drew these red and yellow fires along the surface of your bells; and shaded them deep down into your mysterious breasts whence the curved and curled corolla springs shaded, like a violet in a valley of mosses, or a primrose beneath the shadow of an oak? And, what was the archetype from which He drew such lines of beauty and such blendings and harmonies of color? Where did the model exist? In what garden of Eden did He behold your prototypes? Or, was it from the secret of His own surpassing beauty He devised your loveliness and made you another and a meeker manifestation of that undying principle that underlies every operation of His handmaid, Nature—the principle, that all things round to beauty, and that in the spiral of a vast nebula which covers half the heavens, and in the curve of a little leaf that shelters a tiny insect, order and beauty and proportion and harmony subsist —a reflex of the Mind of the Eternal?

III.

What place has the unconscious chemistry of Nature here? What does blind Nature know of beauty, that she could weave and paint, by instinct only, such unparalleled loveliness? Here are types, here is method, here is a plan, and here must be Mind! Come and sit in this shaded gallery in this ancient city! It is a long gallery, carefully lighted, with but little sun; yet there is a cool shadow in the air that tempers the superabundant light outside into a soft, gray, mellow color as of an autumnal twilight.

A sentinel stands at the door—an Imperial hussar. Yes! there must be something royal and priceless here. You enter. The place is still as a church. It is a reverend place. People speak in whispers. Heads are bowed in an attitude of prayer—the silent, and eloquent prayer of imitation; and all eyes are directed upward to the Holy Thing—the Shrine. And what is it? Only a picture! It occupies that entire wall. The rest of the gallery is bare. No acolyte pictures are grouped around. It would not be fair to them; although no eye could be distracted from that supreme beauty that seems not to be limned, but to hover in front of and above that picture on the wall. Men, hushed in wonder, say in their hearts. It is not human! No earthly pencil painted it! No human mind hath dreamed it! Yet there is the subscription: *Pinxit Raffaelle Sanzio.*

Then it is the work of human hands. And by degrees, as the first wonder subsides, men begin to ponder and think, and imagine how the dream came, how the artist brooded over it; how he mixed his colors; how he drew and drew until the new creation dawned on the brown canvas, and he fell down and worshipped his own work!

IV.

Raffaelle could paint that Lily of Israel, that Rose of Sharon, but he could not create this tiny flower in my fingers. Yet here, too, is type, and method, and plan, and—mind. Who can deny it? If only mind could create a Sistine Madonna, how could chance create that which is greater, lovelier? Chance could not draw a line of her garments, nor give a hue to her cheek. Chance could never put that mother's look in the soft brown eyes; nor that dreamy far-sight into the eyes of the Child. Gather all the azures, and ochres, and browns, and scarlets that are scattered in plant and mineral throughout creation, and cast them down on a palette. Heap together pencils and brushes. Draw the canvas tight, and call on chance to paint a cherub's face or the trumpet of an archangel. You will wait for eternity before chance can come to your beck and call. And how, then, could unconscious chemistry—the mere fortuitous coincidence of atoms—create this floral beauty that springs from the dull, brown clods of my garden-beds? Here is a little water, and a little oil—that is all! Who combined them into such a lovely form? Has water these potencies of color in itself; and has oil in itself that sweet, subtle fragrance? And this outward curve, like a lip turned backwards in the coquetry of anger, who hath given it? And who hath stopped the flame-red that burns from the bottom of the chalice, and toned it away into this beautiful saffron, which itself fades away at the lips? "Chance!" "Unconscious chemistry!" It is against all the traditions of our experience—all the arguments of a reasoning mind.

V.

"We don't know!" Well, that at least is humble—just a shade better than the sneers of a positive infidelity. I have no right to find fault with the wayside beggar whose breast is burdened with the speaking tablet:

I AM BLIND!

It is his misfortune, and an unspeakable one. So, too, when a man says: "I have no faith. I do not know, nor believe," I have hardly the privilege of being angry with him. It is only when he comes to positive assertion or denial that I am privileged not only to pity his ignorance, but to refute it. If such a one came before the Sistine Madonna and said: "It is a daub; the colors are badly laid, and the drawing is but second-hand," the artists sitting around would promptly expel him as a sacrilegious inept And if he went further and said· "Yes, it is pretty here and there; but, mark you, this gallery is draughty, it is but a death-trap," they would say: "Go forth, then, and seek your miserable health elsewhere. What you want is sulphuretted hydrogen, not a divine dream" And if he went further, and declared: "Raffaelle Sanzio never existed What you behold is the fortuitory result of a few pieces of carmine, ochre, and cobalt, which came together by chance, and wrought themselves into the face and figure of a Woman and Child," they would probably hand him over to the Commissioner of Police. Yet all this is what we read in the ravings of Materialism and Positive Philosophy.

VI.

Hip! hip! hurrah! The first swallows have come. I had
been watching for them these last few warm days in early April,
and I scanned the sky every morning and evening for the white
breast and black wings that cut the air like a knife I was disappointed. I saw only a lazy crow winging his dreary way towards
the west; or a great crane slowly laboring with his wide gray
wings towards the sunset; or a thrush or blackbird whir-
ring in alarm towards a sheltering tree, or an indolent sparrow
who pecked at the ground between my feet Then, one evening,
the 16th of April of this year, I looked up suddenly from my
book, and, no ?—yes, indeed, there were my pretty favorites,
tumbling, tossing, gliding, flapping through the air, as in last September, when I bade them farewell, and without sign or warning
they were gone! Gone, too, with some regrets and remorse, for
my gardener and general servant, in a sudden and very unusual
fit of tidiness, had torn down a mud nest beneath the eaves of my
stable, and it was pitiable to see the young swallows swinging
round and round their dilapidated home, having no longer, literally, a place whereon to lay their heads. Fortunately the weather
was warm and the nights were mild, so that none perished; but I
felt a kind of shame in thinking what ideas of our inhospitality
these winged wanderers would carry away to sunny Spain or
Algiers, and I was deeply anxious to know if they would forgive
and forget, unlike ourselves, and grace our little garden and house
once more with their gentle and gracious presence.

VII.

Well, here they are! They passed away silent as ghosts; and
silent as ghosts they have returned. There was no sale of effects as
they departed, no bundling up of *impedimenta*, no display of feeling, not even a farewell! They floated high above my garden on
the evening of September 29th, and on the morrow I looked
in vain for them. And now, again, swiftly and silently, they
have returned What long, lonely wintry hours were they away!
What a mighty multitude of thoughts have swept, like a river,

through my brain! What fears, hopes, anxieties have burned their way into gray ashes since the swallows went! And here are they again, careless of time and human vicissitudes and vexation, here to roll and toss and plow the air like the vibrations of light, so swift and sudden and silent are their movements; caring only for the day and the hour of existence, and only studying alternations of weather, as to whether they shall seek their living food high up in the summer air, or poised above the darkened river, when the heavy clouds bend down weighted with rain, and the flies are languid from the pressure. But here they are, harbingers of Spring, and its most swift and elastic messengers, and here they shall remain during the long summer evenings, and autumn twilights, until the first frost warns them to preen their wings for flight and migrate to foreign latitudes.

VIII

Yet, think of where they have been, and what sights they have seen since last they hovered above my head. With their great strong wings they have cut their way over wood and forest and river; over town and field and hamlet, heedless of the world beneath them, unconscious of all the fever and fret that eat like cankers into the ever turbid, ever restless breast of man. Like exiled seraphs, winging their way back to Heaven, they have passed by night and day over the troubled world, but one instinct in their own breasts—to reach the objective of their autumnal flight. They have paused to gain strength for the effort beneath the white walls of the lighthouse, rested on the ball at the summit, or on the rail of the iron gallery. And then, on the wings of hope and self-reliance they have launched the little barks of their existence above the eternal deep. Brave little voyagers! No mariner's compass directs you, no white sails buoy you above the trembling waves, no haven opens its sheltering arms to receive you, no lighthouse flashes its welcome warning along your line of flight. Beneath you roars the tempest, and great seas lift up their ravening jaws to engulf you, but over all you glide, buoyant and triumphant, for He who made you is your Pilot and your Captain; and He hath given you sense for science, and

curbed all hostile elements that might hinder or endanger your
lonely pilgrimage across His seas And one day, you see beneath
you not the green, barren waters, but yellow fields and purple
vineyards; and you know your journey is at an end, and that here
in the warm and aromatic air, you can plunge and toss at leisure
until the dream of the North comes back, and bids you hie homewards again.

IX.

Of all physical existences on or around this planet, theirs
seems to be the most perfect and joyous Never touching this
dull earth, except to rest or sleep (and then always out of danger),
they seem to have no enemies; and to judge by their movements,
there seems to be the most fraternal and unbroken affection amongst
themselves You never see them peck at one another and quarrel,
like more terrestrial birds They chase one another through the
perfumed air, but it is in sheer joyance of spirit, like the play of
children on summer evenings You never see them eat. They
are too dainty to rest and wrestle with wriggling worms. They
pass through a swarm of midges, and the midges feed them.
But think of the freedom, the ecstasy, the sense of power and
security, the physical delight with which they glide through the
air, with the swiftness almost of spirits; and dart and shoot along
over rivers and meadows, over fresh budding trees and ancient forests, now almost invisible as a skylark ambushed in a cloud, and
now almost touching your cheek as they sweep suddenly from the
skies and pass like a gleam of light above your head But it is
in the evening and especially around old churches that they seem
to be electrified with the very exuberance of existence How
they dart and flash in and out, crossing each other's path by a
hair's breadth, and screaming in the mad convulsions of delight, as
children in the market-place in the summer evening play ! Then,
at twilight far up in the zenith, almost so far as to be invisible, they
hold their diurnal parliament, grouped specks on the gray azure of
the sky ; and then sink down, one by one, to their mud cabins beneath the eaves, until the morning sun calls them forth to another
day of boundless ecstasy and freedom and delight.

X

Yesterday, a great white sea-gull swooped down from the sky, rested for a moment on the brown earth in my garden, and instantly rose, and swept with great beats of his wings over the wall and away. He was a waif in from the marshes and sedgy rivers where flocks of gulls congregate in the cold weather to seek their food. The theory, I believe, is that fish seek the warm depths of the sea, away from the chilled surface in winter and early spring, and that the seabirds must come inland for their food. There is a certain kind of pathos in it. The black crows fraternize with them genially; and it is no uncommon sight to see a ploughed field almost covered with those black and white specks, amicably feeding together. Nay, these sea-waifs actually pick up the tricks of their sable comrades, and perch on the sheep and even cows, seeking their parasites for food. It is a grimy speculation; but it is impossible not to feel a kind of sympathy for those noble seabirds, hanging over a lazy sedgy river instead of the great, green, glorious breakers, which are its natural dominion, and swooping down to a common worm, like a mere sparrow or robin, instead of plunging into their own mighty reservoir, and searching it with their keen, fierce eyes for their natural food. And hence, you never hear them, in their inland winter exile, scream as they do when in the teeth of the storm, and above the roaring of seas, they poise themselves with such exquisite power and grace, and feel that life is a glorious thing, and that infinity of sea and sky are around them and above them, and they must tell their emotions to the vastness above them and the immensities beneath

XI

I remember well what a pretty etching in colors one of these seabirds made many years ago. I was at Ardmore on a sunny day in August. It was a holiday, snatched from much work. Otherwise I would not tell what a lazy, delightful, do-nothing, think-nothing afternoon I had, stretched there on the fragrant purple heather, just sloped enough to enable me to see the great level sea-plain that shone in the sun, and shimmered in the tiny shadows, until at last it faded away in a dreamy mist at the far horizon. A very temperate modest lunch was in the little bag by my side, and I was reading and pondering over that most pathetic poem of that most unhappy poet—the "Nameless" of Clarence Mangan Painted on the otherwise unbroken blue canvas of the deep was a tiny triangular sail, apparently motionless, and only one other speck of white disturbed the monotone of sky and sea. It was a sea-gull, so near me that I felt I could almost touch him; and he was poised motionless, a tiny cloud-like radiance above the deep. Two hundred feet beneath, the deep blue sea fretted itself away in a fringe of foam that crawled up the black cobalt rocks. That was the only sound or motion in nature, for the bird hung motionless without flap of wing or turn of head, though I could see his fierce eyes hungrily devouring the waters beneath. Then, suddenly, like a bolt from the blue, he fell downwards, and struck the waves; and, in an instant, emerged with a great silver fish squirming and flashing in his strong beak. This he beat lifeless against the rocks, and proceeded lazily to devour.

XII.

"Yes," I thought, "there are but two great classes in nature —the victor and the victim—the aggressor and the aggressed. All others resolve themselves into these There is more truth in "Maud" than in "In Memoriam" There is less poetry, but more philosophy in—

For Nature is one with rapine, a harm no preacher can heal;
The May-fly is torn by the swallow, the sparrow speared by the shrike.
And the whole little wood where I sit is a world of plunder and prey,

than in the belief·

> That not a worm is cloven in vain,
>   That not a moth with vain desire
>   Is shrivell'd in a fruitless fire,
> Or but subserves another's gain.

Not only do men not believe it, but all their ill-concealed sympathies are with aggressors, not with the victims. Hence the need of a Revelation! Nothing but the Revelation of God has tamed the savage in man Civilization has not done it, and cannot do it. Nay, civilization is but the net success of brute force—the survival of the strongest Life is warfare. The *élite* are the elect, chosen in the sifting of the battle from the weak and the frail. Strength alone commands admiration, and challenges success.

XIII

All the great world-names are symbolical of strength. Cyrus, Alexander, Hannibal, Cæsar, Napoleon—all stand out from the history of mankind, raised and embossed by pure power of aggression and attack. And no matter how fascinating might be the conquered races in their history, or music, or philosophy, the clash of arms has drowned their appeal for sympathy, and the waving of standards has obscured their national attractions; and the world sees only the victor's heel on the neck of the slave; and hears only the *Væ victis!* as the ultimate pæan and song of conquering humanity. In the Napoleonic wars, for instance, there was something pathetic in the desperate valor with which the Austrian hussars and German legions threw themselves on the invading and aggressive French hordes One's sympathy goes out to them in their heroic efforts to resist the irresistible; but when we see them fleeing before the merciless onslaught of these victorious *sans-culottes*—the lean, hungry wolves of the Revolution, marshalled in a kind of madness, and inspired by the presence of the War-god, the Invincible, insensibly we turn aside from the valor that has failed to the strength that has conquered, and we lift in imagination our bearskins on our bayonets, and stand in our stirrups, and hail the little, pale-faced, delicate-handed god that has hurled for the hundredth time the crashing battle-bolts of his battalions on the fleeing and panic-stricken enemy. Conscience may cry "unjust," "brutal," "aggressive," to this unwarranted invasion, prompted by the lust of ambition, but the lower instinct says "glorious," "marvellous," "sublime;" and the feet of pilgrims wear the flags around the black catafalque with that simple inscription, "Napoleon," beneath the dome of the *Invalides;* and pass by the shrine of saint and scholar to worship at the altar of the Destroyer.

XIV.

And to turn aside from such world-tragedies, we find in the daily lives of the multitude the same aggression, the same weakness, the same worship. The man that asserts himself and attacks is the hero; until all society resolves itself into the two classes—the victors and the conquered. The shopkeeper driving a bargain behind his counter, the lawyer, attacking a victim in the witness-box; the physician, speculating how much he will chaige as fee, whilst he feels the fevered pulse of the patient, the Cabinet-Minister, legislating against turbulent, if justifiable agitation, the opposition, challenging him, the author, attacking an abuse, the Press, attacking him;—all are examples of the universal law

For Nature is one with rapine, a harm no preacher can heal.

And if, in the higher circles of society there is a mute code of morals, called politeness, it is only a tacit armistice, as if they would say Let us sheathe our claws, and forbear from attacking each other, face to face; let us be mutually tolerant, and let us study each other's comfort. Life will be otherwise intolerable. Let us suspend the Law of Nature, not because we love, but just because it is mutually helpful to be mutually tolerant and unaggressive.

XV

But this unwritten code, this tacit understanding, does not apply even in the most civilized society to anyone who steps from the ranks, and assumes an attitude of singularity. Mediocrity alone claims toleration even in the best circles. " Let us be uniform at any cost," so say the Philistines " Whosoever addeth to his stature, addeth to his discomfort " How all the savage in our nature breaks out when a child of destiny steps forward (it may be reluctantly, but destiny is imperative) and says: " I am not as you; my ways are not your ways." What a howl of execration goes out against him, how all the instincts of the circus and the arena break through the fragile crust of civilization, and demand the retribution due to offended mediocrity ' When Gifford in the

Quarterly, for instance, and Terry in *Blackwood*, whipped the soul out of poor Keats, the world laughed, and said. "Serves him right! Why did not he, the apothecary's apprentice, keep to his gallipots, instead of showing us our inferiority by singing his immortal songs?" And the jealous verdicts of an ex-cobbler and an actor were taken as infallible by a world that prided itself on its culture and taste. "Great poetry," says an American critic, "is more intolerable than bad morals" Quite true! The reason is simple, and easy to find The former exasperates us by a sense of superiority, which we are compelled to feel and accept The latter flatter us by a happy intimation of our own perfections The former we condemn and dislike; the latter we also condemn, but they are a wonderful salve to our own self-esteem

XVI.

This is probably one of the reasons why that modern Pagan, Goethe, has so many critics, and such few admirers, of his poetry; yet so many apologists for his morals One of his most recent commentators tells us that at an English university a Goethe student is as rare as a white blackbird Probably Edmond Scherer is the justest and most severe critic of his poetry Matthew Arnold is a cold, cautious worshipper, who would burn a pastil, but not a thurible of incense before this deity Professor Blackie, following the lead of Carlyle, his countryman, is quite Celtic in his fervor But that is all. Yet, when it comes to speak of his life, especially in the great test-case of his attitude towards women, there is such unanimity in seeking excuses for what an old-fashioned chivalry and morality would deem the most flagrant violations of honor and virtue, that one is tempted to think that the world has advanced farther backwards towards pagan ideals than we had hitherto suspected. In fact, we cannot measure the gulf that yawns wider and wider every day between the Church and the world more accurately than by taking their respective estimates, from time to time, of those they consider their heroes and their saints For example, fidelity in the matter of manly friendship has hitherto been considered a noble feature in manly character From the time of Damon and Pythias downward, friendship has been considered a sacred thing. Now, Goethe was notoriously unfaithful to his friends. He dropped them when he tired of them, or they failed to serve him. He had not retained one friend against his old age. Every one knows his treatment of Jacobi and Lavater.

XVII.

Can this be explained? Certainly "Goethe's high sincerity and fidelity to his best *self* compelled him in many instances to sacrifice relations which, though once helpful and mutually stimulating, had become a burden and a hindrance to his growth. This is hardly selfishness, but a duty which every sincere man owes to himself. You can do your friend no good by feigning for him a feeling which no longer possesses you; and all that talk about fidelity under such circumstances is but a remnant of the old feudal ideal "[1] Again, the general sense of mankind hitherto has deemed it dishonorable to trifle with the affections of women, or to betray them. Goethe was notorious for his profligacy in this respect. Even Carlyle gasps a little when speaking of them. Now hear Professor Blackie: "Hence the rich story of Goethe's loves, with which scandal of course and prudery have made their market; but which, when looked into carefully, were just as much part of his genius as 'Faust,' and 'Iphigenia,' a part, indeed, without which 'Faust' and 'Iphigenia' could never have been written. Let no man therefore take offence when I say roundly that Goethe was always falling in love, and that I consider this a great virtue in his character. Had he not done so, he would not have been half the man, nor the tenth part of the poet that he was." The same Professor quotes with approval this extract from the "Journal of Caroline Fox"

"With regard to Goethe's character, the more Sterling examines it, the less he believes in his having wilfully trifled with the feelings of women. With regard to his selfishness, he holds that he did but give the fullest, freest scope for the exercise of his gift, and as we are all gainers thereby, we cannot call it selfishness."

[1] Boyesen's *Essays on German Literature.*

XVIII

This is almost brutal in its candor   It is a distinct apostasy from all that has been hitherto held as honorable amongst Christian and civilized nations   Nay, it would be doing them a dishonor, if I said that Pagans would repudiate such a low standard of ethics in the bosom of civilized society.   Where are we? And what are we to think?   If excuses of this kind can be made for men, on the ground that they are geniuses and exceptional, where shall we draw the line?   Let us look back, and see how we have drifted   It is not so many years since Byron was ostracised and excommunicated by English society, and since Shelley was driven into exile by the Christian communities whose dearest principles he had outraged   To-day, Byron might have the most eligible vacant spot in Westminster Abbey, and Shelley would be the petted darling of half the courts and all the best society of Europe.

XIX

I think it unfair to John Sterling to quote him in the above context   That opinion does not reconcile itself with the truer and saner verdict he had previously passed on Goethe, when his faculties were keener and not yet warped by the insanity of consumption, and when the last shreds of his Christian and clerical character had not been ruthlessly torn from him by Carlyle.   In a letter to the latter, addressed from Funchal, towards the end of the year 1837, he gives a better account of his feelings towards the high priest of naturalism

"I have been looking at *Goethe*, especially the *Life*—much as a shying horse looks at a post   In truth, I am afraid of him   I enjoy and admire him so much, and I feel I could so easily be tempted to go along with him   And yet I have a deeply-rooted and old persuasion that he was the most splendid of anachronisms.   A thoroughly, nay, intensely Pagan life, in an age when it is men's duty to be Christian   I therefore never take him up without a kind of inward check, as if I were trying some forbidden spell; while, on the other hand, there is so infinitely much to be learned from him, and it is so needful to understand the world we live in, and our own age, and espe-

cially our greatest minds, that I cannot bring myself to burn my books
as the converted magicians did, or sink them as did Prospero   There
must have been, I think, some prodigious defect in his mind, to let
him hold such views as his, about women and some other things ; and
in another respect, I find so much coldness and hollowness as to the
highest truths, and feel so strongly that the Heaven he looks up to is
but a vault of ice,—that these two indications, leading to the same
conclusion, go far to convince me that he was a *profoundly immoral
and irreligious spirit,* with as rare faculties of intelligence as ever
belonged to any one ''

XX.

This is the wholly sane and judicious verdict of a man who
still clung to the time-worn but venerable traditions that have
come down to us from all that time and thought have garnered
of the best.   And that is the colder judgment of our own time,
which has allowed the red-hot enthusiasms of the past evaporate
themselves in a worship that is as dead as that of Cybele.   A
piece of pure, cold intellectualism, a Phidian statue in the ice-
grotto of a glacier, lit up occasionally for worship by magnesian
and other lights—that was Goethe !   But intellectualism !   One
of the heresies of the age !   The intellect starving out the heart,
and demanding the sacrifice of all that is most holy and sacred
in human emotions and aspirations, whilst stifling conscience and
all the moral sense—there is the danger, that lies in the path of
all modern reformers and progressivists in the supreme matter
of education !

XXI.

Can you explain it ?   Very easily.   Literature has usurped
the place of religion, as the guide and teacher of mankind, and
religious persons have not been wise enough to retaliate and
carry the war into the enemy's country.   It must be close on fifty
years ago since Carlyle mockingly boasted that the press had
taken the place of the pulpit ; and that religion had been rele-
gated to the organ-loft and psalm-singing   He was speaking of
his own experiences ; or rather of his experiences of Protestantism, for he never entered a church for the purposes of worship.

He was cognizant, however, of the vitality of Catholicity, which
he admitted in so many words, and still more by the fierce viru-
lence with which he attacked it   But the fact remains that literature throughout the whole nineteenth century assumed a didactic
and even dogmatic tone, which ran through novel, essay, poem,
article, and which was, of course, unrestrained except by literary
canons.   Hence, we find, Goethe had a gospel; so had George
Eliot; so had Carlyle; so had Tennyson, so had Browning.
The troubadours of the fifteenth and sixteenth centuries, if they
could return from the shades, would stare aghast at the rhyming
prophets of our age, who preach a kind of pious rogation to a
generation that is sick unto death.

XXII

The strange thing, however, is that these preachers taught
higher doctrine than that which was the rule of their own lives,
as if their early Christian instruction refused to be smothered; or
as if a grave sense of responsibility forced itself into the words of
the teacher, though it was powerless to modify his life.   Hence,
in Goethe, we find recurring frequently the triple search after
happiness, as he supposes that happiness is the *summum bonum*
of life.   Does his hero seek it in voluptuousness?   He fails.   In
intellectualism?   He fails more sadly   In altruism?   He succeeds.   At least he snatches that shadow and wraith of happiness,
called resignation.   So in the novels of George Eliot   Duty here
takes the place of altruism, with the same result.   In Carlyle, the
supreme power is Force manifested in Law, which if you obey,
behold Nirvana'   But what law?   The law of nature, which by
the principle of natural selection sifts out the strongest, and per-
mits them to live, and extinguishes the weak.   He rages against
Darwinism, and—accepts its cardinal doctrine; he anathematizes
evolution, and unconsciously embraces it, repudiating Christianity, he has to fall back on some inner principles in the nature of
things.   He calls them Eternal Verities, whilst—

> Though nature, red in tooth and claw
> With ravine, shrieks against his creed.

XXIII.

It is clear, then, how needful a Revelation was to show us not that "Love is Nature's final law," for it is not; but the final Law of Nature's Creator, which He has framed for, and wishes to be observed by, the rational portion of His creation. Here we break with Evolution. The Gospel flings a sudden light athwart its blind and devious ways, and blocks its progress by a reversal of the universal law—the law that gives survival and success to the strongest. Nature is the religion of force, Christianity, the religion of Love. Nature approves the strong; Christianity covers the weak. The former selects the strong to confound the weak, the latter, in the very imperiousness of its greatness, sifts out the weak and makes of them vessels of election to confound the strong. And nations and individuals drift apart from Christianity and back to savage nature, in proportion as they elect to be proud, victorious, and triumphant, rather than humble, defeated and proscribed. For, in proportion as we accept the law of love, which is Christianity, and reject the law of self, which is Nature, in the same proportion do we cease to be our natural selves,— proud, grasping, and aggressive; and approach the Incarnate Idea of God, who was humble, gentle, and self-immolating.

XXIV.

I never understood why Dante placed Cato near the sedgy lake, and as guardian to the Mount of Purgatory, until I saw the line of Lucan :

Victrix causa deis placuit, sed victa Catoni.

I can sympathize with that. The patron of lost causes, the defender of failures, the foe of Cæsars and conquerors, must have possessed some innate and intrinsic nobility, almost too great for a Pagan. And this, too, at a time when Imperial domination was the dream of every Roman ; and the gods, it was believed, had given the universe into their hands. For, though it was the proud Roman boast that they always spared the conquered and reduced the proud, it was not their religion, nor their rule of conduct. To stand out from one's people or nation, to repudiate their principles, to defy their opinions, and strike out a new noble path for oneself —this is heroism   Perhaps, Dante goes a little far in his *Convito*, when he says. "What man on earth was more worthy to symbolize God than Cato?"   It is the hyperbole of admiration—the emphasis of art, as well as the science of argument   And this was a polemical question, because Dante was accused of a "perverse theology in saving the soul of an idolater and suicide." Yet, here as in all literature, Dante, in Cato, projected his own image. That "victa Catoni" must have appealed to his fancy, who worshipped lowliness in St. Francis; and, surely, he must have written down his own oft-repeated expression, when he placed in the mouth of Cato the words:

non c' è mestier lusinghe !

XXV.

Could any punishment be too great for that great critic in the great Quarterly, who boasted to Harriet Martineau, with a sardonic grin, that he was trying to squeeze out a little more (here he used the gesture) oil of vitriol on the head of a poor poet whose verses had unhappily fallen into his hands?   He said that he and his collaborateurs were rather disappointed because they could not squeeze as much of the burning fluid into their pens as they would like.   And one of them had the reputation of being especially humane in his sympathies , and wept copiously over Burns' address "To a Mouse"   I wonder how would that grim Rhadamanthus, Dante Alighieri, apportion them their places in his *Inferno*?   How would he equalize their punishment to their crime ?   Think of the sinking of heart, bitterness of the spirit, the longing for death, which that poor fellow felt when the cruel, stinging sarcasms met his eyes, and the burning drops fell slowly upon his soul !   How he yearned to hide himself from the world !   How he slunk through the streets, a shadow of shame, and dreaded to meet the eyes of men !   How his friends pitied him, and were ashamed of him , and how his enemies gloated over his discomfiture !   Yes! what would Dante have done with these criminals ?   I think I can imagine !

XXVI.

'And lo! we came unto a horrid lake, black as midnight seas, but still as a mountain pool, which sees naught but the eye of Heaven. Far away on the shore, a spirit doleful read a book, and his words came to us wearily, like the cry of a lonely bird that wings his way at twilight across the sedgy marshes between the city of the leaning tower and the sea. I turned to my Master and said: Sir, who might be this sad spirit, and why is he condemned to read alone unto this dreary and uninhabited lake? And he who had led me thither said Wait and behold! For here are punished the evil souls that in wantonness have wrought dire pain amongst their fellows And lo! as he spoke, the oily surface was agitated, and there appeared, struggling as if suffocated, the inky heads of the tormented. When they had shaken the thick blackness from their eyes, they stared at me and shrieked: Who art thou who comest to this place of torment before thy time? And I trembled all over like one seized with ague, and turned to my guide and said, Let us go hence! But my sweet master reassured me and said, Fear not, they cannot hurt thee! Then turning to them he said, Know you not, you unhappy ones, that I am he who sang at Mantua and Rome the travels of Anchises' son and the loves of the fated Queen, and this is he who sang of life and death, and heaven and hell? But these evil spirits, when they heard that we were poets, gave vent to a hideous howling, and tore their hair, and spat at us, and said: O evil children of an evil calling, why have ye come to torment us further? But my guide said: Be silent, ye unhappy ones; or if you must speak, tell us of your evil crimes and the sad destiny Minos hath appointed ye

XXVII

"And one, lifting himself above his fellows, whilst the inky fluid rolled down his shaggy breast, and he turned from side to side in grievous pain, said. O mortal and immortal, be it known to ye that we once lived in that fairest of European cities in the Hyperborean region, whose walls are washed by the salt waves of Forth, and over whose streets hangs the mighty keep where heroes were incarcerated   In an evil hour we took up our pens and dipped them in vitriolic acid, and poured the contents lavishly on the heads of an evil race of men, called poets.   There was no one to check us in our course of homicide; for all men feared us, and now, alas! we are condemned to this frightful punishment for our iniquities in the light   This lake of Stygian horrors in which we are immersed is a lake of printer's ink, worse ten thousand times than the fetid waters that float their bituminous and stinking waves above the fated cities.   Every half hour there drips from above a tiny rain of vitriol that burns our bald scalps, and streams into our eyes and blinds us; and we are compelled, ever and again, to eat and swallow and disgorge our own writings in the 'yellow and blue.' We had plunged beneath the Stygian waters, when you arrived at the shore, to escape the vitriolic shower, and now again it comes, it comes, oh ! most miserable of wretches we, to bite and burn and torment us.

XXVIII.

" And lo ! as the wretch spoke, I saw a mist gather above their heads, and a thick rain fell. I saw each drop alighting on their bald scalps, and burning a hideous blister there, until their faces ran with blood and fire, and they flung with their hands the inky fluid on their heads to cool the burning torments which they suffered, and then plunged in the slimy waters, and disappeared. And always the sad voice of the dreary poet droned out its clanging discord, and added dreariness of sound to misery of sight in that most unhappy place. Presently the one that interpreted the doleful plight of the other wretched souls, emerged from the slimy blackness; and wiping away the filth and blood from face and eyes, he said in a voice broken by despair, But, alas ! the worst remains to be told.   We could bear the fire and the foul blackness of this abominable pit, for we are a philosophic race, nurtured on a little oatmeal, and one gets inured to everything by habit   But, alas ! (and here his voice rose to a wail) we are also condemned to endure for ever the torture of seeing him who was our victim in the flesh, and of listening to his bad verses throughout eternity.

This is the most maddening of our sufferings; and vainly do we invoke Death, the friend of men, to liberate us   Will ye too listen and pity us?   And lo! the dreary voice, like the howling of the wind at midnight, came over the shuddering and shrinking lake, and my gentle guide turned and wept and said · Alas! this is too much! Hath it not been written:

> mediocribus esse poétis,
> Non homines, non Di, non concessere columnae?

And I, too, weeping turned away; and echoing the dreadful horror, I wrote of that sad poet, as of Cerberus ·—

> Graffia gli spirti, gli scuoia, ed isquarta."[1]

XXIX.

There is more of that subtle music, that carries sense through sound, in that last line than in any poetry outside of Homer. There are more onomatopœic lines in the latter; but for sheer and savage mercilessness, that line stands unmatched.   What a ferocious old Beresark he was!   How he plunges the spurs of his anger into the flanks of his enemies!   If it be true that he took his design for the *Divina Commedia* from St Patrick's Purgatory in Lough Derg, may it not also be true that he imitated the semi-pagan, wholly anti-Christian ferocity of the Irish bards, who exalted their friends to the heaven of heavens and smote their enemies even unto hell?   How could he that wrote that awful line quoted above, and the wail of trumpets hardened into stone in the "Per me si va's," in Canto III; and the thirty lines on Ugolino from *Ed io sente* downwards; and the dread six on Francesca—how could he also have written the last stanzas of the *Paradiso* with their clear farsight into the blisses of eternity, and their superhuman chastity in thought and word?   And yet it is not hard to conceive it.   It is these volcanic natures that pour out lava and scoriæ upon doomed cities and individuals, and, at the same time create for watchers in far-off climes sunsets, clothed in the colors of the Apocalypse—the despair of a Claude Lorraine or a Turner

[1] He rends the spirits, flays, and quarters them   *Inferno*, Canto VI.

XXX.

I know nothing so melancholy as that cenotaph of Dante in the Church of San Marco in Florence It is a perpetual act of contrition and humiliation on the part of that famous municipality; or it is a feeble attempt to clasp the shadow of him whose ashes repose in Ravenna One might condone the former sentiment, and pity the latter. Yet, it is something to see a great people doing penance through the centuries for the crime of their forefathers. It is the old story of aggression and hate triumphant for the moment, and then the Nemesis unsated, eternally dogging their footsteps For this is the one supreme consolation— that injustice, no matter how powerful and supreme, has ever but a temporary and a transient triumph; and that sooner or later the Fate comes hurrying on, veiled from head to foot, and stands silent by the side of the individual or the nation, never to be exorcised, never to be propitiated, until it has wrung out the last drop of retribution appointed by the unseen tribunal that judges the unit and the race What would not the Florentines give to-day to erase two pages from their history—the flame-scorched page of the holocaust of their monk, and the letter of expatriation, which drove their poet to exile and death !

Section II—XXXI.

Some fifty years after the great Florentine's death, there lived in an obscure street in Ravenna one of those artists in iron and brass, of which the towns in Italy then were full You may see their handiwork still in cathedral gates, in the iron fretwork around a shrine, in the gratings around the Sacramental altars in episcopal churches; and if you have not seen them, and entertain any lingering doubts, look up your Ruskin, and he will make you ashamed These were the days when men worked slowly and devoutly, conscious that work was prayer, and that they were laboring for the centuries, and not for mere passing bread We cannot do it now, for we toil in the workshops of Mammon, and neither *fames*, nor fame, can give the inspiration of that mother of art, called faith Well, this artist's name was Jacopo Secconi; and he had an only child, a daughter, whose name was Beatrice, called after the great poet who had made his last home at Ravenna The old man, for he was now old, never tired of speaking to his child of the great exile, and Bice never tired of questioning her father about Beatrice, and the wonders of Purgatory and Heaven. Once a month, however, a dark shadow would fall upon their threshold, a brother of Jacopo's, from Florence, who would come over to see his niece, for he loved her; but she did not love him For, after the midday meal, the conversation of the two brothers invariably turned upon Dante and Florence, and Dante and Ravenna No matter how it commenced, it veered steadily around to the everlasting topic, and on that they held directly contradictory views.

XXXII.

The Florentine stoutly maintained that Dante was in Hell, and eternally damned

"You say here," he would say, pointing his long finger, and sweeping the whole of Ravenna in a circle, "*Eccovi l'uomo che stato all' Inferno !* I say: *Eccovi l'uomo che sta all' Inferno !*"

"*Corpo di Bacco !*" the brother would exclaim, "you deserve to go thither yourself for such a saying God couldn't send such a man to Hell. He could not give such a triumph to Satan !"

"Dante hath sent priests and bishops and cardinals there," the brother would reply. "He hath filled its gloomy caverns with his enemies. He was vengeful and unforgiving. There is no place for such in Heaven !"

"I saw him here in exile," replied Jacopo, "when you, good Florentines, drove him out. I saw him walking our streets, a giave, solitary man. My father used point him out, and say: 'Look well, Jacopone, look well! That's a face that men will worship to the end of time !'"

"A bad, gloomy face, full of sourness and malice to God and man," the Florentine would reply.

"Presence of the Devil ! No, no, no !" cried Jacopo "But a great, solemn, marble face, chiselled as with a point of fire. I mind it well He used to pass our door, always looking forward and upward, his cloak slung around him, and the folded beret on

his head. Men used kneel down and kiss the pavement where
he had trod   God sent his angels and his Beatrice for him when
he died "

XXXIII.

"Pah!" would exclaim his brother   "That's a pious deceit.
There are only ten commandments, brother mine; and one of
these, the greatest : 'Thou shalt love !'   Believe me, your Dante
has read the *Lasciate* more than once since he died !"

"Then where could God put him?" shouted Jacopo.   "Did
He create another circle for him lower down ?   No! no!   God
does not damn such souls as Dante's!   I allow you he may be
in Purgatory for a short time, because we must all go thither for
our sins and imperfections.   But Dante damned!   All Heaven
would cry out against it!"

So the controversy would rage, month after month, and Bice
would listen with wondering, tearful eyes.   But she hated her
uncle cordially, and would refuse to kiss him when he went away.
And for days Jacopo would not be the same, but he swung to his
work in a moody, silent, abstracted way, and sometimes he would
pause, and wipe the sweat from his brow, and say to himself:

"Dante in Hell!   Yes, he was !   We all know that ; but he
is not.   I swear it   He is not!"

And he would bring down his hammer furiously upon the
iron ; and Bice, cooking the midday meal, would tremble and cry.

XXXIV.

But in the cool evening, when her work was done, and father
had had his supper, and was poring over the great black-letter
pages of his great poet, Bice would steal down to the little church
just around the corner, and pray long and earnestly.   For she
was a sweet, innocent child, and loved all things, but most of all
God, as the Supreme Beauty.   Then she played for the soul of
her good mother, who was dead; and lastly, she knelt before a
favorite Madonna, and, remembering her father's words, she prayed
long and earnestly for the dead poet.

"Abandoned and rejected in life," she said, "like all great souls, he must not be neglected in death. God may hear the prayers of a child for the mightiest soul He has made for centuries."

And she always prayed in the poet's own words, for they were as familiar as her *Pater Noster*, or *Ave Maria*, as no evening ever went by but she had to repeat one of the great cantos for her father. And so she used to pray:

Virgin Mother, daughter of thy Son, lowly and uplifted more than any creature, fixed goal of the eternal Counsel . . . . .

. . . .

Thy kindliness not only succoreth whoso requesteth, but doth often-times freely forerun request.

In thee is tenderness, in thee is pity, in thee munificence, in thee united whatever in created being is of excellence.

Now he who from the deepest pool of the universe even to here hath seen the spirit lives one after one,

Imploreth thee, of grace, for so much power as to be able to uplift his eyes more highly towards final bliss,

And I, who never burned for my own vision more than I do for his, proffer thee all the prayers, and pray they be not scant,

That thou do scatter for him every cloud of his mortality with prayers of thine, so that the joy supreme may be unfolded to him.

—*Canto XXXIII.*

XXXV.

Then, one soft summer evening, she fell asleep on the altar-steps immediately after her prayers, and she had a dream. She saw a great sea in the dawn-light, just waking up in the morning breeze, and fluted in long gentle plaits, that caught the pink light from the burning East. And lo! across the waters came a tiny boat, propelled neither by sail nor oar; and standing in the prow was a Soul,—the Soul of a Woman, resplendent as the sun, and glowing in its crystal transparency, for Bice saw the Morning Star through her vesture, as it lay low down in the horizon   And the boat and the Soul came towards the sleeping child, until the latter beckoned and said

"Come hither, O Child of Mercy, and enter with me   I have come for thee!"

And Bice said. "Who art thou?"

And the Soul answered: "I am the spirit of Beatrice.   I have been sent for thee."

And Bice answered: "I cannot go, for my father is old and feeble, and I may not leave him."

And the Soul said: "It is imperative that thou come; for thou alone holdest the keys of that place, where he, whom we love, is detained."

XXXVI.

And Bice entered; and they passed out over the shining waters that trembled beneath them, until they came to a shore, horrid with beetling crags, which seemed to touch the sky, and beneath whose feet the sea swelled and made no sound.   And they rode on the waves to the mouth of a gloomy cavern, vast and impenetrable, for the front was closed by a great iron gate, whose bars seemed red with fire, or the rust of eternity.   And behind the bars was the figure of the great poet, wrapped in his gloomy mantle as of old, and looking out over the shining sea with that same look of settled gloom and despair which Bice knew so well   And the Soul said:

"Go forward, and open the gate, and liberate our Beloved!"

But Bice wept, and said: "Alas!   How can I?   I am but a child, and the gate is heavy, and the task is grievous!"

XXXVII.

But the Soul said: "Loose the keys at thy girdle, and go forward!"

And Bice found two keys at her cincture, and she loosed them.   And one was marked "Charity," and it was of gold, and the other was of silver, and the word " Prayer " was stamped thereon   And going forward she fitted the former into the great rusty lock. The bolt shot backwards, but the gate would not yield   Then she fitted the silver key, and lo ! the great iron barrier swung back heavily. And entering, the child caught the poet's hand, and drew him forth   And the gate swung back with horrid clangor. And, entering the boat, the three sped forward rapidly towards the dawn, which is infinity, which is heaven   And the poet, placing his hand on the child's head, said sweetly and solemnly

"Thrice blessed art thou, thou second Beatrice, for lo ! what my Beatrice accomplished but in vision, thou hast verily wrought ! "

.   .   .   .

" How now ? how now ? giovanetta mia ! " said the aged sacristan, as he rattled his keys above the sleeping child. " What a strange couch hast thou chosen ! But sleep comes lightly to the young *Surge ! filia ! benedicamus Domino !* " he shouted

He bent low and raised the face of the sleeping child.

" Jesu ! Maria ! but she is dead ! "

XXXVIII

Even a philosopher cannot resist the temptation to sacrifice truth to an epigram   Even the mystical Schelling, perhaps because he was so mystical, could not resist the temptation. The reign of dogma, he says, that is, the religion of St. Peter, lasted up to the period of the German Reformation; the reign of grace, the religion of St. Paul, has continued from that time until now. Both are now superseded, and the time has come for the reign of Love, the religion of St John. The first two clauses of the epigram are absurd and untrue   We wish we could say the reverse of the last, but the time has not come. And, alas! the three clauses of the proposition are mutually contradictory and, therefore, unacceptable. If it were true that dogma had disappeared (the hope of all modern agnosticism), charity should disappear with it, for all charity is founded on dogma—the sublime one that charity is charity, because God has ordained it amongst men, as a reflection of His own perfection So, too, if grace disappeared, charity would likewise vanish, for it is not by Nature, which is rapine, we love; but by grace, which compels Nature into its own sweet ways, and files its teeth and claws. But it will be a great day for Humanity, when from pole to pole, and from zone to zone, the great brotherhood, and not the common brutehood of the race is proclaimed; and all the world's weapons of war are piled at the foot of the Cross, never again to be assumed for aggression or defence; for the former will be unknown and the latter unnecessary.

XXXIX.

All the world's great thinkers have been dreaming of this millennium of love Philosophers have defined what it shall be. Its foundation, its internal economy, its laws and institutions, its administration and executive—they have arranged all, there in their studies and laboratories. Every ethical system framed by great thinkers, from Aristotle to Spinoza, from Spinoza to Herbert Spencer, is constructed with a view to the establishment of this Republic of Mankind. Poets dream of it, limn all its beautiful features, chant its triumphs. Shelley visioned it as built upon cloud foundations, with walls of jasper, and ceilings of sapphire, and floors of chalcedony. Tennyson dreamed it more prosaically.

" When the war-drums throb no longer, and the battle-flags are furled
  In the Parliament of men, the Federation of the World."

Political economists strain their eyes towards the far vision, and every theory, Malthusian and other, is directed towards its final fulfilment. Philanthropists and Christian Socialists build this commonwealth in miniature, and " Brook Farms " and Mormon settlements are the temporary embodiments of this idea that is haunting humanity. Meanwhile the world wags on as usual. There is the same inequality in life's conditions, the same chasm between the rich and the poor, only ever deepening and ever widening in the process of the suns; the same poverty and squalor, the same disease and crime. And the battle-drums are rolling, and the rifles are barking as of yore. But the battle-flags are furled, not in the sleep of peace; but the all-grasping belligerent races, whilst coveting everything, have grown economical—in silk and honor!

XL.

And yet the solution of the problem, the realization of the dream, lie beneath men's hands, if men's eyes could only see them. But, as a sick man will have recourse to every kind of quackery, but refuse legitimate and certain remedies, so this civilization of ours, sick unto death, swallows every nostrum of charlatanry, and rejects the one infallible remedy. That remedy could never have been discovered by men. It is the revelation of God. It lies in the voluntary sacrifice of the individual for the sake of the community; in the sacrifice of the class for the welfare of a nation; in the sacrifice of the nation for the benefit of a race, in the sacrifice of a race for the welfare of mankind. But so long as the individual is self-seeking, and the nations strain for self-aggrandizement; and man's life is not a labor according to the primal curse, which is its eternal blessing, but a warfare, with the victory to the strongest, so long will the evolution of the race go forward, not towards final perfection, evolution from the survival of the fittest, but towards final destruction with the elimination of all that is sweetest and most beautiful. And yet, in its fiercest and most aggressive spirit, the world would hardly choose to go back to Beresarks and Vikings, to Alarics and Attilas! Yet, thitherwards most surely it is tending, in that neo-heathenism which sings the soft hymns of Christianity whilst pursuing its pagan career of conquest and aggression.

XLI.

But here comes in the complex question: Can the really humble rule? And must there not be the pride of strength in those who are called to govern? The question concerns individuals, limited communities, whole nations. Is humility, self-effacement, a qualification for the father of a family, the superior of a

religious house, the captain of a great army, the premier of a
world-ruling parliament? If it is, there seems to be no power of
ruling, which means the enforcement of one's own will on the will
of others A family, a community, a commonwealth, without a
strong, self-reliant hand to guide it, lapses into anarchy. On the
other hand, how can humility consist with the absolute exercise
of unlimited power? The problem may be put in other terms We
have seen how the world, and our lower nature, worship strength,
even brute strength We all admire the famous Abbot Sampson,
who reduced an unruly community to order, defied a king, in-
sisted on the rights of his order, braved force from without and
rebellion from within In our own days, the same hand that canonized Abbot Sampson deified Oliver Cromwell Yet, if ever there
was a brute, it was this latter adventurer. Say what we like, the
vast majority of mankind worship brute force. " We like a strong
man," is the cry of every one But it is the cry of a low nature,
still akin to the brute and the serpent; or it is the norm and
standard demand of an advanced and perfected civilization

XLII.

On the other hand, gentle, refined natures love simple and
lowly lives, and humble and pleading actions. That sentence in
the " Sentimental Journey," in which Sterne depicts his own feelings, when the shamed Franciscan monk turned away and looked
down at his brown, threadbare sleeve, finds a responsive echo in
all human hearts. The characters in the novels of that great
dramatist, Dickens, which appeal most to our sympathy and love,
are such humble beings as Tom Pinch, and Little Nell, and Little
Dorrit, and Florence Dombey, and Peggotty, etc. Ah, yes! but
that is fiction Precisely. But if we met these gentle, pleading
beings in real life, would we feel similarly towards them? Yes, if
we were like them, not otherwise. If we were simple, and lowly,
and gentle, we would love them in flesh and blood, as well as we
love their spectral forms in literature But if we were base and
ignoble, if we worshipped strength and distinction, we would
despise them heartily as beneath us. Why? Because, in the
solitude of our rooms we have no eye of public opinion upon us

to rebuke us for our weakness in loving the weak. But, with the Argus eyes of society upon us, it would be a grave test of our integrity to walk a crowded street with the ragged companion of our school-days , or to stand up in a heated ball-room with the homely rustic, and face a hundred eyes of criticism and contempt

XLIII.

But the really humble can rule, and can rule with firmness and success, if unaggressive. There is a world of difference between strength and aggression, between power and the pride of power. It is the sheathed strength, that underlies all real humility, which we worship. And it will invariably be found that those meek, yielding characters, who never assert themselves, who willingly efface themselves, exhibit the fortitude of endurance and the swiftness of strong resource, when in crises of life and death, great personal or state emergencies, such qualities of mind and soul are demanded by the exigencies of the weak, or the panic of the pretentious and the boastful. And, if raised to power by the suffrages of subjects, or the command of some higher authority, they invariably develop unsuspected resources of spiritual strength and agility ; whilst their sense of humility and self-nothingness prevents them from infringing on the rights of the weak. They can be imperative without being aggressive. They can guide without hurting. They can stretch forth the shepherd's crook and lead into line the vagrant and the self-willed without plucking one wisp of wool or forcing one pitiful bleat. And they are content to govern and guide their own without throwing covetous eyes on alien property , or seeking in some reflex axiom, which is generally an unacknowledged sophism, an excuse for conquest or aggression.

XLIV.

Indeed, if we look close, we shall find that it is the Omnipotence of Christ, even more than His Mercy, that enchained the multitude and kept close to Him His most capricious disciples. "Show us a sign," was the cry of the curious and selfish mob. If

our Lord had merely preached, He would have left no converts.
If He had wrought miracles without having preached, He would
have bequeathed to us no Gospel   It is His power that prevails.
"He hath done all things well"   It is His positive, dogmatic,
assertive teaching that convinces   "Surely man never spake like
this Man." The multitude wondered and worshipped. The chosen
ones worshipped and loved. And we, in the far-off times, we, too,
are entrained amongst His worshippers and lovers, because we
feel that here is Omnipotence, and that when all things else are
as fragile as a broken reed, we can fall back upon and lean our
weakness on the unyielding strength of Jesus Christ   And this
awful commanding power was so unaggressive. He smote no one
—He coveted nothing   "Put up thy sword." It is the Meek and
the Lowly One, who holds in leash the elements of invincible
might, that commands that instinct of admiration, which as well
as pity is the first condition of love.

XLV.

And yet, while we wonder at and worship His invincible power,
it is the consciousness of its possession, rather than its arbitrary
exercise, that demands our admiration. It is the reticence in
speech, and the restraint in action, that we adore. And this exquisite self-balancing, this absence of all passion, the submission
to calmness and reason, under the greatest provocation, were
manifested towards His brethren more conspicuously than towards
His Jewish enemies.

I know nothing more pathetic than that sentence of the Evangelist: "He rebuked their incredulity." When ? Just as He was
about to ascend into Heaven   Incredulity at such a moment, and
after such experience !

Alas! yes   They had seen Him put forth proof after proof
of His Divinity in His many and marvellous miracles; they had
seen the wonder of His Death, and the splendors of His Resurrection; they had marvelled at His divine equanimity, and it is
not difficult to imagine their looks of bewildered admiration, curiosity, and doubt, as they saw to-day proofs of His Godhead, and
to-morrow evidences of His Manhood, He had appeared to them

again and again after His Resurrection, spoken to them, eaten
with them, to prove He was no spirit. And yet, weak and in-
credulous to the last moment, they stared at Him, there on the
hillside of Olivet, with mute, blank, unintelligent wonder, until He
was obliged to repeat that old formula of His pity and sorrow,
" *O stulti et tardi corde ! Quousque ! Quousque?* " He rebuked
their incredulity; and then—a cloud hid Him from their sight.

XLVI.

Paganism conquered by aggression. Christianity conquers
by submission, and her victories are more lasting. Attila and
Leo, Gregory and Henry, Napoleon and Pius VII; Bismarck
and Pius IX. What mighty duellists they were; and how the
feeble priests, in the end, by the might that is from above, prevailed over the mail-clad warriors, with their legions behind them.
Yes! the end is always certain: victory is to the just. But what
almost infinite patience is required to watch for that end, and to
be satisfied with the fruition of victory! For one naturally argues:
Can victory give back all that we have lost by being unjustly as-
sailed? Can it recompense us for the weary suspense, the sleep-
less anxiety, the bruised feelings, the ignominy, the shame, the
sorrow? And, on the other hand, will a mere black mark in the
judgment-roll of History be accounted sufficient retribution for
pride, injustice, and aggression? Doth not the whole man arise
in protest against wrong? And is there not something fiercer in
the human heart in its revolt against injustice than the plaintive
wail of the .exiled Pontiff: " I have loved justice, and hated iniquity; therefore I die in exile "?

XLVII.

Human nature is unchangeable; and to-day there are few who
have been in contact with men, that do not suffer an almost irresistible temptation to despise them The law of rapine, which is
self, so predominates amongst them, their little souls are held in
leash by so fragile a tenement; their time is so short; and they
play their wretched little parts so badly, that one is tempted to

hiss the whole company from the stage forever   Human history
is but a record of human weakness and brutality.   The Cross has
been planted in the Coliseum, but the evil spirits that lashed with
lust and fury the sixty thousand spectators, who seemed to drink
with their eyes the blood of their victims, have sought better-
swept and cleaner places   But they are by no means exorcised
or banished from the earth   Let the battlefields of the world, the
cries of the oppressed, pæans of the victors, the broken hearts, the
wrecked lives, testify to it.   What then?   Are we to grow impatient with these little minnies?   Are we to dream of a greater and
stronger and more spiritual race than we behold on our planet?
Perhaps so!   Yet it would be better to restrain our judgments,
and imitate "the soft yearnings of infinite pity," conscious that
the key to the mystery of so much meanness and so much weakness is somewhere.   "Tout comprendre c'est tout pardonner!"

XLVIII.

It is this divine resemblance to the toleration of His Father,
this reflex of divine magnanimity that should put all question of
our Lord's Divinity quite outside the pale of controversy.   He
was amongst men, but not of them.   Their querulousness, their
jealousy, their doubts, their powerlessness to lift themselves above
the merely human are perpetuated in human lives to this day;
and are not the characteristics of any race or nation, but are
the common and universal inheritance of all.   Yet, how calmly
God looks down not only upon this provoking meanness and
littleness, but even more, upon the mighty mass of iniquity
that seethes in great cities and in country hamlets, and steams
up a sickening holocaust before His throne!   And how infinite
is His toleration and even benevolence in view of such ingrati-
tude, for His times and seasons revolve as if earth were an altar
of sweet-smelling sacrifice, and His sun shines, and His dews fall
alike on the saint and sinner!   Behold the patience and love of
our Lord reflected in the larger operations of His Father!   No
wonder that men should say. He hath done all things well!   No
wonder that the lonely prisoner in St. Helena, once the Impera-
tor and world Cæsar, should exclaim: "I know men well; and I
say that Jesus Christ was not a man!"

XLIX

On passing to and from the schools these spring days, I saw a strange and pathetic sight. Our Irish boys are passionately fond of birds and dogs, and beneath the thatched eaves of the simple cabins you may count by the dozen goldfinches and linnets, seemingly happy in their captivity, as they jump from perch to perch and trill out their little melodies. Occasionally, some more ambitious youngster, generally a shoemaker, has a large wicker cage outside his door, where a brown thrush, or a red-beaked blackbird wakens up the whole neighborhood these lovely mornings with his melody "He's as good as the chapel-bell, to call people to Mass," says an old woman, admiringly. But in one cage was a solitary prisoner, and he was mute. Crouched in a corner of his prison on a sod of grass, which was once wet and dewy and sweet, but is now dry and sodden, he sat in one posture day by day, silent, dreaming, miserable, with his large, beaded, black eyes steadily gazing upwards to the sky. It was a picture of misery that nothing could extenuate or relieve He could not be frightened You might touch him, and he would not move or flutter aside. He took no notice of the lesser souls in the adjoining cages, who hugged their captivity, and sang their little songs of Sion for their masters. He felt his chains galling him, and the thoughts of freedom maddened him. It was a captive lark.

L.

His thoughts were as readable as print You could see of what he was dreaming—the dewy meadow, the deep, round, warm nest, the fragrant cowslip bending over it, the sweet-scented hay all around, the daisy and the harebell, and the long lush grass, and jets of matin song springing up all around him, and far up in the sky, as if Mother Nature from her teeming breasts sent up fountain after fountain of musical spray, and seemed to bathe the clouds with melody. And the light of morning and the awakening, the first spring upwards into the cool, clean air, the beating and fluttering of wings, and then the clear carol, growing in shrillness and varied cadences every moment as the exuberance

of life intoxicated him and he felt new pulsations as of an emancipated spirit, as he mounted higher and higher towards the infinite azure, till he was lost in a cloud and his song was extinguished for a moment, only to be revived as he approached earth
again, and saw far beneath him his little home, and carolled to
his brown mate or the little ones whose yellow beaks opened
towards the Hand that feeds all His creation; and then one
sudden plunge sideways, lest evil eyes should discover his little
home in the universe, and a final creep back to home and warmth
and the life of little loves and cares again! And here, ah, yes!
here were the wicker bars, as stout against freedom as if they
were iron, and there is the narrow roof above him; and here
beneath is the mockery of meadow-grass and flowers, and fragrance, and freedom, and delight!

LI.

It was too bad! I watched him three mornings in succession,
and then determined to give him his liberty.

"Why doesn't the lark sing?" I said to the young barbarian
who had captured him

"He isn't used to the cage a-yet," he replied

"And will he sing when he gets used to it?" I asked.

"He will," said the captor

"What's the use of that dry sod?" I said

"He thinks 'tis his nist," said he

"I'm going to liberate that bird," I said. He set up a pillalu,
which is a fair equivalent for the most dismal howl that ever
emanated from human lips.

"Never mind, I'll pay you," I said "Bring that cage and bird
down to my garden at once"

He did so reluctantly and wonderingly. We placed the cage
in the midst of the flower-plots. The lark woke up to a new life.
I opened the wicker gate and stood aside The poor little prisoner
gazed at the avenue to freedom, incredulously it seemed, for he
appeared reluctant to take advantage of it. Then tentatively he
hopped on to the threshold of his prison, looked dubiously around.
Then, with one swift flutter of his wings, he shot like a meteor
over my garden wall

" He's gone," said the boy, as if he doubted his senses.

" Yes," I said. " How would you like to be in gaol ? " The thought never struck him before, for he appeared ashamed of himself   He took up the cage dubiously, and, as if conscious that he had no right to a reward, but rather to a whipping, he was going away in a repentant mood   I called him back

" You haven't waited for your money ? " I said   He was silent, I handed him a half-crown.   It broke the spell of repentance. I saw him put it deep down in his pocket and hold it fast there, with one hand, whilst he swung the empty cage in the other. Then he winked with his right eye at some imaginary individual, and then with his left

" Look here ! " I cried.

He became suddenly demure and impassive.   " If ever again you capture and imprison a skylark, I'll take the half-crown's worth of licking out of you.   Do you understand ? "

He said he did, and I believed him.

LII.

Then I gave myself up to thinking and dreaming of what the poor bird felt on his release from captivity.   I knew that for the rest of the evening he would be so dazed with his sudden recovery of liberty that he could neither sing, nor fly, nor even seek his food, but would hide deep down in the young grass, and think and ponder and wonder if it were true.   But next morning, ah me ! the first shock of waking in the belief that he was yet in captivity ; the disbelief in his priceless privilege of freedom ; the fear of using his wings lest he should dash himself against his prison walls, the sudden rush of emotion on finding that he *was* free, the little tentative flights, to prove the new privilege ; the momentary jealousy of his mates, as they sprang upwards in the morning sunlight ; and then one swift, exultant spring into the air, the palpitation of his wings, as they struck madly for strength to mount into the empyrean, one or two little chirruped prologues ; and then a great stream of exultant melody, as he mounts higher and higher into the blue dome above him, and earth recedes beneath ; and up, up, up into the white bosom of a cloud, till he becomes a "sightless song," and is intoxicated with the raptures of life and love and freedom.   And then the slower return homeward, down, down, still making melodious music from his overflowing heart, and closing the little matin programme with a silver tremolo, as he looks eagerly around for his little bed in the lush grass, and hovers and sinks at last into his new life of freedom, and happiness, and love !

LIII.

It is a wonderful thing—that same freedom, or, to use a more classical term—Liberty   It is always first in the programme of existent or aspiring nationalities   Poets have hymned it, orators glorified it, artists embodied it, as the right indefeasible, the privilege inadmissible, of humanity.   And yet, between liberty and tyranny, how thin the dividing line !   How easily the divine and the dæmonic merge in each other !   How swiftly the Phrygian cap passes under the guillotine, and the pikes of Liberty are hammered into the sword of conquest and aggression !   No !   There are but two classes of humanity—the aggressors and the aggressed !   The slave of to-day becomes the tyrant of to-morrow.   Poor Rouget de Lisle !

> "Liberté, Liberté, chérie,
>   Combats avec tes defenseurs "

The goddess came at his beck, and almost led him to the scaffold. And the defenders of Freedom became destroyers of Freedom from end to end of Europe   The fact is, there is no such deity as Liberty   It is a dream of the race, especially of poets and humanitarians.   So long as human nature remains what it is, the weak will be oppressed by the strong, and the cries of a Poland, or an Ireland, will sound in the ears of a conquering world, as the cracking of bones and the moans of victims beneath the artillery wagons of Napoleon were lost in the ears of the ribboned Conqueror, who only heard the *Vive l'Empereur !* of his own dying veterans.

LIV.

Individual liberties, too, scarcely exist in the most professedly independent state. Every man has a hundred masters The laws of his country hedge him around on every side; and these laws are very often oppressive and unjust The employment or profession in which he is engaged has a hundred restrictions on his freedom. The circle of society in which he moves draws its silent and tacit legislation around him, ever fretting him into mute and servile obedience; the press frames his opinion for him, and he bows like a slave to its behests, his family ties bind him with withes of straw that are strong as iron fetters, his actions are controlled by his doctor, his agent, his broker, his wife, his child; his tongue is governed by all the minute and silent legislation that regulates the "minor moralities" of life; his very dress is ordered according to an imperative fashion; his gait is guided by law; his speech must be attuned to regulations, as arbitrary as they are absurd; and the only sensation of freedom he ever feels is when down by the seaside for a week or two of emancipation from the treadmills of life he flings himself in his shirt-sleeves upon the heather above the sea, stretches his arms, and cries Heigh-ho! lights a cigar, and declares in the teeth of an angry civilization that he *will* be a boy for at least one hour of his weary life!

LV.

Do you remember who was that fine poet—and, if I mistake not, he was a great one, too—who used to fly from the tyranny of civilization once a year to the remotest seaside village in Cornwall and there abandon himself to absolute, unrestricted freedom ? I remember how it struck me—his delightful habit before bathing, of burying himself deep in the warm sand and remaining in that gritty bath for an hour or so, and then plunging into the cool breakers and taking his douche after the improvised Turkish—primitive, unrestricted, free No handing up of watches and coins to the proprietor, no turning in on the burning tiles, no cadaverous or swollen humanities around you ; no *masseur* to pound you into jelly. But Nature! dear old mother and nurse, combining all in her own dear old self, and doing her work without fee or reward. But I think he said it was the sense of absolute freedom that made the experience an ecstasy—the thought that there was no one within miles of you, that the Sunday tripper had never come hither, that there were no bands, no Christy Minstrels, no Pierrots or Pierrottes, no stripping and dressing ten times a day; and, above all, no staring, wondering, insolent eye to gauge and measure you, but the blue eye of heaven, and the " unnumbered laughter " of the deep, and all the wild, free, savage, beautiful things that haunt solitude, and flee from civilization.

LVI.

I can thoroughly sympathize with Henry Thoreau; and I cannot think he was a madman. Emerson believed in him, and that counts for much   But I can easily understand his raptures in the loneliness of his lake-home, just as I can easily understand the delights that thronged around the daily lives of the great hermits or cænobites of old   In fact, all great souls love solitude; and if old Burton does warn us against it, mark, he puts solitude and idleness together, and they are by no means essential companions.   Just as Emerson found that the best place for lonely, uninterrupted work was a front chamber in a New York hotel, so it may be that a solitary life would have great cares and great labors, although apparently free from the ordinary distractions of humanity   But it may be a question whether the absolute freedom of the desert is a fair exchange for the more convenient tyranny of civilization. Yes! Rousseau won't do! We cannot go back to barbarism   If there be one thing more certain than another it is that we cannot put back the hand on the dial   Last evening, I was telling an old priest how I had sped to Dublin the week before—144 miles in three hours   " I remember well," he said, " when it took me three days, and on the outside of a coach, in winter, travelling night and day, with bad meals, and many stops. It was not pleasant." " But," I said, " you were all the better and happier for the experience. You were a strong generation, and could call on Nature freely. We are weaklings" — He looked at me in such a way that I did not pursue the subject

LVII.

What a singular thing it is, that the world's greatest literature is tinged with melancholy! All deep thought is sombre thought. Sadness is the handmaiden of philosophy. What a low, sad wail seems to moan all through the historical books and psalms of the Old Testament, until it culminates in the woes and desolation of Isaias, when " Moab shall howl to Moab," and " I will lament with the weeping of Iazer the vineyard of Sabama ; and water thee with my tears, O Hesebon, and Eleale ! " And then, at its culmination, it passes on to the terrors of Ezechiel, and the threnodies of Jeremias, and seems to die away in the burden of the weeping of the wind in the minor prophecies of Amos and Aggaeus And even in the New Testament, the testament of love and mercy, the same sadness predominates. The thunders of John the Baptist, fresh from the deserts of Bashan, subside to the " soft wailings of infinite pity" of Him of whom he was Precursor and Prophet; until they, too, grow and swell into that terrible *crescendo* that startled the darkness of Golgotha, and broke into the final cry of desolation · " Eloi, Eloi, lamma Sabacthani ! " So, too, in the Epistles of St. Paul, if we meet here and there with a " Gaudete, item dico, gaudete !" somehow or other, it seems forced by the pity and charity of the great saint for his followers. The truer expression of his habitual sentiments would be : " Cupio dissolvi, et esse cum Christo ! "

LVIII.

The Homeric ballads, too, commence with a tragedy, and seem to ring with defeat Βῆ δ'ἀκέων moves on to that strange line :

Αἱ μὲν ἔτι ζωὸν γόον Ἑκτορα ᾧ ἐνί οἴκῳ

Again, all the great Greek drama is tragical with its eternal lesson of Nemesis dogging the feet of crime. The grinning face of Aristophanes seems as much out of place in Grecian literature as that of a mimic in a house of mourning. The more modern Virgilian verse, too, sweeps on in a great dark torrent, with Sybils and Parcæ here and there, foretelling or compassing the ruin of nations

and individuals; and the lighter poets, such as Horace or Catul-
lus, drift into the same melancholy the moment they take the
bowl from their lips, and commence to philosophize.   What shall
we say of the melancholy of Dante and Milton, of the genius of
Shakspere best manifested in such successions of horrors as are
depicted in Othello, Macbeth, Hamlet, and Lear ?   How the
same note obtains in all the pages of Tennyson, and permeates
all the poetry of Matthew Arnold, that truest interpreter of the
modern infelicity and weariness of life —

> And then we suffer, and amongst us one,
> Who most has suffered, takes dejectedly
> His seat upon the intellectual throne;
> And all his store of sad experience he
>   Lays bare of wretched days;
> Tells us his misery's birth and growth and signs,
> And how the dying spark of hope was fed,
> And how the breast was soothed, how the head,
> And all his hourly varied anodynes.

LIX.

There was some meaning, then, in that half-comical remark
of his cheerful friend to the melancholy Johnson: "You are a
philosopher, Dr. Johnson.   I have tried, too, in my time, to be a
philosopher, but, I don't know how, cheerfulness was always
breaking in."   That's just it!   Cheerfulness and philosophy won't
go hand in hand.   The moment you think, you begin to sink;
just as a swimmer afloat on the surface of the water has to struggle
to save himself from sinking, if he attempts to draw the least
breath.   "The weight and burden of all this unintelligible world"
is too much for us   We can only bear it by not thinking of it
Just as physical agony is not only tolerable, but actually forgotten,
the moment the mind is abstracted by sleep, or greater absorption,
or an anæsthetic; so, if life is to be happy and pleasurable, we
must cease to view it too closely, or to watch too minutely the
ticking away of time, or the varied pulsations of everyday experience.   Of course, there is a class set apart for these things—those

"intellectually throned"; they *must* suffer, but probably they have
their reward   For ordinary mortals, it is wisest to face the little
drama of each day with hopeful hearts, perform its duties, enjoy
its pleasures, suffer its trials; and place the sum-total at the feet
of Him who is the dramatic Censor of all the alternate tragedy
and comedy into which life is divided.

LX

It has been said, too, that the reading of a great book has a
tendency to make the reader gloomy and despondent   Probably
it puts so high an ideal before him that he becomes quite discontented with the humdrum existence around him, and passes gradually from a first feeling of discontent to one of self-contempt, and
a grave undervaluing of all that he had esteemed in others.   It is
a grave disturbance of homely, happy thoughts and customs that
were pursued with a certain feeling of satisfaction that there was
no obligation to reach higher.   There is, of course, a certain
exhilaration in feeling that we have seized on higher possibilities,
and lighted ourselves to a higher plane.   But then we bid good-
bye to the pleasant valleys beneath us, where in humble associations and with very commonplace views of life we had managed
to jog along pleasantly through the greater part of life.   Here, too,
are there compensation and loss, the eternal interchange between
the positive and negative forces of life.   For high thought we have
to sacrifice lowly pleasures; for exaltation of mind we have to
yield up content, and whether the exchange is to our profit we
shall never determine   But we must go on; there is no halting,
unless we wish to be crushed or pushed aside, or be faithless to
our vocation.

LXI

We had a big fire, last night.   Something mysterious woke me
up from a deep sleep just as the clock was chiming midnight.   It
was some time before I could gather my thoughts together   Then
I noticed a curious light, palpitating against the blind of my
northern window   I thought it was the moon, but instantly

remembered that the moon never appears in the northern horizon, and that the moon shines steadily, and not with this pulsating light   I rose up, and raised the blind.   Across the river, and not two hundred yards away, the mill, a vast building, six stories high, built as a flour mill, years before American competition drove Irish flour even from Irish markets, was on fire   Every coign and crevice was caught in the flames, which leaped through its seventy windows and reared themselves thirty feet above the roof.   I could feel the heat in my bedroom, but could not hear a sound   The wind blew from the east, and carried the roar of the conflagration far out to the west, and over the river and beyond the trees   Not a soul was stirring, although the single street was lighted as if by a hundred electric arcs.   The very dogs, which never cease barking on ordinary nights, were silent. I was anxious for my stables, and when I found these were safe, I roused the village.   It was no easy task.   They slept the sleep of innocence and exhaustion.   Then they grew alarmed, and no wonder, for half the village is thatched, and nothing could have saved it if the wind blew from the north or west.

LXII.

As it was, there was but one building imperilled, and that was the Convent, which lay right in the track of the burning debris that was flung high in the air from the seething cauldron beneath, and was then caught by the wind, and carried hundreds of yards in a westerly direction.   We could see great flakes of fire falling on the Convent roofs, and lodging in the branches of the trees around   It seemed only a matter of minutes before the whole building would be wrapped in fire and smoke.   There were plenty of willing hands to help, however; and, although they had to dodge the burning flakes of slate and timber that fell noiselessly upon the grass, they soon extinguished the burning fragments on roof and trees; and, in a few minutes, all danger was over.   I returned home; and, as there was no possibility of sleep with such a conflagration lighting up the heavens and the earth, I went up into my garden, and sat down, and watched the flowers under that light I should probably never see again.

LXIII

There was no color, but a kind of soft brown atmosphere over all This was the reflection flung downwards from the heavy clouds overhead, which now were reddened as in a winter sunset, when the light falls lurid and glaring, and the angry sky forebodes stormy weather. The shadows were deep and black; but, in the open this strange color hung down over all the garden-beds and tinted hyacinth, tulip, and daffodil in the same monastic and uniform tints. Then, early in that spring morning, I noticed for the first time the meekness of the flowers It had never struck me before. Now, they looked like little children awakened from sleep under a sudden terror; and they seemed so helpless, so gentle, there whilst the horrors of the conflagration were round about them, and the roar and the flame were startling all the darkness of the night. I remained there till the faint Spring dawn lit up the eastern sky, and in a few moments dulled and almost extinguished the splendors of the furnace that had now become a well of redhot metals and stones. Presently, the sun arose; and all the flowers began to turn their gentle and wistful faces towards him It was as the face of a mother bending over the cradle of children awakened in terror of the night.

SECTION III.—LXIV.

I have often studied that curious aspect of gentleness and meekness in flowers of which I have made mention before Here, and here alone, is the lie given direct to the poet :

For Nature is one with rapine.

Whatever be said of bird, beast, fish, or insect, of which it may perhaps be true that they subsist by plunder and violence, here is the great exception A little water and a little air, and behold! they perform their part in the universe of things, and not an unimportant part, if beauty and fragrance are essential ends in that great evolution that works upwards from the clod to the star. And not only are they unaggressive, but they are infinitely forbearing and long-suffering. Sky and earth and air combine against them ; and they suffer all meekly. The angry and wanton winds toss them to and fro, the fierce whips of the rain lash them, till they droop their meek heads, and weep like chidden children ; the teeming earth sends up its little parasites, that heedless of beauty nestle beneath the loveliest leaf or stamen, and consume its vitality. There is no defence and no protest It is as if an acid were flung on a panel by Angelico, or a Murillo exposed to sun and rain

But no angry remonstrance arises from Man or Nature. The great mother is so prolific of her beauties, that no one heeds the prodigality and waste.

LXV.

It is true indeed that there are carnivorous plants beneath the tropics, and upas-leaves of death beneath which the tiny animal creation, so destructive of flowers in temperate climates, suffer retributive justice from their victims. But then, everything is made fierce by that terrible tropical sun ; and the meekest things forego their natural inclinations beneath his maddening influences It is also true, I am told by experts, that the most gentle-seeming flowers exhale a poisonous, miasmatic breath, so that their sisters droop beneath their aromatic, but treacherous breathing But these are exceptions, proving that the fairest things may be the most deadly; and that, as we so often read in the histories of men, death may lurk in the vintage of the Apennines, sparkling through Venetian crystal But I only speak of what I know, and that is that flowers are the fairest and gentlest things the Hand of God hath fashioned from His elements of Nature, and one would almost hope they had souls to be reborn forever in the sunlit valleys of Paradise.

LXVI

One thing also I never realized before,—and that was the terrific beauty and loveliness of fire. Dealing with it in ordinary life, it is, I suppose, too much of a slave to us to command our admiration It is only when it starts up and assumes the mastership, that we recognize its majestic, if destructive power It is as if a company of galley-slaves broke their bounds, and carried ruin and terror all along before them ; then fell down lifeless under the ruin they had made   But it is a mighty element—all the more to be dreaded, because it is latent, yet operative everywhere —nay, it is the great central energy which everywhere works through space.   That blue jet of flame in my grate is lighted by the sun , and it is diluted but real sun-force that lights this paper which I am just now darkening   The same mysterious power has bleached the linen in my sleeve, and browned the cuticle of my hand.   It has cooked that meat before me, and enamelled the plate on which it lies.   It built the temples of the gods in Persia, for itself was the deity worshipped ; and in the Irish valleys it raised these dolmens and cromlechs that have withstood the storms of three thousand years

LXVII

But if you would like to trace this mighty element, not on the earth, where its footsteps are so deeply impressed , but even in the Heaven of Heavens, and through even immaterial things, such as human thought and the soul of man, up through the tortuous paths of philosophy, and even to the throne of the Eternal, read that wonderful treatise of Bishop Berkeley's, which he quaintly calls *Siris*   Here he takes you from the exudations of the pine-tree to their latent energies; from these to their source, the Sun , thence to Light and Fire, real and symbolical , thence to first principles of Being, to first objects of worship; thence to Chaldæan religions and Persian fire-temples ; or through Platonism to the Hebrew Prophecies and Psalms, where fire has always figured largely as symbol, as vesture, as metaphor ; thence, again, through Pagan adumbrations of the Trinity up to the great central mystery of Creation, until in the highest altitudes of thought, he suddenly remembers its origin, and goes back to the homely virtues of tar-water.

LXVIII.

Is there a more pathetic scene in literary biography than that which took place between Berkeley and Malebranche in the cell of the Oratorian in Paris? The fine old priest, with his wonderful ideas about God, bending over the pipkin on the fire that held the decoction that was to cure the inflammation of the lungs from which he was suffering ; and the grave English philosopher, with his new idealism occupying every cranny and nook of his brain! Malebranche could not accept such visionary notions as an explanation of the mystery of Being, and argued, reasoned, expostulated, whilst he stirred the medicine in the pipkin His Gallic impetuosity was too much for him Inflamed lungs will not stand much pressure even from philosophy. The phlegmatic Englishman hied him homeward to his country, the Oratorian was dead in a few days, martyred by his devotion to what he deemed truth.

LXIX.

Talking of this beneficent, and symbolical, and dread element, I came across a curious expression a few days ago On turning over the leaves of certain autobiographies of famous persons, I saw that one of them gave, under the head of " Recreations," the following :

"Variation of occupation, *playing with fire,*" etc. How did he amuse himself playing with fire ? Did he swallow live-hot coals, like a stage-conjuror, or put a lighted candle in his mouth, as we all did when we were boys, or was he an amateur pyrotechnist, amusing himself in his back-garden on winter nights, and delighting all the small boys in his neighborhood? I suspect there was a little affectation in this " playing with fire," as indeed there is in most autobiographies I remember how affected I used be by Carlyle's letters to his wife, until I found she accused him of writing all these affectionate epistles with a view to their future publication, and for the edification of posterity But I came across one little note, which was thoroughly naïve and genuine; and another which was pathetic The former was written by a lady-authoress; and a very distinguished one Under the head of " Recreations," she mentions three things. Reading, writing, and—talking! God bless her! There's no nonsense there! No "archæological explorations," " Alpine climbing," " deciphering Assyrian inscriptions, " but " talking," a plain, honest avowal of a harmless amusement.

LXX.

I would give a good deal to be one of the circle around the tea-table of that lady, some winter night, when the wind was threatening the final cataclysm on all things outside, and the merry blazes were dancing up the chimney—you know the rest! The ghost of Dickens rises up before me, with a raised forefinger "I have said all that a thousand times better than you" God bless you, Charles! So you have; and made us all your debtors forever! But let us suppose a Dickens' picture, and that good lady presiding; and let us suppose that she has done the honors, and is now free—to talk. I can imagine myself listening in the shade of a great lamp, or under the shelter of a Grand piano—listening, listening, whilst the stream of calm, graceful eloquence rolled smoothly from that lady's lips. And, if I am to judge by her written language, it is no idle gossip either; but gentle, liberal views on things and places and persons, that are very interesting; of strange scenes she has visited abroad, of distinguished persons she has met, of rare intellectual tournaments between the giants of intellect of our own day; and not a word to wound charity. For, where Intellect rules, Charity is always inviolate.

LXXI.

The pathos in these brief autobiographies came in thus ·

"*Recreations. In former days*, golfing and tennis, cycling and swimming."—Alas! my poor friend, going down the slope of life, thou must now take things gently· Thou hast no longer the elasticity of spirit, nor the suppleness of limb, nor that *élan*, which helped thee in youth to despise consequences and rush at the immediate. That twinge in thy shoulder reminds thee that tennis-bats and golf-mallets cannot now be swung with impunity; and a fall from a cycle, *in former days* to be laughed at as a trifle, might mean something serious now In fact, friend, thou hast passed under the ferule of that dread schoolmaster, experience, and his lessons there is no despising nor ignoring Thou hast the heart of a boy, for I perceive there is a note of admiration, the admiration of regret, beneath that phrase *in former days;* but thou hast the mind of a man, tutored and experienced by many a rough accident in the uphill struggle of life; and thou art conquered! The splendid disdain of youth has vanished; thou hast learned to respect destiny, and thou hast become cautious, and let us hope modest withal

LXXII.

But is all this regrettable? Certainly not The best part of life is unquestionably its decline, just as the mellow autumn is the fruit-bearer and peace harbinger of the year. I cannot for a moment envy these young athletes who sweep past my window here, flash across my vision for a moment and are gone. I feel glad of their courage, their splendid animal spirits, the exhilaration of youth and exercise, their enjoyment of the living present. But I do not envy them I never go into a school-room without half wishing, like John Bright, to shed a tear over these young lives, with all the dread problems of life before them Hence, too, I think we should pour into these young lives all the wine and oil of gladness we may, consistently with the discipline that will fit them for the future struggle. I cannot bear to see a child weeping. I almost feel, like Cardinal Manning, that "every tear shed by a child is a blood-stain on the earth" Yes! give them all the enjoyment they can hold The struggle is before them. The ascending slope of life is a *Via Dolorosa*, a mounting of Calvary heights, if not an actual crucifixion Want, despair, sin, sickness, disappointment, are waiting in the hidden caverns to leap out and waylay them And many, how many? will fall by the wayside, and find in the arms of merciful death, the final relief from the struggle and burden of life.

LXXIII.

Hence, undoubtedly, the evening of life is best. We have toilfully mounted the hillside; the setting sun is behind us, and soon we, too, shall go down into the great sea to awake again, we hope, in the dawn of a brighter morrow. Many of our comrades have fallen by the way, we regret them, we think gently and compas-

sionately of them, but we cannot help just a little self-complacency
in the reflection that we have emerged victorious on the summit
of life, whilst so many have fainted by the way We have realized at least, too, that the worries of life are mere incidents—the
inevitable concomitants of an imperfect state of being; and we
now make no more of them than of the wind-buffettings and the
rain-drenchings that brought the color to our cheeks and sent the
warm blood leaping through every capillary and nerve of our
system Yes! youth is the preparation for age; age is the
fruition of youth How well that kindly optimist, Robert Browning, knew it:

> Grow old along with me !
> The best is yet to be,
> The last of life, for which the first was made ;
> Our times are in His hand,
> Who saith, " A whole I planned,
> Youth shows but half: trust God:
> See all ; nor be afraid! "

LXXIV.

And then, behind all and crowning all, there remains the
Earth-Cure—the great solemn enfolding in the arms of Mother
Nature of her weary and worn children. From her breast they
sprang, little jets of organic life, and mounted higher and higher
in the sun and light, making sweet sprays of pearls as the sunshine caught them and played with their crystal splendors; or,
alas! perhaps, muddy and discolored from a too great mixture of
clay. But, clear or turbid, they have touched their altitudes,
and now break lower down and lower, until they are caught to
the breast of Mother Nature again, and lost in her final embrace.
And she is merciful, and knows nothing of her weak or wayward
children She folds them up with all their perverseness, and
gently covers them all over, and is silent, till they pass into the
charity of oblivion. But, meanwhile, she puts forth her tender
grass and wild flowers above the most erring as well as the most
faithful of her children ; and allows her willows to weep down-

ward, and her ubiquitous ivy to drape their headstones, as if even these were too loud-tongued for her wishes, and, as if in answer to the poor querulous desire of mortals to be remembered, she allows Time to pass his iron finger across their names, and whispers, " Be forgotten, be forgiven, and rest! "

LXXV

But here Mother Church breaks with Mother Nature, and emphatically demands some perpetuation of memory She will not silence the pitiful pleadings from the tomb. All is *not* over. And all is not at rest as yet. The weary brain is stilled; no more troublous and restless thoughts flash across it The limbs are at rest. No pain shall evermore rack them; no pleasure disturb them. But the spark of the Divinity which they imprisoned is still pursuing its way, through penal fires and across the dark airs of other worlds to its final resting-place whence it set out, and it seeks peace, peace and rest! Even the rather libertine fancies of Lord Byron were touched by the simple, Christian epitaphs in the cemetery at Ferrara ·

> Martini Luigi
> Implora Pace.
>
> Lucrezia Picini
> Implora Eterna Quiete.

" The dead had had enough of life," he says, " and all they wanted was rest, and that they *implore!* There is all the helplessness, and humble hope, and deathlike prayer, that can arise from the grave—'implora pace.' I hope whoever will survive me, and shall see me put in the foreigners' burying-ground at the Lido, within the fortress by the Adriatic, will see these two words, and no more, put over me."

LXXVI

There is no doubt but that all the thought of the world has been used up long since, and that the most a modern writer can do is to present the thoughts that were familiar to Hebrew, Greek, or Roman, in new forms and more intelligible language Here, for example, is a fine piece of philosophy, put by two minds extremely remote from each other by time, space, and habit, and couched in characteristic phraseology .

"He (Lamennais) also said to us on hearing the clock strike, 'If one were to say to this clock that in an instant it would be destroyed, it would none the less strike its hour until that instant had arrived. My children, be like the clock; whatever is to happen, always strike your hour'" [3]

The more modern counterpart of this is from the "Aes Triplex" of Robert Louis Stevenson :

"It is best to begin your folio; even if the doctor does not give you a year, even if he hesitates about a month, make one brave push, see what can be finished in a week . . . All who have meant good work with their whole heart, have done good work, although they may die before they have time to sign it. . . . Life goes down with a better grace, foaming in full tide over a precipice, than miserably struggling to an end in sandy deltas That is the true meaning of the saying about those whom the gods love. At whatever age death may come, the man who does so, dies young"

And are not both sentiments purloined from Montaigne : "Nous sommes nayz pour agir. Le veux qu'on agisse, et qu'on alonge les offices de la vie, tant qu'on peult; et que la mort me treuve plantant mes choulx, mais nonchalant d'elle, et encores plus de mon jardin imparfaict." [4]

LXXVII.

There is something heroic in these expressions of the same idea For we must remember that just as he spoke those words there loomed up before Lamennais that awful cloud, which came down upon him swiftly and never lifted—in whose tenebrous folds his clock of life sounded and was shattered , and before the other the shadow of that death that ever crept closer and closer, until it enveloped him, and hurried him away from a world he loved, and which loved him in turn.   But really the idea is com-

[3] *Journal of Maurice de Guérin*   [4] First Book, Chapt. XIX

mon to all fine minds   Look forward fearlessly, and do not penetrate, or seek to penetrate, too closely behind the veil!   Drown
all doubts and fears in the duties of the present and solve all difficulties by steady, persistent work.   Take up problems, if you like,
for intellectual pleasure or profit, but always remember the solution of them is beyond the grave.   Hold fast by the certainties
that are revealed, but seek not the solution of mysteries which of
their nature are insoluble   And keep on the harness of battle to
the end.   So sings a kindred spirit, Robert Browning:

> I was ever a fighter, so—one fight more,
> > The best and the last !
> I would hate that death bandaged my eyes, and forbore,
> > And let me creep past
> No ! let me taste the whole of it, fare like my peers,
> > The heroes of old,
> Bear the brunt, in a minute pay glad life's arrears
> > Of pain, darkness, and cold.

LXXVIII

There is a curious similarity, not only between the thoughts
that surge through the minds of men, but even between the physical features of many who, for good or ill, have left the impress of
their presence on the world   There is a startling resemblance, for
example, between the faces of two beings so utterly dissimilar as
Voltaire and the Curé of Ars, between Rabelais and St. Benedict Joseph Labré, between Savonarola and George Eliot   How
is it accounted for ?   Were both originally cast in the same physical and mental mould, then when the latter came to be acted
upon by outer influences, it yielded to the pressure; and whilst
the facial expression remained unchanged, as the flesh is less plas-
tic than the spirit, the spiritual elements were shaped into the
symmetry of the Saint or the distorted lineaments of an abortive
or misshapen genius ?   Yet, the similarity is startling, although
there is certainly in the face of the Saints a curious enamelling,
a surface of sanctified beauty, that make the wrinkles beneath
something far different from those that thought has indented on the
face of the philosopher !

LXXIX.

Benedict Joseph Labré! Saint? Yes. Canonized? Yes. The superb defiance flung by the great Empire Church in the face of modern Sybaritism! I confess to a certain sense of shrinking and squeamishness every time I stumbled across the words " crosus insectis," in the lessons of the Second Nocturne of his Office. I could not understand it. Is not cleanliness next to godliness? What about St. Bernard's: " I love poverty, but not dirt?" And St. Jerome? Were not all our dear Saints remarkable for this exquisite sense of corporal, as symbolical of internal, purity? And are not all our monastic, and conventual institutions, spotless and speckless, from attic to cellar? Would not a young postulant, in any of our nunneries, be promptly dismissed for the least symptoms of untidiness? And here is a beggar, a tramp, with just enough rags to cover him, but not to protect him, and these filthy in the extreme, raised on the altars of the Church for the veneration of the faithful! What about the Church keeping abreast of progress, and leavening civilization, when she defiantly canonizes this revolting pilgrim and vagrant, who repudiates every canon of sanitary science, and goes around, from shrine to shrine, with his rags and vermin, in the days of Russian and Turkish baths, massage, superfine *lingerie*, and vermicides, and insecticides *ad infinitum!*

LXXX.

It was as great and as interesting a problem as Free-will and Fore-knowledge, Ideas Innate or Acquired, or any other psychological question that might interest the ever inquisitive mind of man I thought I should probe it to the end I took up his life, written, *mirabile dictu!* by the superfine Anglican converts of the 'forties. It seemed to make matters infinitely worse. The habits of this Saint were simply appalling. He was a moving mass of vermin. He slept on dunghills He ate the refuse of the poorest Italian cabins. He refused bread, and lived on cabbage stalks, orange-peel, and fragments of culinary refuse. Abominable! Loathsome! No, my curled and perfumed and unguented friend!

Is there not something in Scripture about certain people that resemble platters, well cleaned on the outside, but very filthy within? And something about whited sepulchres? May it not happen also that this strange loathsome figure, externally defiled, may have a splendor and purity all his own; and that He who sees beneath the surface of things may discern sanctities beneath these grewsome surroundings, that would compel Him to send His angels from the high heavens to guard so resplendent a soul in so humble and defiled a tabernacle?

LXXXI.

Defiled? No I retract that word There was no defilement there. Nothing but the most exquisite and delicate purity of soul and body, so exquisite that it is almost certain this Saint never lost his baptismal innocence, and was kept absolutely free during his short life from that particular ensoiling which is especially antagonistic to Christian holiness and sanctity. His humility was perfect. When fine ladies stood up from the altar rails, and retired (we cannot blame them), when the Saint approached to receive Holy Communion, he bore the reproach with meek dignity, and besought the priest to communicate him apart from the congregation. He rejoiced that men shrank from him and loathed him He sought humiliations as fools sought honors, he courted affronts, as men court flattery. Modest, mortified, chaste as an angel, mortified more than Anthony, more hidden than an Alexis, as meek as Francis de Sales, as seraphic as the angel of Assisi—how now the ethereal splendors of his beautiful soul shine through the tattered and broken integument of flesh and garments; and consecrate, as by some liturgical unction, the very things which seemed to the purely natural man an offence and a scandal to society!

LXXXII.

This poor beggar died He was picked up from the streets, fainting, and carried to a neighboring house. He never recovered He passed out of the visible world, and saw God! And then? And then, all Rome went wild about the dead Saint. There was a tumult in the Eternal City. Messenger boys ran wildly through the streets crying. The Saint is dead! The Saint is dead! Crowds thronged the chamber where he lay, with the beatitude of Heaven on his face The fine ladies who had shrunk away as he passed and gathered up closely their perfumed silks, actually fought for one of those vile rags, which seemed so loathsome on the living frame; but were now converted, by the magic of death, into precious relics to be kept in all their sordidness, and honored, both as souvenirs and talismans The cry went forth demanding his canonization Miracles are wrought by the dead body, as erstwhile by the living He is beatified, and known as the Blessed Benedict Joseph for a century. And, finally, the great Pope, the reconciler of civilization and the Church, the writer of the great Encyclicals, and the sublime *Carmina*, the stately representative of all that is most cultured and refined in Catholicity, puts his final *imprimatur* on the pilgrim and the beggar, and confirms the verdict of the faithful by the official canonization of the Church. And this in the very teeth of the greatest of all the centuries!

LXXXIII

What a strange, sublime, unhuman thing is that saintly desire for contempt! It is a reversal of all the processes and passions of men Nine hundred and ninety-nine thousand nine hundred and ninety-nine human beings are consumed with the desire for honor, for human respect, for the esteem of their fellow-beings. The passion is universal and intense. The courage of the warrior, the ambition of the statesman, the vanity of the poet, the slavery to fashion, the delirium of love—all are created and stimulated by that one central desire—the esteem of men And lo! here is one who, without affectation or hypocrisy, segregates himself from humanity, and places himself in the dust beneath the feet of men on the highways of the world They take him at his word, trample on him, despise him, mock at him, leave him finally a mass of bruised compost; and then in the awful revelation of death they discern the Saint, the peculiar one, and they go on their knees, and lift up the bruised and mangled figure, and kiss the wounds they themselves have made, and almost dismember it in their passion for relics; and finally clamor to the great High-Priest at Rome to elevate that bruised figure on the altars of the Church, and to say that it was sacrosanct and holy. And, perhaps, under all this enthusiasm may be discerned that very vanity and self-seeking to which the life and death of the Saint were the keenest reproach.

LXXXIV.

But often (it should be oftener), those meek, self-effacing spirits, who think the potsherds and dunghills too good for them, do command esteem even in this world   I can imagine with reverence and awe, the smitten monk, leaving his stall at a nod, and going up humbly to prostrate himself before the altar   I can imagine the Sister sharply chidden in Chapter, the hot blood mounting to the cheek and brow, but sternly ordered back by the voice of humility, and I can see the smile, genuine and unaffected, with which that hurt and grieved soul will immediately afterwards do some little kindly, humble office for the one that smote her. These are the things that bring us to our knees, and compel us to kiss the ground where saints have trod.   And if we ourselves are yet unchastened, and would quiver beneath the rod, at least it is something to know that we can reverence in others what is wanting to ourselves.   Thank God! no one yet, however antagonistic to the Church, has ever ventured to paint a sullen monk or an angry and disobedient nun   It is a negative tribute to the genuineness of Catholicity, as the religion of Christ.

LXXXV.

But what about the folly of the majority, who pursue this phantom, and even stretch their mouldering hands from the grave to grasp it   Brought to the test of reason, can there be anything so ridiculous as to seek the good opinion of fellow-mortals like ourselves?   For, mark you, we seldom deceive ourselves as to our own insignificance.   Whatever we appear or try to appear before the world, we cast a true, too true a reflection on the deep mirror of our own souls.   And there we are not flattered.

How do we measure *our* opinion of others? As a something not to be noted Did we hear that a far-off author, or singer, or painter, was distressed by our poor opinion of him, it would make him simply ridiculous in our eyes, however flattering to our vanity it might be And how does the judgment of others upon us differ from our judgment upon them? Not by a hair's breadth. But are quantities not to be taken into account by any sensible man? For, what am I, or you, or any one, to nine-tenths of those who have heard of us? A name—a certain collocation of a few letters, and no more Of the I, or the THOU, they know nothing, or care less. A fall in stocks, a gray hair, an ill-fitting frock, is of far more consequence.

LXXXVI

Why then are we disturbed, elated, or depressed, by praise or contempt? Why, but because passion is more with us than reason, to say nothing of grace. Argue as we will, this human opinion weighs with us. It should not disturb the serenity of our thoughts even for an instant. Nay, even if one of those passionate, incontinent, undisciplined spirits should loom upon us out of his welcome invisibility, and say to our face what others speak against our mere name, how should it affect us? Clearly not at all! Let the creature carry his half inarticulate, savage hate away with him into the darkness again ! He has come like a shadow, and like a shadow he departs. Let his evil words pass with him Let them haunt his soul, and not thine Thus, too, we should allow that most uncouth being, the flatterer, to depart Let the treacle stick to his soul, and not to thine. Ay, but can we? Yes! if we were all saints and philosophers. Aye! but if we were all saints and philosophers, would the wheels of the universe continue to revolve?

LXXXVII.

Mid-May, and the virgin Spring in all her tender, and modest, and chaste beauties My little garden is now "full." All the bareness of Winter has vanished ; and every tree and nook and corner is replete with rich vegetation The rain, too, has fallen, soft, rich, "wet" rain, and the ground is spongy and soft, and the leaves are glistening, and the blossoms are filled with the clear, pearly dew You can see Nature and her children drinking from the fountains of the heavens, and growing lush and lusty and vigorous under the benevolence of the skies. And what a picture! The apple-trees are laden with pink and white blossoms, and they seem to stand out against the dark background of the forests behind, as clear as in a stereoscope; but colored with the magic blending of petals that seem to hang in air, so delicate and beautiful are their colors The tulips are just beginning to die away in a blaze of colors; and the round balls of the peonies seem eager to break into their great, thick, glossy leaves, which in a week will make burning spots of color against the dark or speckled laurel Overhead, the swallows, with wet wings, are cutting the ether into all manner of perfect segments and arcs, and from the wet trees, the blackbirds and thrushes are pouring forth their deep, rich bell-tones, to call into existence the little lives that are hidden in the speckled or blue eggs lying nested beneath.

LXXXVIII.

But I think the greatest pleasure of these beautiful rich May mornings is that of listening to the music that bursts from every copse and tree from the throats of blackbirds and throstles, and seems to make the pure virgin air vibrate with melody. From the thick bosky verdure in the forest beyond, where the young leaves are still tender and silky; from the top branch of firs and pines; from neighboring gardens, where the bird has become an "unseen song;" from the ivy over my head, pours a stream of melody, so rich, so varied, so sweet and joyous, that it would make the veriest pessimist thank God for the mere pleasure of existence For, surely, those little creatures with their speckled breasts, or blue-black coats and scarlet beaks must feel that life is worth living, when they can pour out such rapturous music from their full hearts, careless as to who is listening, or how the world takes their improvisations, only anxious to get out the full tide of imprisoned melody before it chokes them with its impetuosity or breaks their little hearts in despair And they do not know where they will get their noontide or evening meal: they only feel that some Hand feeds them and their little ones · and they pour out their gratitude blindly at His feet

LXXXIX.

But this glad matin oratorio, with its chorus of a hundred male voices, sinks into the commonplace, almost, when in the evening, the trees black against the saffron sunset, a single missel-thrush takes his place on the highest naked branch of an apple tree or a pine tree, and whilst all around is hushed, tolls across the valley the *Angelus* of his own creation One could listen to him forever, and believe the old monastic legend, so sweet and far away in these raucous and rabid ages, of the monk who followed the singing bird to immortality, and came back to his monastery after a century had passed which he thought an hour or a day. It is inexpressibly beautiful, these calm Spring evenings—clear, blue sky overhead, absolute silence all around, the hush of Nature going to rest, and this vesperal hymn alone waking up echoes across the river, and waking, perhaps, sleepy birds who querulouly demand: "Is this the dawn?" One would give a good deal to be able to describe its enchantment I know but one who has adequately done so I think Crashaw's "Music's Duel" the finest—(well, I must not talk in superlatives) but amongst the finest—(which is only a comparative-superlative) of poems in the English language I think it is almost worthy of this evening solo of my missel-thrush; and I cannot say more That great Catholic poet received his reward, even in this world: He died—Canon of Loreto !

XC.

I confess I feel a sense of personal aggrievement when I see this spiritual song, embodied in so frail a form, stoop down to the commonplaces of life I never could understand how people could talk about a great sermon, or how any preacher could listen ever to adulation, when he has just come down from Sinai, with the sun in his face and the glory around his head. It seems a horrible anti-climax to tell such a man: That was a beautiful sermon! Silence is the only legitimate comment So, too, how can you reconcile a great performance, say by Kubelik on the violin, with the miserable chit-chat of the audience? And worst of all, what a horrible disillusion to turn from the inspirations of some great poet to his "Letters." The life of a poet should never be written The world should be content with what he has given them. There should be no inquiries as to the how or the why. There is his work, and take it with gratitude The life of Edgar Allan Poe, for instance! Who would not wish it unwritten, with all its terrible squalor and imbecility—a great dark night, lighted only by two stars—his gentle wife; and the incomparable woman to whom he wrote those sublime lines—My Mother!

XCI.

Yet what delicacy, what purity, runs through all his verse. Not a line, not a word, to shock the tenderest sensibilities. Contrasted with his life, sunk in all kinds of sottishness, it seems difficult to believe that the profligate of college life, and the ingrate to his best benefactor, could have written those lines, which might be hung like an amulet around the neck of a child, and which he inscribed · To Helen! But I find that this was the case with all the mystical poets. Coleridge, Blake, Mangan, Poe; and in our own time, Francis Thompson—are all singularly pure in their verses. How is it explained? There is but one reading of the riddle, namely, that these men were poets, dowered with the insanity of genius, and absolutely oblivious in the raptures of inspiration of anything, in word or deed, that could be deemed gross and sensual On the other hand, the dramatist or mere rhetorician, who cuts up so much eloquence into metrical lines, or who deals with exclusively human subjects, invariably slips into that prurency and salaciousness which denotes the step-child, but not the direct offspring of the Muses

XCII

The most timid and reserved of young men might read the works of the poets just mentioned right through at a Boston Literary Circle, or in a family party after tea, or to a group of ladies on some balcony at a seaside hotel,—might read through without a blush, or a stammer, or a single look in advance, tentative of a rude word, or a dangerous line. But the same reader cannot take up a page at random of Shakspere, Byron, Goethe, or Burns, and read twenty lines without wishing he had bitten off his tongue Yet, such is the force of national prejudices, that these are the demigods of their respective nations There are more monuments to Burns in Scotland than to Dante in Italy, and if Byron's remains had to be buried in Newstead Abbey under a nation's excommunication, the censure has long since been reversed. "What is the secret of these men's popularity?" I once asked a Scotchman "They represent in their writings the virtues of their respective nations," was his reply.

XCIII.

The great question to be solved, or rather presented for solution in our generation is, whether we are to accept universally the ideal when it comes into conflict with the actual; or whether we are to accept the actual, and put aside the ideal, when they fail to harmonize, as they are pretty certain to do in modern ethics This is the race question, the religious question, the question of creed, the question of *ethos*, to all "tribes, and races, and peoples, and tongues." The world on this broad ground challenges the Church "Give up your ideals," it says, "and become even as me." The Parisian Gavroche says the same to the Breton peasant. "Give up your faith, and take our positivism, your faith in saints, and take our heroes, your purity and sweetness, for our gaiety and licentiousness, your absurd ideas of chivalry and honor for our theories of expediency and profit." In the streets of Rome the contadini from the mountains meet a similar challenge. The Czech or Tyrolese will hear the same on the streets of Vienna, the moudjik on the pavements of Moscow; and it is repeated in a thousand ways, by word, rebuke, statute, coercion law, plank bed, and hard labor, to the Irish peasant and laborer, who has been driving his fist into the face of this temptation for nigh seven hundred years. The difference now, however, is that friends, as well as foes, seem to combine for the compromise, and say to the Martyr for the Ideal, "Thou fool, rise from thy gridiron, and be thou as we."

XCIV.

It is just possible that the question will settle itself eventually, nay that it is settling itself by the abandonment of the ideal for the actual "We cannot subsist, much less succeed," is the cry from the markets of commerce through the world, "if you insist on your ideals" "If I were to accept your theories of commercial honesty," said a certain merchant to the present writer not long ago, "I should close my place of business, and enter the workhouse with my wife and family." He abandoned the ideal for the actual, and appears to be happy in the compromise But as an academical question, how is it to be arranged? The one postulate of conscience and Commandments is adamantine. You can by no means fit it in with libertinism which modern freedom demands, nor with dishonesty and overreaching which commerce demands, nor with brutality which successful pushfulness demands; nor with callousness of conscience, and hardness of heart which are essential conditions of worldly success; nor with prevarication, which is the lever of life to the ambitious You cannot do it. Reflex principles will not help you It was on stone, not on water, the Commandments were written, and the "still small voice" thunders above the clamor that would stifle it. And so thou, O Breton fisherman, with thy saints and thy faith, and thy scruples, thou, too, O Irish peasant, with thy seven century traditions, must take a hindmost place in the noisy procession of thy race towards ———.

XCV.

That word can only be supplied when the mad rush of the modern world shall break itself to pieces against the inevitable. Then comes reconstruction, most probably on the higher basis of Christianity Meanwhile, to all pure and holy souls, and there are many such everywhere—students in universities, young men climbing painfully into their professions, and somewhat disgusted

at the means they have to employ to reach them; young ladies
in the world, whose hearts are sick with its hollowness and their
own degradation; grave, bearded men, who have seen life and been
disillusioned,—all these will fly from the Actual, at least in spirit,
and seek happiness, or rather honor, in the Ideal   And to these
the Church will appeal, not so much by its dogmas, for theirs will
not be intellectual, but moral wants; but through its *ethos*, as alone
holding in itself all that men have ever dreamed of perfection
These, the unhappy, but elect, will be forced to admit that in the
Sisters of Charity bending over the wounded on the battlefield,
over the leper in his hut, over the cancerous and gangrened in the
City Hospital, humanity has reached its apogee; and in the Catholic
girl, or wife, or mother, the culmination of that civilization which,
springing from the chivalrous ideal, has ever sought its lost loyal-
ties in the person of a pure and cultured womanhood.

XCVI

φώνησει συνετοῖσιν! She, the Church, will speak to the
Elect, and the Elect will hear! Souls sick unto death with
the modern atrophy of scepticism or unbelief, will lift their weary
eyes to her, Mother and Mistress of Peoples, and she will be
to them what the brazen serpent in the desert was to the bitten
and poisoned Israelites. And they shall be healed. Learned
men, with all the higher powers dried up and impoverished by
the exclusive exercise of the critical faculty, will turn to the fountains of her philosophy, where truth forever sweetens the bitter
waters of Marah! Young students, whose fresh enthusiasm for
all that is sublime and most perfect has not yet been stifled by
their contact with the Actual, will pass into her cloisters, and find
there the peace and refreshment which a well-reasoned, prophetic
anticipation of life tells them is not to be sought for nor found in
the mad struggle into which the ambition and selfishness of men
have turned our short pilgrimage of life. But above all, the pure
of heart, whose reward is to see God, shall see Him even whilst
they are yet in the flesh, in that strange presentment of His life
and doctrine, which the daily life of the Church exhibits; and
they predestined by their purity of life, and led and defended by

legions of angels, like the Lady in Comus, shall find all that the
spirit demands in the fine exaltation of austere lives, fleshless
loves, restrained imaginings, and all bounded by limitless horizon
of everlasting union with the regenerated and perfected elect!

XCVII.

For the more one studies the expression of popular ideas
or feelings in modern literature, the more clearly is it seen
that it is the desire to get back to Pagan license of life that
is at the root of all modern irreligion Disputes about dogmas
and creeds are but the tactical and strategic movements designed
to cover the retreat of Humanity towards its long-lost Pagan
ideals. Once and again a candid poet or philosopher or cynic,
like Goethe, or Renan, or Heine, will admit it   The rest of the
world deems such admissions premature, but secretly likes them.
The intense devotion, the sweetness, the delicacy, the elevation of
thought, that belong to Catholicity are beginning to fall on a
world that every day is becoming more egotistic, more selfish,
more sensual.   But to all pure and lofty minds, to the humble, the
mortified, the pure of spirit, the seekers after God in every one of
the dissolving and disappearing creeds that sprang from the fatal
Reformation, the divine and holy spirit which breathes through
the testaments of Christ, will still appeal; and they will find all
their concepts and ideals of holiness, sweetness, purity and charity,
in the faith, which alone professes to declare with the certainty
of a special revelation, that its children did in very deed, touch
these summits of sanctity, whilst on earth, and have been gathered, as a reward, into the ineffable blisses of Heaven.

XCVIII.

So, too, all that rage against Christianity find their apology in
its restraints, not so much on the human intellect, as on human
passion and pride.   Deep down in their hearts is the secret desire
of unlimited license   In fact, when one comes to consider what
is the one doctrine or rather precept of the Church against which
the Gentiles rage, and the people meditate vain things, it is found

in that one word, *Restrain ! Control !* It is this cold discipline that exasperates the world; and still more, the felicity of those who, in practising that discipline, have found the secret of all human happiness But apart from divine grace, it needs not only a certain elevation of thought, but a certain sense of refinement and delicacy, to understand this. It is in this connection it has been said that vulgarity is inconsistent with Catholicity. For the essence of vulgarity is self-esteem and self-love, and the essence of Catholicity is self-effacement. Hence, too, in the vocabulary of our religious communities, the mundane word "politeness" is never mentioned Its place is taken by its mother, who is "Charity."

XCIX.

I think that a very cursory research in the pages of such literature as we possess, would very easily prove this Materialism, not only in doctrine, but in principle and practice, is the very antithesis of the Church's teaching. It leads of necessity to grossness and license; whilst the truths of Christianity develop, without effort, the sense of delicacy and refinement, which is the reputed flower of civilization, but which has really sprung from the teachings of the Church Hence, all purely materialistic literature degenerates, as if unconsciously, into unclean and unholy expressions, whilst all Catholic literature is redolent of the immaculate sweetness and delicacy of pure and unsullied minds. It is extremely plain, and as easy of proof as of assertion. Yet, it will help a little to quote the admission from the lips of an antagonist, who could never shake himself entirely free from the enchantment of his Catholic childhood. It is Ernest Renan, who says in the close of his last letter to the Abbé Cognat: "What you say of the antagonists of Christianity is very true. I have, as it happens, made some curious researches on this point, which, when completed, might form a somewhat interesting narrative The consequences would appear triumphant to the orthodox; and especially the first, viz, that Christianity has rarely been attacked hitherto, except in the name of immorality, and of the abject doctrines of materialism—by blackguards in so many words. This is a fact, and I am prepared to prove it."

PART IV

SUMMER

SUMMER.

What a curious thing is our sense of beauty and proportion! How far we take it, and then tire of it! The ambition
of every amateur gardener is to imitate in his flower-beds tapestries
or wall-papers—what is technically known as carpet-gardening.
Few attain to its perfection, which generally consists in an
outer rim or embankment of gray garden leeks, with their pretty
blossoms, which are ruthlessly snipped off because they spoil
the proportion of colors, an inner border of blue or white
lobelia, with its delicate medicinal blossoms; then a deep purple
circle of beetroot, within which are ranged row after row of geraniums of all forms and colors, until the central oriflamme of yellow
or deep-bronzed calecolarias is finally reached   The compactness,
leaving no space of brown earth visible; the evenness, which will
allow no blossom to spring beyond the common level; the gra-
dations of color, contrasting with the emerald of the closely-
cropped sward all around, are the elements and constituents of
the beauty achieved with infinite pain and care.   Then, suddenly
your eye rests on a page from Florence or Rome, contemptuously
decrying this well-ordered and prim perfection in contrast with
the tropical luxuriance of Italy run wild; and lo ! you accept the
verdict, and turn away from your " English " garden, and pine for
a wild flower in the forest, or the colored mosses by some mountain stream

II.

It is the eternal protest of Nature against its great rival, Art;
and somehow the untamed heart of man responds to it. It is a
tradition, probably well-founded, that a savage who has been re-
claimed even in infancy, clothed, fed, educated in the lap of civilization, will, if ever he get the chance of going back to his tribe,

fling aside the trappings of civilized life, and, taking up his blanket, revert to the primitive conditions of savagery again. And no doubt Nature itself, instead of moving onwards to artificial perfection according to the theory of the evolutionists, is ever seeking to get back to its savage state Let the hand of man be taken from her for a moment, and back she goes to prairies, and "forests primeval," and tangled bushwoods, and takes once more her savage cubs to her breast And is there not something half-akin to this in our own yearnings to leave behind the prim, Quaker-like perfection of the lawn and the garden, and the trim drawing-room with all its pretty appurtenances, and spend one day at least on the breast of Mother Nature in all her savage solitude, her mosses our couch, her forest-trees our canopy, her streams and seas our music, and her vast silence our medicine to nerves and brain fretted by all the noises and artificialities of life?

III.

The pathos of great cities is overwhelming The submerged, shuffling along the pavements, side by side with their brothers and sisters who float just now with the tide, but some of whom are certainly destined to be themselves submerged; the anxiety of the young to attain to position and wealth; the anxiety of the middle-aged to retain these slippery treasures; the loungers in the parks not knowing well how to kill time, the ministers to human vanity in the shops, the stricken ones, wearily plodding along with mothers or sisters to seek help in the back, dark parlor of some noted physician, the many colossal and forbidding mansions of disease, or sin, or death, the alarm-bell of the ambulance with its horrible freight of wrecked and broken humanity, the Courts of Justice and condemned cells; and perhaps, worst of all, the stately, gaslit apartments, where men and women, in despair of happiness, seek its meretricious rival, excitement—all is melancholy and overpowering It is the aggregate of misery that strikes you In the country, unhappiness is fairly divided. Here and there a mortal, fretting under his load, and seeking in vain relief But he is only a speck against the azure In cities, unhappiness seems a cloud that blots out heaven altogether.

IV.

But, somehow one of the most pathetic things in a great city is the aspect of an evergreen shrub, which, planted within a black iron railing just outside some fashionable drawing-room window, seeks to wear out its wretched life in that prison Just above it perhaps, in a square, decorated box, are hyacinths in spring, or white begonias in summer; and every morning, some fair, jewelled hand, or perhaps the white, pure finger of a child, is stretched out shyly to give them the little water that keeps up their artificial life. No face bends over them That's as much against our conventionalities, as if every house was a harem. But no one heeds that poor shrub With dry, sapless roots, tainted and blackened leaves, it looks wearily at the sun, until, as in a kind of leprosy, leaves droop, and wither, and fall down; then the wrinkled little branches become dry sticks; and one day it is seen that only a blackened skeleton remains. It has pined for its forest life, for winds and rains, for the soft burden of the snow; for the pleasant, if hurried visit of the blackbird or thrush; perhaps for the soft nest where the young of both are laid. It is an exile in the wilderness of brick It eats out its heart and dies.

V.

The most lonely thing in cities is a summer twilight. Summer twilights, however beautiful, are supremely melancholy. The vesperal song of birds, the swift groupings of swallows overhead, the return of the rooks in stately procession, the steely blueness or purple of eastern skies, the branched trees, black against the daffodil sky where the sunlight yet lingers, the swift whir of the bats, the dancing of midges, the closing of the flowers, are all harbingers of night, and, as yet, we deem Night a kind of Death, until we know better. It is all very sweet, and tender, and beautiful, but there is a note of sadness somewhere. Hence, I have heard many say, that in these beautiful twilights, that, with us, stretch up to ten o'clock and further, they yearn for the cosy fireside of winter, and the companionship of blazing logs, and the book, and the music, and the tea-urn. It is quite clear that this feeling is begotten of the common natural impulse to regret the end, or the departure, or the close of anything which has become familiar to us. It is the sadness of all "Farewells,"—at the railway station, at the pier, at the door, at the marriage service, and most of all at the grave. Especially, when those without faith say the final farewell, as poor Huxley over his dead child   It is less poignant with us who, as in Swiss cemeteries, always write on the tombstones: *Auf Wiedersehen !*

VI.

This must have been what the Psalmist had in his mind when he said, or sang. "In the evening weeping shall have place, and in the morning gladness." For, in the morning, we come out of the far land of dreams and mystery, and emerge into the glad realities of life. In the evening, the realities begin to fade all around us, and we are about to enter into the unknown and trackless ways of sleep and oblivion. There is a certain reluctance in all human hearts to venture on the mysterious or unexperienced   We cling to what we know. We dread the unrevealed. Children invariably hate to be taken away from the company of the living, and to be left with the companionship of the dark. All day long they played in the sunshine   Now shadows impenetrable gather around them   They are alone—and alone with the impalpable and mysterious   And they dread it   The feeling is shared even by grown-up people. The mysteries of Night, however beautiful, are mysteries, and we pine for the visible and the real   Hence, too, is prayer more suitable for the evening than for the morning   The swift delight of coming out of the shadowy land into the sunshine does not predispose to prayer   But, at night, we move into the shadows again; and the awe and reverence that are all around us, penetrate our souls   We kneel, and think, and become reverent   And then we pray.

VII

How did Blanco White come to write his famous sonnet, "To Night" (probably the only instance in literature where Fame has

been summoned by one poem in fourteen lines), if he had then
abandoned his faith? His comparison of Night and Death is a
purely Catholic idea   The natural trembling of humanity for

> This glorious canopy,
> This lovely frame of light and blue,

is what we still feel at the approach of night, until we perceive that
the sun was the real veil, drawn for a moment over countless
splendors, and that he goes down into the sea only to make way
for " Hesperus with all the host of heaven." And so it is with
Death   Life is the day-star, the sun of our petty existence, veil-
ing from our eyes the splendors of eternity. Death is the interpreter, the revealer. our last breath is our apocalypse. But yet
so controlled are we by our senses, that there is always an unde-
finable feeling of loneliness at sunset and at death. We are
parting with the familiar, and going out to the unfamiliar, for
night, with all its starry splendors, is unknown to us. We know
the gas-jets of the ball-room and saloon, the electric arcs in the
theatre. We never see the countless suns of the universe. And
death is unfamiliar, with all our experience of its surroundings.
We must pass through its gates to understand its tremendous
revelations

VIII.

But to come back   I think the city twilights are the most
pathetic of all. The sinking, yellow sun streaming along such
great thoroughfares as Trafalgar Square and the Strand in London, or down along the *Champs Elysées* in Paris, and lingering
on window, or column, or roof, has an aspect of extreme loneliness, emphasized by the little, twinkling eyes of star-jets or arcs,
in café or restaurant, or even beneath the solemn trees. Man is
summoned from labor to rest, and if one can pass by what he
sees is the evening amusement of those " whose lines are cast in
pleasant places," and watch the proletariat, the weary, bent, and
broken masses of humanity, shuffling by with hod or mattock on
shoulder, and probably envying the " elect of the earth " who
sit within their gorgeous clubs or cosy corners in the fashionable
restaurant ; and then follow them further to their foul haunts in

by-street or tenement house, and think of all the squalor and destitution and low mental and moral environments, one regrets that
sunlight or twilight should pierce through and reveal the surroundings of toiling humanity; and would wish rather for the
merciful darkness of winter that seems more in keeping with, and
certainly covers more effectually, the sordid aspect which life
turns towards her suffering and unhappy children.

IX.

This thought broke suddenly upon me (nor can I remove
the haunting fascination of it to this day), one summer evening
very many years ago.   It was not in a great city, but on a sunny
island, "a summer isle of Eden," which, by some tasteless ingenuity, had been made a penal settlement.   A mission was being
conducted there by Regulars from the city; and we had been
invited over to hear the convicts' confessions.   It was pretty late
when we finished, and on our way to dinner we had to pass
through the dormitory or sleeping apartments of the prisoners   It
was just five o'clock, and the summer sun was streaming across
the bay, lighting up the headlands all around and the deep hulls
of the ships, and casting great long shadows of buildings, and
masts, and wooded promontories across the darkening sea   All
was sunshine, and life, and sweetness without, all was darkness
and desolation here   For we saw but strong cages, tier over tier,
walls and partitions of corrugated iron, and a net of strong wire
or iron in front of each cage, through which alone the little air,
and the little light from the outer hall penetrated   Each cell was
eight feet by four, and each, even at that early hour, on that
sweet summer evening, had its human occupant.   Some were in
bed; others sat drearily on the wretched wooden stool and stared
like wild beasts at us   All were locked in.   It was a human
menagerie   I have often seen prisoners since then, even under
worse circumstances.   But, somehow, those wire cages haunted my
imagination.   And then we stepped, free and unembarrassed, and
honored by the very warders, who held in their hands the keys
of these human cages   The summer sun was oppressive in its
heat and light.   A pleasure steamer, well filled with all the fash-

ion and style of a great city, panted by   A band was playing.
No one gave a thought to the entombment of their fellow-mortals
just a few yards away.

X

Some evenings later, I, too, was locked in at a comparatively
early hour in some such solemn twilight as I loved   It was at a
Cistercian monastery   The bells had ceased their interminable
tolling, the rumbling of the organ was hushed; the pattering of
feet had ceased, the very birds, as if respecting the Trappist rule,
were silent   I sat and looked out across the darkening twilight
at the white statues glimmering against the deep background of
pines and laurels   If there be any spot on earth where there is
peace, and rest, surely it is here   Some day, a tired world will
demand monasticism as a luxury, or necessity.   But that was
not my thought as I sat there, and put my hand on some such
work of Catholic philosophy, as the *Imitation*, or the *Soliloquia* of
St Augustine.   My thoughts swiftly reverted to the penal settlement on the "isle of Eden" and the cages, and their occupants.
What an enormous gulf separated one condition from the other!
There the one feeling uppermost was the degradation of humanity, here, you experienced its elevation   It was the nadir and
zenith of the race.   And yet, the conditions of life did not differ
so much.   Nay, so far as physical comfort or enjoyment, the
prisoners are much better off than the monks   The latter rise
earlier, have much coarser and more meagre fare, work harder,
keep perpetual silence, sleep on harder couches, submit to greater
humiliations   And yet, there is the whole width of the horizon of
heaven between them   There you pitied, or compassionated,
here you are reverent and envious.   Despair seemed to hover
over the prison, but it is the wings of angels that lift the fringes
of the pines that sentinel the mountain abbey

XI

But there is something more curious even than this.   I should
not like to say that those poor, squalid prisoners would gladly
exchange their lot with the monks.   That is doubtful   But there

can be no doubt that the monks, if called upon, would assume the garb and chains of the felon, and in the terrible transmutation experience only the greater joy   And the attraction would be, the very degradation and contempt and loss of caste and honor, which is the peculiar lot of the convict   Does the world deem this credible ?   Well, we have proofs   If saints seek contempt as ordinary mortals seek honors ; if they have regarded themselves as the *peripsema* and offscouring of humanity ; if they have begged to be laid on ashes in their dying moments; or that they may be privileged to die on dunghills, remote from all human observation ; if a Vincent de Paul did go down to the galleys and suffer the cannon-ball to be riveted to his ankles, as you can see in that famous picture by Bonnat—why may not all this be repeated, when the spirit and teachings of Christianity are the same, and when from countless human hearts made invincible by charity rises ever and ever that prayer of St. Teresa, " *Aut pati, aut mori ?* "

XII.

I wonder is the secret to be discovered in that saying of Emerson's . " The hope of man resides in the private heart, and what it can achieve by translating that into sense. And that hope in our reasonable moments is always immense and refuses to be diminished by any deduction of experience."   But that immutability of hope, my dear philosopher of Concord, demands the monk or the saint, or some such childlike and unspoiled temperament as thine own. The "deductions of experience" point all the other way.   To keep one's heart unhardened until death is the achievement of a saint. Every stroke of the hammer of experience tends to anneal it.   The two great impulses of nature, even in its lowest forms, are self-preservation and reproduction, and both demand the wisdom of the serpent more than the meekness of the dove.   And these impulses are accentuated and intensified by experience   Every man stands solitary, with all other men's hands against him   He must fight for existence. Failure, defeat, is the one hell to be dreaded   Success is the supposed Elysium   Nay, all our modern systems of education tend thitherward.   For what is all this terrible and complicated apparatus of education intended? What is the meaning of all this competition, rivalry, gaining of prizes, etc.? What but the preparation for the greater struggle? And struggle means rivalry, and rivalry, enmity. "One alone can attain supremacy" And that one must be thou, and no other How are the best feelings of the heart translated into sense here?

XIII.

Nay, in such a struggle, where the watchword appears to be· "We neither ask, nor give quarter!" would not the uncontrolled impulses of the heart be the great traitors? Could there be any hope of success for a man who would be, above all things, generous, compassionate, self-sacrificing, kind? It is all right for you, my Crœsus-friend, whom I see labelled "multi-millionaire and philanthropist!" You can be lavish now, as much as you please Nay, you must get rid of much of that glittering ballast, else it will sink your stately argosy. For gold is a weighty metal, you know, and you cannot steer well the ship of your fortunes so long as you have so much of a dead weight in the hold. But "philanthropist"? It is a pretty euphemism; and I don't want to quarrel with it But I should have liked to know how you fared in the good ship Argo, as you set out in pursuit of the golden fleece For I notice that Jason was very generous, and considerate and pious to the gods, after his many adventures and trials. He built a splendid mausoleum to the island-king whom he accidentally killed, and sacrificed a sheep or two, after he, in concert with the amiable enchantress, Medea, had strewn the waters of the Euxine with the dismembered remains of the young Absyrtus.

XIV.

I will suggest something to you, "multi-millionaire and philanthropist," which may obviate such expiations by suspending the possibility of your errors, at least for a lustrum. What would you think of building and endowing a new species of educational institution, to be called the *Collegium Christi?* It will have for

its motto . *S'effacer;* and " Bear ye one another's burdens " may
be inscribed over the lecture-rostrums in the class-halls. It shall
have all the latest appliances of science for the further conquest
of Nature, and advancement of mankind.   The extirpation of disease, the destruction of social evils, the bridging of the mighty
gulf between rich and poor, the lifting up of fallen humanity,
the study of criminology from the standpoint of Christ, the ven-
tilation of grievances not as subjects for parliamentary eloquence,
but as subjects to be grappled with, and destroyed and removed—
these shall form the curriculum of studies.   We shall by no means
exclude even Pagan ideals   You may have busts of Crates and
Cincinnatus, but not of Crœsus, Minerva and Apollo may grace
your corridors, but the long perspective must not be bounded by
glittering *idola* of Mammon and Plutus. For the former are
merely symbols, and, alas! rarely pass beyond their symbolic
state. But these latter are the dread divinities that haunt the
steps of mankind from the cradle to the grave.

XV

But it is quite clear that to yield to heart-impulses and generous emotions is to court failure in the struggle for existence,
which has become with us synonymous with the struggle for
wealth   Life is a masked ball, ending in success or failure. If
you raise your domino, you might as well order your carriage,
or droshky, or cab, and go home. You have revealed your
identity, and the revelation is fatal. Unknown you might have
moved safely amongst the unknown. But when everyone else
knows you, whilst they remain unrevealed, what chance have
you? You have lifted your visor in the tournament, and exposed
yourself to deadly blows. Yes, get away from the tumult as
quickly as you can, and, with the experience of so terrible a lesson, get away amongst the world's *anonymi,* and hide yourself.
Or take some other mask, and wear it closely ; and keep a close
hand upon those traitorous, if generous emotions which are the
fatal gifts of your heritage   It is all very melancholy ; yet it is
consoling to know that men still have hearts to feel, and if they
must stifle their appeals, they cannot altogether still their beat-

ings And, now and again, secretly and with misgivings, they may yield to the luxury of fine, pure emotions without the danger of ultimate betrayal.

XVI.

Hence, if you want to know what a man really is, watch him alone in the company of children. Here he can show himself as he is, because here he has nothing to fear and nothing to gain Elsewhere, even in the society of his intimates and relations, he cannot reveal himself Brother is a mystery to brother ; and father to child In the drawing-room, in the council chamber, in the club, in the easy undress of an after-dinner, one would suppose that men are off their guard, and wear their hearts on their sleeves. No! assuredly no ! Wherever there is a something to dread, the petals of the soul close in, as the petals of flowers at the coming of night , and open reluctantly only when the light appears again. What a history of mankind in miniature is that little story of a certain Queen-Regent of France, who was down on her knees, groping around with hands and feet, playing Bo-peep with her little children in the nursery amidst shouts, and shrieking, and laughter Suddenly, the ambassador of a great state is announced. The mother stands suddenly erect, and is transformed into the Regent. Stately, and stiff, and ceremonious, she steels her face against even a smile. That must be impenetrable The domino is suddenly pulled down She speaks in riddles, and answers in enigmas. She watches every line of his face to read it ; she heeds not his words. They mean nothing So too with him. He is studying her eyes, her features. Both are playing a part , and both know it. They separate with mutual compliments and distrust He goes back to his cabinet and mutters: "A clever woman ! " She goes back to her nursery, and resumes her play with her children. Here is the whole world in miniature

XVII

Pitiable ! Yes, perhaps so ! But, *que voulez-vous ?* You have outgrown your childhood, and mankind has got out of its nursery and small clothes. You talk pitifully of the world's

childhood, of its myths, and legends, and superstitions You speak
of its heroes as of great big children of generous hearts and
narrow minds. Your twentieth-centuried scientist is painfully like
the grandiose hero of Locksley Hall

> I to herd with narrow foreheads, vacant of our glorious gains,
> Like a beast with lower pleasures, like a beast with lower pains.

Yes! he has gone a step higher. He is illuminated He has
electric cars and railway murders. He has romantic novels and
divorces. He has the Stock Exchange, and suicides. We are
moving at break-neck speed, and the wheel of existence revolves
so rapidly but few gain the summit of the tire: the many are precipitated into the mire below. Inequalities between rich and poor
yawn every day wider than the chaos between Dives and Lazarus.
But on the wheel must go. He would be reputed a madman
or, what is worse, an obscurantist, who would cry · "Slow down,
O wheel of life, and let the fallen arise! There is room for all,
within you and around you ! Slow down, or break into splintered
wood and twisted iron in the end ! "

XVIII.

One cannot help thinking of such things when memory recalls that prison-cage and its occupants, and the long streamers of
the yellow sun gilding all nature with their beauty. But these
are sombre reflections, twilight thoughts For hath not the ever-
true Psalmist said. "In the evening weeping shall have place,
and in the morning gladness?" Yes, let us carry, if we can, the
"wild freshness of morning" with us through the entire day.
From the *Subhi kázib*, the False Dawn, the morning twilight,
when sleepy little birds wake up reluctantly and ask each other,
Is it day? to the *Subhi sádik*, the True Dawn, when all the
woods are vocal with the deep, rich music of blackbirds and
thrushes; from that dawn to the fuller solar light, when already
nature is sheltering itself from his rays; from that brilliance of
morning to midday, when no sound is heard but the *Coo, Coo,
Coo*, of the solitary ringdove, hidden away in deep umbrageous
fastnesses; on to the evening twilight, with its call to rest, let us

keep the heart of the morning with its gladness, and make of the melancholy of twilight a palinode of the music of the dawn. For there is no night in these summer months, but a great ring of light, with a blank agate in the centre. And even that is shot through with light-waves fiom the faint auroras of the setting and the rising sun.

XIX.

It is strange that Nature, so fond of using its blue pigment, in other ways, is slow to waste it upon its most perfect handiwork, the flower She lavishes and squandeis it with the most incontinent profusion on hei two great fields of color, the sky and the sea. But she is singularly economic in its use in the forest, the field, or the flowei-garden At least she only uses it on her tiniest creations, violets, or pansies, or forget-me-nots. These latter indeed aie the only really blue flowers ; for there is a strong infusion of Tyrian and regal purple in the violet and the pansy. But who evei heard of a blue rose, or a sapphire tulip or dahlia ? Nay, I am not betraying my ignorance. I know well what wonderful things our modern gardeners can effect ; and how by the aid of chemistry they can obtain what colors they please in their flowers. But I am speaking of Mother Nature. I want to know why she economizes that lovely color here ; and I want to know whether the "grand old gardener and his wife" had, without the aid of chemistry, which I suppose was then unknown, such a thing as a blue rose in the garden of Eden And if not, why ? It is an interesting speculation Has Nature used all the pigment up in her skies and seas, so that none is left for her children ? Well, there is a compensation. "What is rare, is dear," said the old logic-treatise. And we cannot help loving the tiny, blue-eyed little children that look all so modest beside their regal and florid sisters

XX.

I think this must be the reason why that truly mystical German poet, Novalis, chose a blue flower as his symbol of poetry, poetry itself being the supieme ait in which all others are com-

bined. And this was no tiny childkin of Nature, peeping shyly
out of a mass of broad leaves, but a great, tall, pearly garden-
queen, with a mass of broad, glittering petals, and springing from
the moist earth near a stream. " Round it stood innumerable
flowers of all kinds and colors, and the sweetest perfume filled the
air   He saw nothing but the Blue Flower, and gazed on it long
with nameless tenderness   At last, he was for approaching, when
all at once it began to move and change; the leaves grew more
resplendent, and clasped themselves around the waxen stem ; the
Flower bent itself towards him ; and the petals showed like a blue
spreading ruff, in which hovered a lovely face"   So after innumerable adventures, and wanderings through lonely, if beautiful places, he found the object of his life's search, and lo ! it was
all but a dream. So, too, was his vision of the deep-blue river in
which he, embodied in his hero, Heinrich, sunk, swallowed in the
vortices, and beneath which he meets once more Matilda, who
put a wondrous secret word in his mouth, and it pierced through
all his being. He was about to repeat it, when someone called,
and he awoke   He would have given his life to remember that
word   What was it ? The Blue Flower is Poetry   What is the
Word ?

XXI

It is not a little singular that such a thinker, dreamer, mystic,
yet mathematician and realist should be so little known even in
his own country   Still more singular is it that we have never
utilized his most powerful and penetrating work, *Europe and
Christianity*. There is such a dearth amongst us, not of apologies (of these we have enough), but of poetic and philosophical
presentments of the aspects of Catholicity that present themselves
so attractively to fine, spiritual natures, that one would have supposed we would seize on so eloquent a picture of what the Church
is and does for humanity by putting before it the most sacred and
poetic ideals[1] The fact alone that it was selected by Schlegel for

1 "These were beautiful, brilliant days when Europe was a Christian land,—
when one Christianity occupied the Continent   Rightfully did the wise head of the
Church oppose the insolent education of men at the expense of their holy sense, and
untimely, dangerous discoveries in the realm of knowledge   . . This great,

publication in the *Athenæum*, but suppressed by Goethe, is an
eloquent argument in its favor, and if anything were wanting
to such an argument, its magnificent defence of Catholic devotion
to our Blessed Lady, so detested by materialists and neo-pagans,
like Goethe, should prepossess us in its favor. He is but one of
the many non-Catholic poets who have dreamed of perfect spiritual beauty, and found that dream realized in :

Maria, lieblich ausgedrückt.

XXII

There is a wide difference between Novalis, writing such hymns
as this Fifteenth, and writing from a bed of sickness, with all the
ghastly forerunners of death showing themselves in violent hemor-
rhages, and his fellow-countryman Heinrich Heine, rising from his
mattress-bed in the Rue d'Amsterdam, semi-paralyzed and almost
blind, to make his way to the Louvre to pay his valedictory visit
to the Venus de Milo. "Alas !" so he thought the mutilated
statue replied, " how can I help you ? Do you not see that I, too,
am powerless and armless, as yourself ? " It seems like an excess
of affectation—this farewell to the marble Aphrodite. There is

interior schism (Protestantism), which destroying wars accompanied, was a remarkable
sign of the hurtfulness of culture. The insurgents separated the inseparable, divided
the indivisible Church, and tore themselves wickedly out of the universal Christian
union, through which, and in which alone, genuine and enduring regeneration was
possible Luther treated Christianity in general arbitrarily, mistook its spirit, introduced another letter and another religion, the sacred universal sufficiency of the Bible
namely. With the Reformation, Christianity went to destruction Fortunately for
the old Constitution, a newly-arisen order, the Jesuits, now appeared, upon which
the dying spirit of the hierarchy seemed to have poured out its last gifts In Germany,
we can already point out with full certainty the traces of a new world,—a great time
of reconciliation, a new golden age, a Saviour dwelling among men, under countless
forms visible to the believers, eaten as Bread and Wine, embraced as the Beloved,
breathed as air, and heard as word and song The old Catholic belief was Christianity applied, become living Its presence everywhere in life, its love for art, its
deep humanity, the indissolubility of its marriages, its human sympathy, its joy in
poverty, obedience and fidelity, make it unmistakably a genuine religion It is
made pure by the stream of time, it will eternally make happy this earth. Shall not
Protestantism finally cease, and give place to a new, more durable Church ? " (*Extract from Novalis, quoted by Hofmer, who always maintained that Novalis was certainly a Catholic, and quotes a number of authorities to support that statement.*)

no parallel to it, except in the prayer of Ernest Renan to Minerva
in the Acropolis ·

"Je n'aimerai que toi   Je vais apprendre ta langue, désap-
prendre la reste. J'arracherai de mon cœur tout fibre qui n'est
pas raison et art pur. . . . Le monde ne sera sauvé qu'en
revenant à toi, en repudiant ses attaches barbares. Courons,
venons en troupe."

But then, as with Venus, comes the minor note of despair:
"Tout n'est ici-bas que symbole, et que songe."

XXIII

Venus was of but little help to Heine; Minerva of less help to
Renan. But how strangely and irregularly move the minds of
men! The German-Franco Jew scoffs, like his progenitors, scoffs
at everything sacred and holy. He has one idol, and but one—
Napoleon. The Breton Catholic does not sneer. Herein he differs
much from his countrymen. He only laments. He bewails lost
gods and present beliefs in the living and eternal divinity   Yet it
might be doubted whether Voltairean gibes at Christianity would
do more harm than his pathetic mourning over human credulity,
although, in some mysterious manner, his critical faculty cannot
altogether subdue some secret yearning after a spirit of faith
which it has vainly exorcised   And lo! the Lutheran[2] Novalis
finds in Catholicity, although he never embraced it, "the only
saving faith," and thinks the Reformation a "most unqualified
evil"   It only proves for the hundredth time that the impulses of
a generous and pure heart are more than the "artistic sense," and
lead farther and deeper than the "critical faculty," no matter how
highly developed.

XXIV.

Probably no more interesting conversation was ever heard
than that which took place between Novalis, on his death-bed,
and his brother, Charles Hardenberg, and which eventuated in the
conversion of the latter to Catholicity. These conversations, too,

[2] See former statement, and authorities quoted by Hofmer.

afterwards gathered up and embodied, became the famous book
of which we have spoken, *Europe and Christianity*. Novalis has
been styled the German Pascal, and it would seem as if he had
some idea of constructing a great scheme of ethical and philosophical principles on the same lines as his great French compeer.
Like the latter, he had to leave his scheme unfinished, with just
such pithy and pregnant apothegms as would lead us to conjecture what might have been the grandeur of the completed work.
But the above-named essay remains almost entire; and to such
minds as have the taste for such things, and can follow this mystic
through the intricacies of unfamiliar thoughts, woven into untrans-
latable language, the work, which aroused Tieck and Schlegel's
enthusiasm, might be found not altogether unworthy or useless.
For we do need a certain airy and poetic vesture for dry bones of
doctrine, and Theology, if the Queen of the Sciences, needs to be
draped in royal robes to attract the homage of her subjects and
the reverence of those who are not yet her vassals or ministers.

XXV.

 " Poetry is absolute reality. This is the kernel of my philosophy The more poetic, the truer." How this profession of
Novalis jars upon the senses of those who see nothing but facts
and hear nothing but arguments ! How it chimes with the more
Catholic idea, which protests there is always something higher
than reason, and that something, the *donum descendens desursum*
from the Father of all light.   Yes ! faith and poetry are near akin.
The mere reasoner will never touch the altitudes of the former ;
the mere scientist, nay even the mere artist, can never reach the
Pisgah-heights of the latter.   There is something more than mere
perception of judgment or taste ; and there are places where these
faculties or gifts have to play a very subordinate part "*Credo,
quia impossibile* " is not unreasonable. It merely confesses a higher
power, and a higher region of sentiment or thought " Poetry is
absolute reality " Yes, if it be the poetry, unsensual and transcendental, which penetrates beneath the surface of things, and sees
their essence, which looks beyond art to that which it embodies ;
which beholds man, the mystery, interpreted by God, the ever-

lasting Reality ; and which understands that the mysteries of life
and time are explained by Death and Eternity !

XXVI.

Quite in contrast with that highly-mystical and spiritual temperament, as represented by Tieck, Fouqué, and Novalis, is the
dread realism of our day   Before the echoes of the Easter bells,
ringing out their glad Alleluias have died away, we read that Tolstoi's *Resurrection* had been placed on the stage in London, and
that its representation, mainly owing to the acting of the lady who
took the part of Katusha in the novel, has been an almost unpre-
cedented success.   It is a sign of the times—the eternal drifting,
drifting of the world from pure and lofty ideals ; and its rapid
descent towards the newly-awakened sympathy with all that is
spiritually deformed and obscure.   Fifteen years ago, ten years
ago, five years ago, no manager dare put such a drama of vice
and loathsomeness on the stage.   The public censor would in-
hibit it, and public opinion, if it escaped his censure, would condemn it   To-day people throng the theatres to witness the most
loathsome and degrading spectacle of a woman that even such a
lurid imagination as Zola's could conceive ; and the change is explained by the argument that the spirit of charity is now more
abroad than ever ; and that even the purest minds may sympathize with the fearful degradation to which womanhood may be
reduced by the habit of vice

XXVII.

Such a plea is too pitifully transparent   To present an immoral
and degrading spectacle on the score of morality, and to invite
the virtuous and clean of mind to witness such grossness on the
plea of awakening their sympathy, is too hollow a pretence to
need refutation   Something else is needed, and it is forthcoming
in the ancient formula: Art for its own sake, and Art independent
of morality.   This is intelligible   One can argue with it   No
one would waste ink in refuting the former defence.   It is the
final apology for realism.   It is the ethics of materialism worked

out to a logical conclusion   But Art for its own sake !   How
often have we heard it, how the changes have been rung upon it,
in painting, in sculpture, in poetry.   It is the region where "there
ain't no Ten Commandments," and where licentiousness may revel
without license.   And Tolstoi's *Resurrection* is Art   There is no
question of it   Nehlúdoff and Maslova are as terribly real as the
infernal princes in *Paradise Lost,* but, alas ! they represent passions which are far more infectious and dangerous, because more
human and common.   It is indeed possible that their dreadful consequences may be a deterrent against vice; but the principle is an
old one and a safe one .   It is better to attract towards the positive,
than repel from the negative.   And it is doubtful if vice can ever
be painted in such hideous colors as to exorcise the passions of
mankind.

XXVIII

But, Art for its own sake !   Art as teacher, because of its
own intrinsic perfection; and because perfection of any kind is
morality !   This is a great and subtle heresy.   I heard it once
refuted by a parable, founded on fact.

A young student, not enamoured of art for its own sake, but
anxious to see two things—a certain painting of Turner's, and
Burton's drawing of the head and face of Clarence Mangan, as he
lay dead in the Meath Hospital—visited the National Gallery
in Dublin.   It was the old gallery, and this was many years ago.
Having feasted his eyes on Turner, and sketched with a pencil
roughly the head of the dead poet, he turned to depart.   The
gallery was well filled with sightseers,—city-loungers, strolling
from picture to picture, and from statue to statue; a few country
cousins, staring with open mouths at the art-nudities that filled
up the centre of the gallery; here and there, a student copying;
not a few others affecting art-studies, and standing before large
easels, or unfolding massive portfolios.   But the student's work
was done, and he hastened to leave.   Just as he stood at the
head of the broad staircase, a lady with her two daughters came
up the steps with that eager look which people assume when they
expect something delightful   The three stood on the top step,
looked at the nude Venuses and Apollos for a moment, seemed

transfixed into marble themselves, so tense were their surprise and horror; and then, with a simultaneous movement, they rushed down the staircase, and out into the open air

XXIX.

" Obscurantists," " reactionaries," " prudes," I fancy I hear some one saying. But let me suppose that that lady and her two girls, brought out suddenly from the sweet seclusion of a refined home, and with all kinds of modest and delicate ideas, did yield to such a clamor, and did go around, coolly and critically surveying these marble figures or plaster-casts, could we consider it really a gain ? It would be quite in accordance with all we read about the advance of education, the march of progress, the *Zeitgeist ,* but would we like it ? Or, rather, would we not share the feelings of that student, who, on witnessing this glorious retreat of modest women, and all it conveyed more eloquently than the most impassioned oratory, did lift his hat above his head, and mutter deep down in his heart : Thanks be to God ?

XXX.

Here was the fundamental difference between Goethe and Novalis The former was a Pagan, who worshipped Art for its own sake. The latter a Christian, who believed Art should be the handmaid of religion. To the former all the mediæval churches in Christendom were not worth a Greek torso dug from the ruins of the Acropolis ; to the latter, these churches were not only monuments of faith, but temples whose sacred gloom shot through and through by heavenly lights, transfused through the consecrated figures of virgins and martyrs, made an aureole on the mosaic of the floor, and around the daily lives of countless multitudes, who held that life had essential duties, but that their futures were safeguarded by the diligent combination of work and worship here. The former thought Christianity a development of priest-craft, happily checked and stayed by the Reformation. The latter, though a Lutheran, believed that the visible Church was the seamless robe of Christ ; and that the capital crime of the Reformers was "separating the inseparable, dividing the indivisible Church." And hence, like his modern disciples, the former regarded the French Revolution as a "truth, clad in hellfire;" the latter, the logical outcome and consequence of the moral and intellectual libertinism which commenced in the Reformation.

XXXI.

And philosophy! How he loathes that mock philosophy of France, which eliminating all that was gracious in the past, religion and enthusiasm and self-sacrifice, makes of the universe a mill, and all the music of the spheres the rumble and clatter of machinery! And how he rises as on wings of light to a right conception of its sphere, as postulating for man a universe and surroundings congruous with his higher wants and aspirations.

"Philosophy can make no bread, but she can procure for us God, freedom, immortality. Which then is more practical, philosophy or economy?"

"Philosophy is properly home-sickness, the wish to be everywhere at home."

"The true philosophical act is self-annihilation. This is the real beginning of all philosophy, all requisites for being a disciple of philosophy point hither."

"The first man is the first spirit-seer; all appears to him as spirit. What are children, but first men? The fresh gaze of a child is richer in significance than the forecasting of the most indubitable seer."

XXXII.

But, with all his sorrow over German reformations, French revolutions, and other disastrous signs of steady decadence in human affairs, he does not despond. He was too young and inexperienced to despair. It is only those who have reached the middle term of life that can afford to be pessimists The young have the morning sun of gladness in their eyes; the old, the setting sun of tranquillity. The gray sky hangs above life's meridian Hence, Novalis is hopeful. He believes we yet shall see,

"a new Europe, an all-embracing, divine place. When will it be?
We cannot say Only let us have patience It will come; it must
come ' "

A century has gone by since he wrote these words; and who
shall say his prophecy has been verified? Or where, if anywhere, can we look around and say that the dream of this
poet-philosopher has come true?

Section II —XXXIII.

The problem suggested itself, and a possible solution one day
two summers agone, as I sat in a cleft of red sandstone, in a
cathedra, or chair, improvised by the action of the sea far down in
what are known as the Diamond Rocks at a certain watering-place.
I was out of the shadow of the cedars , and my limited horizon had
faded out and lengthened into the boundless expanses of the
ocean.   Here, beneath my feet, boiled the surges; and there was
no break in the continuity of that mighty element, which tossed
up yellow flecks on these rocks, washed the shores of Labrador
out yonder, and hid in warm sunny nooks beneath the palms of
Sorrento, or under the domes and minarets of Stamboul.   Somehow, one's mind expands with this glorious element, and the great
dome of the sky leans down north, south, east, and west, un-
marred and unlatticed by branches or foliage ; whilst the constellations repeat their splendors in the false firmament that is created
beneath these dark-blue waves It is a place where one may
think a good deal and without interruption, unless Nature is in a
capricious temper, and is determined to woo your mind from
abstract thought to her ever-attractive interplay of wind and
wave.

XXXIV.

I had come down from another popular resort on the same
coast, along the savage sea-line that is jagged and bitten into
mercilessly by the unrestrained Atlantic ; and here, on the warm
summer mornings, before the visitors at the hotel had finished
their morning papers and correspondence, I had Nature, in her

most lovely and attractive and terrible aspects, all alone to myself. Yet, it was not solitude How could it be when there were beauty and music all around—the savage, untamed beauty of sea and rock and cliff; and the more tender beauty of deepsea pools here and there in the crevices—seapools, clear and green as the most fleckless emerald, and in their depths purple mollusks, whose deep, rich Tyrian dyes contrasted with the limpid water, and wonderful algæ of every shape and color, floating and coiling and waving their long, cool flags, as the wind rippled the waters around them. And lest there should be here aught to mar the freshness and sweetness and purity of these tiny lakelets, twice a day the great mother-sea poured in her living waters in deep channels, and flushed the cisterns with foam, which melted into glittering globes and sweetened and purified the rock-wells down to their lowest depths. And sea-gulls gleamed white and gray above the surges, and speckled sea-swallows dipped and flashed here and there from wave to rock, and from rock to wave.

XXXV.

There could be no solitude here, for voices were ever calling, calling to you; and you had to shade your eyes from the glare of sunlit foam, that not only dazzled and blinded at your feet, but floated up in a kind of sea-dust that filled all the air with sun-mists, and was shot through and through with rainbows that melted and appeared again, and vanished as the sunlight fell or the wind caught the smoke of the breakers and flung it back against the steel-blue, darkened sea without Far up along the coast, you could see the same glorious phenomenon—a fringe of golden foam breaking helplessly against iron barriers, and, here and there, where a great rock stood alone and motionless, cut loose from the mainland by centuries of attrition, you might behold cataract after cataract of molten gold pouring out and over it, covering it for a moment in the glittering sheet of waters, and then diminishing into threads of silver as the spent waves divided into tiny cataracts and fell It was again the eternal war of Nature, the aggressive sea, flinging its tremendous tonnage of waters on the land, and the patient rocks, washed and beaten and tortured, for ever turning their patient faces to the sea.

XXXVI.

Why doesn't all the world come to Ireland at least for the few days of quiet breathing and torpor which summer brings, and which even the most exacting Shylock of the modern world must allow? If I were a Crœsus-philanthropist, such as I have already described, I would take from out all the factories and workshops of the world those pale mechanics, those anæmic and wasted women, and bring them here. I would take them from the stifling atmosphere where they breathe poison, and fill their lungs with the strong clean salt air from the sea. For the rumble and thunder of machinery I would give them the ever soothing sounds of winds and waves   For the smell of oil and rags, and the odors of streets and slums, I would give them the intoxicating perfume of winds odorous from their march over purple heather and yellow broom, and the subtle scents that breathe from seaweeds washed with brine, and exhaling its sweetness and strength. And I would say to them . Here, rest and forget! Plunge in these breakers, sleep on this heathy hillock, read, and pause, and think all day! The cares of life have no place here! They have "folded their tents like the Arabs" There is nothing over you here but the blue dome of Heaven, and the Eye of God looking through!

XXXVII.

The English have long ago discovered these nooks of paradise on the Irish coast. They have so completely monopolized one or two down there in the kingdom of Kerry that they feel quite resentful since the natives have found out those beauty spots, and are actually courageous enough to demand a right to share them. And here on this wild coast you will see a solitary Briton, a bewildered and almost panic-stricken mortal, pale-faced, thinly bearded, spectacled, with the field glass slung around his shoulders and something like an alpenstock in his hand He looks rather fearfully around. He is outside civilization, and he does not know what is going to happen He is quite astonished at the temerity of these young gentlemen in white flannels, and these young ladies in tennis costume, swinging their bats gaily, as they mount the declivity towards the broad plateau above the sea. By and by, his nerves cool down ; and if he can pick up courage enough to answer your kindly greetings, you will find him a bright, clear, intelligent soul He is just come from the Bodleian, or the British Museum The smell of books and mummies hangs around him. He, too, needs the sea!

XXXVIII

But all these bronzed and ruddy Irish, with health and life in every movement, feet that spring lightly from the turf, clean, ruddy bodies, as you see when they plunge from rock or spring-board and cut their way, like natives of the element, across the sea, what are they doing here? Taking their holidays? There are no holidays in Ireland, for every day is a holiday. We take the best out of life, and laugh at the world pursuing its phantoms across the weary wastes bleached with the bones of the unsuccessful and the fallen. We don't teach the philosophy of the schools well, but we practise the philosophy of life perfectly. So thinks, evidently, my statuesque Englishman, whose nerves are somewhat startled by our exuberant spirits. So think these German lads, who, amazed at Irish generosity, believe the donors of these innumerable sixpences millionaires, although the donors may be as poor as themselves So think these two lonely Italian brothers, who vend their pretty artistic paper-weights at fabulous prices. They are Garibaldians, if you please, brought up to believe that a government of priests is the worst in the world. They have been beaten into orthodoxy by the old Irishwoman, who feeds them as if they were her own children, and thinks she has a right therefore to chastise their irreligion But all carry back to their homes the idea that the Irish are the freest, gayest, most irresponsible people on the surface of the earth.

XXXIX.

It is evening here The sun has just gone down over there towards America, with all the pomp and splendor of cloud curtains and aerial tapestries, and the sea swings calm, acknowledging the prescriptive right of the vesperal-time to peace. The wealthy classes, who have just dined, the more modest people, who have just had tea, are all gathered pell-mell here before the handsome villas that crest the summit of these cliffs above the sea   Just here, inside the sea-wall, between two priests, sits an aged Archbishop, the weight of eighty winters bending his broad shoulders as he looks across the darkening bay and thinks of many things. Undeterred by rank or splendor, for there is a kind of glorious communion here, crowds of young lads and girls throng the sea-wall   A German band is playing Strauss and Waldteufel waltzes. But it is not dance music these Irish want.   They demand the *Lieder* of the Fatherland.   For every penny they give for a waltz, they will give sixpence for a German song.   A young Bavarian, fair-haired, blue-eyed, will oblige them   And there, above the Atlantic surges, on this wild coast, the strange, sweet melodies, learned far away in some woodman's hut in the Black Forest, are entrancing Irish hearts, which understand not a single articulate guttural or labial of the foreigners, but feel the magic of the music stealing their senses away.   And then the strangers reciprocate. And a hundred voices sing· *Come back to Erin, mavourneen, mavourneen!* to the accompaniment of violoncello and bassoon.

X L.

Passing along the corridor of my hotel that night on the way to my own room I was accosted by a friend   After a few minutes' conversation he invited me to his room   Oysters and champagne? No.   A game of nap?   No   A whole family, three generations of them, were gathered into the father's bedroom   They were saying their night-prayers before separating for the night   The aged grandmother was reciting the first decade of the Rosary as we entered   We knelt.   When she had finished the decade, she looked around and said "Alice, go on!"   Alice was a tiny tot of seven summers   Grandmamma promptly took up the recitation, repeated the form of the meditation, as found in Catholic prayer-books, and slowly and sweetly "gave out" the decade to the end. The grandmother looked around again and called out   "Go on,

Willy!" Willy was the father, a gray-haired man of fifty-seven. To the mother's imagination he was but the child she carried in her arms half a century ago Willy finished; and the aged mistress of ceremonies called out, now a grandchild, now the mother, until all were finished Then the children kissed "good-night!" and departed. Across the yard, which is also garden,

> All night have the roses heard
> The flute, violin, bassoon ;
> All night has the casement jessamine stirred
> To the dancers dancing in tune.

They kept me awake

> Till a silence fell with the waking bird
> And a hush with the setting moon.

XLI.

And this was the subject of my meditation the following morning, as I sat in my perch there above the sea. Here is the world's great secret solved. Here is the dream of the gentle mystic, Novalis, realized Not that the scheme has yet rounded to absolute perfection here. The material and subordinate element has to be developed as yet to supplement the spiritual forces that are alive and active But all the possibilities of such a perfect scheme of human happiness as Novalis dreamed of, are here,— Nature with all her magic beauty, Art in embryo, but with every promise of speedy and perfect development, and Religion, holy and mysterious mother, overshadowing all Comfort without wealth, perfect physical health without passion, ambition without cruelty, love without desire, the enjoyment of life without forgetfulness of eternity, the combination of temporal and spiritual interests, gaiety without levity, the laugh that never hurts, the smile that is never deceptive,—clean bodies, keen minds, pure hearts,—what better would can philosopher construct, or poet dream of ?

XLII.

I choose this watering-place rather than the former as both the type and theatre of what we may expect, when some great constructive spirit comes along from eternity to harmonize apparently rival elements, and bring all into the perfect symmetry of a *Civitas Dei in terra.* Because here there was a leaven of worldliness and pleasure; there religion dominated and interpenetrated everything The place seems more a shrine than a fashionable resort. If one did not know otherwise, he might mistake that lonely hamlet, undistinguished except for a few monster hotels, there on the brown moorland, seven miles from a railway station, and with only the thin sea-line in the distance, for a La Salette or a Lourdes How otherwise shall you account for those gray-haired priests waiting from four o'clock this summer morning for the sacristy door to be opened? How will you explain the constant succession of Masses at five different altars from five o'clock to ten, each Mass followed by an immense and fervent congregation? How will you interpret the constant stream of devout worshippers that passes into that church all day long, to make visits, follow the Stations of the Cross, recite the Rosary, etc? Pleasure-seekers and health-seekers, where are they? God-seekers and soul-seekers rather, for never a mission or retreat was attended with such passionate fervor and piety as these well-dressed worshippers exhibit, as they seem to grudge the time at the spa or at the sea, or on the far cliffs, as so much stolen from God.

XLIII

And just there, look! Across that light of sea sleep the three islands that link us with the past, and whose traditions, were we otherwise, would shame us They are *Aran-na-naomh,* Arran of the Saints, where rests the dust of thousands whose lives were heroic. You are at the end of civilization, and the beginning of heaven. There is not in the world so savage a spot as that where I stand It is a huge plateau or shelf of limestone rock, pitted and marked by immense holes where the eternal rains have worn the soft limestone Beneath my feet the devouring sea is thundering and bellowing through deep sea-caves where all the finny monsters of the sea might hide forever, and never be found There is no gentleness here! It is not

> The blind wave feeling round his long sea hall
> In silence

you hear, but the savage waves leaping and tearing with aggressive fury through every vantage point created by their ceaseless
and never-ending attacks   It is a place for the hermit and the
saint; and mark you ! O world-dreamer, and far-seer, the hermit
and the saint must again resume their rightful places in the economy of new orders and systems !   You cannot do without them.
They symbolize the rest and the gracious peace which the world
will ever stand in need of.

XLIV.

But here in this more fashionable place there is something more
of the human element; and it makes things more interesting to a
student of humanity, although they may not reach such sublimity
in idea or feeling.   And as it is this commingling of the human
and divine that will form the great principle or organic constituent
of the commonwealth that is to be, it makes an apter subject for
study than society where religion not only predominates, but is
everything.   For it is easy to solve the problem, Religion alone;
and it is easy to solve the problem, Humanity alone !   But to
combine both in one great republic of reason, each fitting in and
harmonizing with the other, with no repellent principles under-
lying the structure of either, but both cooperating to develop
all that is best in nature, and to eliminate all that is evil—here is
the great problem to be solved by some master-mind under the
distinctly unfavorable circumstances of modern European life ; or
to be solved naturally from some such condition of society as that
which we have described, and which seems to be the peculiar
prerogative of this Catholic land of ours.

XLV.

I think all unbiased minds, anxious for this union of culture
and religion, would choose this our country for the experiment
All conditions seem happily placed for the working-out of the
gigantic problem.   It would be no place certainly for a Voltairean
scoffer; for the omniscient, yet agnostic scientist, or for a modern
Ibsenite, who would pin his faith to the prophets of naturalism.

I am quite sure that if I were to place this book of Tolstoi's in
the hands of any young girl who is now sitting on those crags
that overhang the Atlantic, she would fling it into the sea before
she had read a dozen pages   I am quite sure, if I told any of
these ecclesiastics who mingle so freely amongst their people
here, the story of Parson Brand, he would at once say that the
stoning and subsequent interment of that idealist in an avalanche
was richly deserved   For, somehow, eccentricities of any kind
are laughed out of court here; and for a sentimental people, it is
wonderful how they have caught and retained the sense of that
juste milieu that lies at the bottom of all reason and all order.

XLVI.

The two things that seem to have preserved the buoyancy of
this people hitherto are the total absence of the habit of introspection, and their ignorance of the neurotic literature of the age.
It is quite true that their feelings, with surprising and painful
quickness, leap from depression to exaltation, and *vice versa ;* but
this swift succession of feeling is emotional, and not intellectual.
Except on the occasion of confession, in which they are strongly
advised to be brief and definite, they never look inwards to
scrutinize motives or impulses.   They know nothing of psychological analysis of themselves, and they are content to measure
others by what they see, without desiring to unveil and pry into
the hidden sanctuary where rests that Holy of Holies—the human
soul!   And hence there can be no morbidity here.   They look,
like children, at the surfaces of things, and as these surfaces are
mostly smooth, and it is only beneath there is the ruffling of
tempests, they are content to take life even so, and say, All is
revealed, and all is well!

XLVII.

It is a negative constituent of happiness, too, that hitherto
they have never heard of the strange modern literature that, com-
mencing with this morbid analysis of human thoughts and motives, ends in revolting realism and dreary pessimism.   They

know nothing of the *Weltschmerz*, have never heard of Parson Manders or Rosmer Solness with his dreary verdict on his life: "As I look backwards, I have really built nothing, and sacrificed nothing to be able to build." Oswald Alving is as yet a stranger; and happily the sculptor Rubek with his Irene and Maia are unknown names They would not class the creator of such types with Shakspere, even if they knew them. In fact, they are a healthy people, and just as they never will be taught to appreciate high venison or rotten Stilton, so, too, they have not reached as yet that intellectual status where nerves seem to be everything, and healthy thought is not only unrefined but morbid In fact, some one has called it:

Mundus mundulus in mundo immundo.

XLVIII.

Will all this last? Ah, there is the problem I am trying to solve here on this rock-shelf above the immaculate sea. Will not the *Zeitgeist* come along and seize these island people, as it has seized the world without ? How can we stop the process of the suns, or turn back the hand on the dial of time? And if education has to advance, as it is advancing by leaps and bounds, must not the literature of introspection and bad nerves and pessimism creep in gradually, and affect the whole mental and moral life of the country? And then, what becomes of your physical and spiritual health, and the beautiful happy balance and poise of faculties, neither enervated by disease nor warped by intellectual misdirection? It is a big problem; and push it as far back as we like, it will loom up suddenly some day, and demand a solution , or an unmolested influence, such as we see unhappily bearing bitter fruit in other and less favored lands.

XLIX.

It is hard to imagine such a revolution in a nation's ideas as this supposes; and, as I study this strange people, here in their humid climate and surrounded by a misty and melancholy ocean;

as I see them watching dreamily the sunsets over the western ocean, as only a poetic people may; dancing in ball-rooms to-night until twelve o'clock; reverently worshipping at the morning Mass; returning to their hotels, dripping brine from dress and hair; spending the day in excursions and amusements, but always ending it in the parish church; and, as I think you cannot move in any circle of society here, or change your location, or stir hand or foot without coming bolt upright against God; I conclude that a genius so varied and exalted will never long suffer itself to be linked with the spirit of the age or any other spirit of darkness, but will always rise above mere materialism on the wings of the poetic idea, and always keep within touch of reality through its moral and religious instinct. I doubt if Ireland will ever produce an Amiel, or a Senancour, or a Rousseau.

L.

But the Man of Letters will come, and the Man of Letters will always set himself in opposition to what he is pleased to designate sacerdotalism. Literature and dogma have never yet been taught to go hand in hand. For Literature has a dogmatic influence of its own; and believes its highest form to be the didactic. Unlike Art, whose central principle is "Art for its own sake alone," Literature assumes and has assumed in all ages, but more especially in modern times, the privilege of "guide, philosopher, and friend" to the world. Hence, we find that the worst forms of literature are excused on the ground that they teach a lesson "Anna Karénina," "Resurrection," "Ghosts," "Lourdes," "Rome," "Paris," are all sermons, told with all the emphasis, not of voice and accent, but of a horrible realism that affects one's nerves more terribly than the most torrential eloquence. And now that literature is pledged to preaching, it is doubtful if it ever will drop the rôle. And so the Man of Letters will come to Ireland, as he has come to France, to England, to Germany, and with him the seven other spirits, *Zeitgeist*, *Weltschmerz*, etc., to abide and take up their home, or to be exorcised and banished summarily and forever!

LI.

And all the spirits have one enemy, and but one—the spirit of religion. This was the *L'Infame* of Voltaire, who dreaded it so much that he would banish from his republic of atheism even the ancillary arts of poetry and music and painting. Everything that savored of idealism, and appealed to aught but the senses, was ruthlessly ostracized. The fight in that unhappy country of his between the man of letters and the priest, between literature and dogma, lasts to this day, with such lurid manifestations, as French Revolutions, Carmagnoles, etc. Then came the man of letters in the shape of the scientist, also banishing from human thought everything that savored of the ideal, everything that could not be peered at in a microscope, or examined in a test-tube. He has passed, too, but left his mark on the religious tone of England. Now comes the man of letters, with his religion of humanity, from the steppes of Russia to the Scandinavian mountains, and thence to the mud-dykes of Holland, and he, too, comes in the name of religion, with priests and ritual and ceremonies—above all, with dogma—the dogma that man is supreme, and there is no one like him in heaven or on earth.

LII

And I can forecast the time when this people of destiny, here by the wild seas of the north, and right in the gangway of the modern world, will have to face and examine the dogma of this modern literature. Nay, I can even see certain vacillations and soul-tremblings under the magic of the sweet and delicious music of language, attuned and attenuated in accordance with the canons of modern, perfect taste. But I know that the sturdy character of the people, stubborn after their eight hundred years of fight, and their religious instincts which nothing can uproot, and their power of adapting all that is best in life with all that is useful for eternity, and, above all, their sense of humor, will help them, after the first shock, to vibrate back towards their traditional and historical ideals, and finally settle down into the perfect poise of reason and religion combined. They never will accept literature as dogma; but they may turn the tables, and make their dogmatic beliefs expand into a world-wide literature.

LIII.

That is just the point   Can literature be made our ally, as it has hitherto been our enemy?   Are literature and Catholic dogma irreconcilable?   He would be a bold man who would assert it, with Calderon and Dante before his eyes.   But we do not sufficiently realize and understand that poetry, romance, art —everything that idealizes, is on our side.   If Voltaire banished from the republic of letters everything that savored of chivalry, enthusiasm, poetry, heroism, it is quite clear that these must have been recognized as the allies of religion   And when the inevitable reaction took place, one by one these ambassadors were recalled, and at length religion was accepted and enthroned in the very places where she had abdicated or been expelled   So, Walter Scott's Waverly Novels prepared the way for the Tractarian Movement, and became its initial impulse, and Tieck, Novalis, the Schlegels, who formed the romantic school in Germany, prepared men's minds for Catholicism by recalling the ancient glories that filled every city of Europe with churches and cathedrals, and the galleries of Italy with priceless and immortal art.

LIV.

Just as I scratched these words in pencil in a note-book, I became aware of a figure beneath me, standing in a hesitating way on a great shelf of rock that sloped down into a crystal pool of sea-water.   It was a young student, and I thought: "He wants to bathe, and no wonder.   Yonder bath of crystalline purity, improvised by Mother Nature, would tempt a hydrophobic patient. He is shy about disrobing in my presence, so I will leave him alone with the luxury"   No! he didn't want to bathe   He wanted a chat.   Might he take the liberty, etc , etc.? By all means.   He was very young, but I am not one of those who believe that to be a young man is a crime. If the ideas of youth have not an autumnal mellowness, at least they have all the freshness and elasticity of spring. It is good and wholesome to talk with the young, not for what they may learn, but for what they impart. It is good to see young hopes unfolding, and young ambitions ripening, and young eyes looking boldly and unflinchingly along the road which we have trodden, where we have leaped some pitfalls and fallen into others, and have now very little left of the weary journey but its dust, and sweat, and languor   And my young friend was buoyant.   He wanted to know everything, and to try everything. The red light of the dawn was on his wings, as he tried to soar in the empyrean

LV.

All was on his side—youth, enthusiasm, health, hope; he felt he lacked but one thing—knowledge. Not wisdom, mind! What youth ever deemed he lacked wisdom? But he felt there were certain things hidden from him, and but dimly revealed; and he wanted to tear away the veil and see them in all their naked truth. He intended leaving Ireland and going abroad. It did not matter where   He wanted work, and arduous work, and difficulties and trials   Otherwise he could never find his manhood. Missionary life in Ireland is merely running a knife through a cheese. You couldn't call that work—could you, now? But he felt—he was modest enough to admit it—that the difficulties he sought to confront and conquer were of an intricate nature, inasmuch as they sprang from souls, and he was reverent enough to say that man's soul, be it the soul of a poet or a hind, is a kind of Holy of Holies, only to be approached with a certain awe, and, above all, with the shoes off the feet, by which I think he meant purity of intention. And, furthermore, as it was not likely that he would go amongst savages to teach them to wear blankets and abstain from roast baby-fingers, he thought that the souls he wished to conquer might need reasoning with, if one were ever to understand the crypts and labyrinths that wind their dark and devious ways through modern human thought.

LVI

Would it not be well, then, to make a study of such souls, to try to understand them, above all, to get on to their standpoint and to see through their eyes? How do they regard us? How do they deal with all those complex situations in which men will find themselves, in spite of every effort to keep themselves free or disentangle themselves? And surely, if progress means passing out from the homogeneous to the heterogeneous, and if this is the most progressive of ages, the multitude of thoughts that vex, emotions that stir, principles that guide, passions that mislead, must be beyond counting. But these we can never understand, so utterly different are our own surroundings, unless we have the faculty of going out of ourselves and entering the minds of others. Experience alone can thoroughly teach this, but experience of this kind comes to one priest in a million. How, then, shall we know these secrets? Well, the literature of a world is the mind of the world placed articulately before us. Literature is the world's general confession, because it is the revelation of certain minds, which owe all their success to the fact that they have caught up the spirit of the age and rendered its voiceless agony articulate.

LVII.

Now, the malady of this age is Ennui—the eternal getting tired of, and wearying of monotony—in religion, art, science, and literature itself. Heresy is ennui of the sameness of rite, ceremonial, and prayer. Hence we see many who have entered the Church from emotional or æsthetic impulses very soon tire of such monotony and drift back to the "variety theatre" of their youth. Furthermore, infidelity is the delight of despair. There is a certain paroxysm of pride in defying or denying God. Milton has put it in the souls of the rebel angels. It is the ecstasy of the lost. Dante never understood it. Hence, amongst all his reprobate, there are no defiant souls. All are despairful, or admit the justice of their punishment. Why? Because infidelity did not exist in Dante's time; and to his great Catholic mind it was inconceivable. But if any Dante or Milton could arise now, he could impersonate another phase of the malady in the ennuyés and the defiant Yes, the passion for change and the revolt of the intellect are amongst the many symptoms of this overwrought and frenzied age.

LVIII.

It is one of the reasons, my young student-friend, why theories and systems are always acceptable to the human mind, dogmas, never! The former place no shackles on the intellect. You can move easily to and fro beneath them, or cast them aside altogether. But dogma binds the intellect, and the intellect chafes beneath it You must break the neck of *non serviam!* before the head bows beneath the keystone of the arch. And, strangely enough, this is just what modern science, nay, even what modern literature is doing, it may be unconsciously The man of letters is the Samson of the New Revolution. He preaches man's perfectibility, and shouts liberty, fraternity, equality, whilst allowing his axe to fall on his unhappy victims And the world will one day wake from the horrid dream, and demand a return to common sense, and a sane understanding of man's relations with the universe. The hermits in the deserts of science must be also visionaries; and the apparitions are for the most part diabolic.

LIX.

What, then, have we to teach the world, that is, if the world will condescend to listen ? Simply a return to common sense and a little repose of the spirit To this end, men must seek God and Nature a little more, self and society a little less. The great Master and Model, after His day's labor in the squalid towns, or along the dusty roads of Judea, went up at night into the mountains to pray Even He sought solitude as a balm and sedative for tired brain and nerves. Hence I hold that monasticism sprang from a necessity of nature, as well as from the decree of God. The deserts of Nitria and Libya were little paradises of peace after the maddening whirl and excitement of Greek or Roman cities. But, even in the desert, even here, my young student-friend, be-

side the barren sea, we must keep away from analysis and introspection, and maintain our souls on the perfect poise which we
witness everywhere in nature. Mark the swing of that sea, the
return of that star. All is obedient to law. There is no liberty
anywhere   The tides are chained to the moon; the star runs in
its appointed groove. They do not ask the why or the wherefore   They are content with their equilibrium   Why should
man's mind alone be lawless and untamed?

LX.

My young student didn't quite see the bearing of the parallel
on the question he had originally propounded. But he will later
on   He went his way, I am afraid, dissatisfied. And immediately beneath me, fifty feet or so, and on the shelf of rock where
I had seen him, stood a youth and a young girl. They were
conversing earnestly. And then the former knelt on the rock,
and with some sharp instrument cut deep into the stone, his companion watching intently. They, too, went their ways, and I was
curious enough to see what he had cut in the rock. It was a
circle within which were the magic letters A and R. It was the
first act in a little drama   Next morning we were horrified at
breakfast to hear that a young law-student from Dublin had just
been drowned in the bay   He had been an expert swimmer, had
slept late, and essayed to swim across the neck of waters that
connected the inner bay with the ocean. He had been seen to
cross half way over, then to fling up his hands and sink   There
was no help at hand. All the great swimmers had gone back to
their hotels

LXI

There was great gloom all day over the little place. In the
evening I was in my usual perch in the cliffs. The sun was setting amidst all the gorgeous magnificence of a clouded but not
darkened sky. One solitary figure fifty feet beneath me watched
it. Then I saw that infinitely pathetic human gesture, the secret
wiping away of a tear. She turned, and bending down she traced

with the sharp end of her parasol the letters on the rock, and then the round circle that clasped them, several times. There was no mistaking Act II in the little drama. " Here last evening we stood, and here, etc., etc. And now I am alone, and he—." An hour later I entered the parish church to say my evening prayer. My student was making the Stations of the Cross ; and the young bereaved one was kneeling at the feet of *Christus Consolator* I did not hear a word But I knew what she was saying They were the words of Martha and Mary " Lord, if Thou hadst been there! But now I know that whatever Thou askest of God, He will grant Thee " What did she want ? His poor body was out at sea, half-eaten by the sharks That she should never see more What then ? What these Irish, student or soul-friend, seem to be ever dreaming about—One Soul!

LXII.

Here was a direct exemplification of that saying of Novalis : "Absolute love, independent of the heart, and grounded upon faith, is religion. Love can pass through absolute will, into re- ligion We become worthy of the highest being only through death, atoning death." To a superficial mind it sounds sentimen- tal. We must understand how deeply those mystics felt, as well as how serenely they thought, before we can see the occult meanings that lie deep down beneath their expressions of feeling, or the embodiments of their ideas In all cases, they seem to have thought with the heart rather than with the brain. Their ideas came forth not cut, chiselled, and chilled by mere mental evolu- tion, but rough and warm from the mould of the deep sympathy that lay between them and nature and God Nor is this emo- tionalism by any means foreign to the spirit of religion Nay, rather it is its spirit and its form The absence of natural affection is considered by St. Paul one of the distinguishing characteristics of Paganism ; and he who had earned that most illustrious of all titles, " the beloved disciple," and whose picture by Albrecht Durer of Nurnberg is taken to be an exact portrait of Novalis, is also the apostle of love. There is something in it after all, and cold intellectualism might do well to study its effects and mani-

festations   How well it would be for us all if we could believe,
in his own spirit of splendid optimism, with Novalis, that "love is
the final end of the world's history, the Amen of the universe"

Section III.—LXIII.

I have always to undergo a certain species of humiliation
when I return home from the autumn holidays   People will ask:
"Where did you go this year?" And I have to answer: "Only to
Kilkee or Tramore!" Some gentle and modest questioner will
say: "I hope you enjoyed yourself and had good weather" But
there is a large and ever-growing class, who, when they receive
that reply, suddenly drop or change the conversation, as if it were
too painful to be pursued   You know them well.   They are the
world-explorers or globe-trotters, who have climbed the Pyramids
and seen the Iceland geysers; who have glimpsed the interiors of
the Lamaseries of Thibet, and visited Siberian prisons; who have
wondered (that is, if they can wonder at anything) at the giant
recumbent statue of Buddha in Ceylon, and read Aztec inscriptions in the ruined temples of Mexico, and to whom a dash at
Constantinople or Cairo, or a run across the States to Vancouver,
is considered a mere preliminary canter to a six-months' holiday
across the planet.   They are formidable folk to meet, and
modest people shrink away into a kind of coveted annihilation,
until they get beyond the shadow of such experienced and
ubiquitous neighbors.

LXIV.

There is a minor species of travelled people, however, who
are more intolerant, and intolerable   They are the less enterpris-
ing, but more impressive holiday-makers, who are modest enough
to admit that they have only climbed Mont Blanc and seen the
Passion-Play; but who always ask you with a singular kind of
pitiful contempt: "Is it possible you have never seen Spain?
Really now you ought to go to Spain!" And you feel very humble,
and indeed half-criminal, and you then and there resolve that
your ultimate salvation depends on your having seen Spain, and that

you must make the attempt, if it costs your life   And you regard these experienced people with a kind of admiring wonder; and think how unhappily nature has dealt with you in not inspiring you with such glorious and profitable ambitions, and endowing you instead with a kind of hopeless inertia, that makes the packing of a trunk, or the purchase of a Cook's ticket, a work to be dreaded and shunned.   You admit how feebly you are equipped for life's serious work, and you make a desperate resolution that, come what will, you will see Spain and,—no, or die !

LXV

On more sober reflection, however, and when the awful sense of your inferiority has vanished, you may be disposed to reflect; and reflecting to ask yourself, Is travelling abroad really essential to existence? or to health and long life? or to education?   And is it some innate or congenital defect in your own nature that creates that repugnance to going abroad for your holidays?   For really, it is just there that self-contempt comes in   And, as you reflect, you probably will recall the case of the vast multitudes who never leave their own country, nay, their own village, or townland, and whose lives are quite as laborious as yours   Here are nuns, for example, who for fifty years have never gone outside these convent walls, who have seen the same little span of sky, the same little patch of stars, during all that time, whose lives have been lives of unremitting labor, and who now, in the evening of life, take as cheerful an outlook over life and eternity as the most philosophical, or rather eupeptic, optimist   They listen to all recitals of foreign travels with a certain amount of interest, but without much envy.   They have been content to live, to work, and are content to die.   And they have never known, even for a moment, that sensation of ennui which will attack people in the hotels of Cairo, or the seraglios of Stamboul.   Clearly then, travelling abroad is not an essential of existence, or even of health

LXVI

Then, again, here are three or four thousand people in this remote parish, whose lives, too, are draped in the same sober monotone of place and scene and unintermittent toil, and somehow they never think it a necessity of existence to leave their homes, and see strange faces and foreign climes. And they live, and have perfect health and nerves and spirits, and thank God for His blessings, nay even for His visitations, when He does come to them under the disguise of sorrow Moreover, our forefathers and our predecessors who had the same class of work to accomplish, with greater labor and more worries, never dreamed of an autumn holiday in France or Spain And they lived to ripe old age, and dropped peacefully into peaceful graves. Ah, but! we get depressed, and the springs of all mental and bodily activity get dulled or broken, and the doctor says: " You must really go abroad and see strange faces and live under different circumstances, and pick up fresh elasticity of spirits by change, change !" Alas! it is the eternal question of nerves again.   Nervous irritability is genius , nervous ennui, heresy ; nervous literature, Ibsens and Mæterlincks ; and one and only one remedy,—which is never more than a palliative, for the disease is deep-rooted—and that is change, change, change !

LXVII.

But education ? Is not travel here at least an essential ? This, too, may be doubted. How very few celebrities, after all, made the " grand tour " ! Did Shakspere or Spenser cross the English Channel ? Of those who did venture aboard in those days, how many repeated the experiment ? Even in our times, let it be remembered that Byron and Shelley, Landor and Browning, were voluntary exiles, not travellers , and that if George Eliot could not get on without her annual trip to the Continent, Tennyson on the other hand rarely ventured from home.   And Carlyle—ah! Carlyle, what it cost him to leave even his unhappy home at Chelsea, and get away amongst friends who were prepared to put pillows of roses under his nerve-distracted head !   How he fumed

and raged till he got back to his own dismal quarters again!
And the two or three continental trips! *Ach Gott!* as he would
say. Here is a specimen.

"We got to Putbus, doing picturesquely the way   A beautiful Putbus indeed! where I had such a night as should be long
memorable to me ; big loud hotel, sea-bathing, lodgers with their
noises, including plenteous coach-horses under my window, followed by noises of cats, brood-sows, and at 2 P M by the simultaneous explosion of two Cochin-China cocks, who continued to
play henceforth, and left me what sleep you can fancy in such
quarters . .   Adieu ! *Kul Kissen*, sloppy, greasy victual, all
cold, too, especially the coffee and tea   Adieu, Teutschland!
Adieu, travelling altogether, now and forevermore !"

LXVIII.

Really, this kind of thing reconciles you to your lot, if you
are unable, or unwilling, to leave your own land   And if you have
the least experience in travelling, and understand ever so little of
its worries and annoyances, even in these days of luxury, you begin to think, that except for the extremely mercurial, who cannot
sit still, and the extremely depressed, who require frequent change,
the game is hardly worth the candle. For after all, in the whole of
Europe this moment, how many things are there which you would
really like to see ?   I do not say, how many places and things are
there which you would like to be able to boast you saw.   But
how many things, persons, places, do you really covet with the
eyes of your imagination ?   Lord Bacon gives you a handsome
list for selection.   He tells every traveller what he ought to see.
Here is the list: " The courts of princes, especially when they
give audience to ambassadors ; the courts of justice, while they
sit and hear causes ; ecclesiastical consistories ; the churches and
monasteries, with the monuments which are therein extant ; the
walls and fortifications of cities and towns, havens and harbors,
antiquities and ruins, libraries, colleges, disputations, and lectures,
shipping and navies, houses and gardens of state and pleasure
near great cities ; armories, arsenals, magazines, exchanges,
bourses, warehouses, exercises of horsemanship, fencing, soldiers

and the like ; comedies ; treasures of jewels and robes ; cabinets
and ranties ; and to conclude, whatever is memorable in the places
where they go."

LXIX.

Of all of these, about nine-tenths, I should say, are inaccessible to the ordinary traveller   Of those that are accessible, I confess the churches and monasteries alone would interest me , and
one thing more, which the writer has omitted,—the haunts and
graves of great men   The room in the Roman College where
St Aloysius died would have more attraction for me than the
Forum ; and the places consecrated by the presence and minis-
trations of that sweet saint, Philip Neri, would drag me away
from the spot where the mighty Cæsar fell.   I would of course
visit the Colosseum, but I would see only the mangled remains
of the young Christian athletes and virgins whose limbs were rent
asunder down there in its arena for the name of Christ.   And I
would see it by moonlight also, but only to observe the shadowy
figures who steal through the dark aisles and gather for sacred
burial these hallowed remains.   I would not give one precious
quarter of an hour that I might spend in the Sacred Catacombs,
to study the ruins of Pœstum, or trace the broken splendors of
Hadrian's villa ; but I would rise with the dawn to be able to say
Mass in that Mamertine prison, where the great apostles were
incarcerated, and where they baptized their gaolers with the water
of that miraculous spring that flows there in the dark beneath my
feet.

LXX.

But education ?   We are wandering a little, as befits the subject   Travelling is essential to education ?   Perhaps so.   But the
most one can ever hope to extract from a travelled man is the
exclamation : I saw that !   For example :

You —" The Parthenon which after so many thousand years
is yet the noblest temple—"

Traveller.—" Oh, yes ! we saw the Parthenon, and the Acropolis ! "

You.—"It cannot be any longer maintained that the Moorish or Saracenic influence was hostile to the arts of civilization when that magnificent relic of their architecture, the Alhambra—"

Traveller.—"The Alhambra! Oh we saw the Alhambra! 'Twas lovely!"

You—"And so if you want to see at their best Fountains' or Melrose—"

Traveller.—"Oh, yes! We were there We saw both! They are exquisite!"

You—"I was just saying that if you want to see Fountains' or Melrose, visit them by moonlight. And you shall never know the vastness and sublimity of the Colosseum, until you startle the bats at midnight from its drapery of ivy, and—"

Traveller—"Oh, yes! That's Byron, you know! No, Scott! Let me see:

> If you would see the—hem—aright,
> Visit it by the pale moonlight.

"Isn't that it? No? Well, then, 'twas Byron who said: 'Whilst stands the Colosseum,' etc, etc."

Who does not remember those two little girls whom Ruskin has pilloried forever in his *Fors Clavigera*,—who read trashy novels, and eat sugared lemons all the way between Venice and Verona, and whose only remarks on the scenery and associations were:

> "Don't those snow-caps make you cool?"
> "No—I wish they did."

Are they types?

LXXI.

Ah, but the memory of people, places, scenes, you have beheld! Isn't that worth preserving? Yes! I make the concession candidly. You have hit the bull's-eye this time. The memory of travel is the real gain and blessing of travel, just as our memories of youth, and middle-age, have a charm which our experiences did not possess. It is a curious fact and well worth investigating Sitting here by the fireside, the eye of memory

travels with an acute, and a certain kind of pathetic pleasure, over
all the accidents and vicissitudes of our long journey   How little
it makes of the worries and embarrassments , how greatly it en-
hances the pleasures.   You smile now at the inconveniences of
that long, dusty, tiresome railway journey, which you thought
would never end, at the incivility of the porters or waiters, who
contemptuously passed you by for greater folk , at the polite
rudeness of the hotel-keeper, who told you at twelve o'clock at
night, when you stumbled half-dazed from the railway carriage,
that he had not a single room available ; at the long avenue of
waiters and waitresses who filed along the hotel corridor at your
departure expectant of much backsheesh, and ungrateful for little ; at the cold of Alpine heights, and the heat of Italian cities in the
dog-days; at the little black-eyed beggar who served your Mass
for a bajocco, and turned somersaults at the altar free gratis; at
the crush and the crowd, and the hustling and the elbowing in
St. Peter's , at the awful extortions, made with the utmost politeness, by those charming and intolerable natives, of the eternal
peculation by the bland and smiling officials, etc., etc.

LXXII.

And you recall, with a pleasure you never felt in the experience, the long, amber-colored ranges of snow-clad mountains
sweeping into sight as the train rushes through horrid gorges, or
creeps slowly up some Alpine spur that slopes its declivities to meet
the demands of science; the vast vistas of snow-white palaces above
the ever-blue Mediterranean , the long days spent in the cool
galleries face to face with immortal paintings, the twilight of
great churches with all their half-veiled splendors of marbles and
pictures , that evening, when you watched the sun set across the
Val d'Arno, and the strange blue twilight crept down before it,
deepened into the purple black of the night; the hour you spent
above the graves of Shelley and Keats beneath the pyramid of
Caius Cestius, that organ recital in the great Italian Cathedral,
when you thought you saw the heavens opened and the angels
ascending and descending ; the shock and terror at the sudden
rocking of the earth at Sorrento; the cool quadrangle in the

Dominican Convent, the play of the fountain, and the white-robed monks in the gallery overhead, the home-coming; the sight of ruddy English faces instead of the dusky, black-eyed Greek or Italian; the unpacking of your treasures, the steady settling down into the old groove of life, and the resumption of ancient habits

LXXIII.

There is no doubt but that here is pleasure, deep, unalloyed pleasure, independent of the vanity of being able to say · I was there! How do you account for it? Thus, my travelled friend! You see, wherever you went, you yourself were part and parcel of all you saw and felt, and you cast the shadow of self over all. And even a Lucretian philosopher will admit that self is the ever-present trouble, dimming and darkening all eternal splendors of space and time, and mingling its own bitter myrrh of thought and feeling with the brightest and most sparkling wine of life. Yes, you were worried here, and fretted there, the memory of your little annoyance was fresh, and you took it with you, and here you were the victim of weariness and ennui, and you sang *Home, sweet home!* in your heart. And your fellow-travellers, you remember, were sometimes disagreeable. You did not get on well together. It was all their fault, of course; they were so horribly impatient, and even ignorant. What pleased you, displeased them. You would have wished to linger over that immortal canvas, which you knew you would never see again; or you would have liked to try your imperfect Italian on that laughing little nigger who rolled out his musical language so softly as he twisted the macaroni between his dirty fingers, but you were hurried on, on by your friends, and you found it hard to forgive them. They wanted to linger over dainty goods in shop-windows here and there, or to listen to a barrel organ. You said, very naturally Can't they see and hear these things at home? Why do such people ever travel abroad?

LXXIV.

That, too, is simple of explanation. They have splendid physical health, and no minds worth speaking of. They cannot rest at home, just as the untamed animal spirits of a boy will not permit him to sit still for a moment. Now, Nature is a most even and impartial mother She doles out her gifts with rigid impartiality She has given some the affluence of great health and spirits, unburdened by imagination and unstinted by reflection To others (shall we say they are her favorites?) she gives the superior gifts of mentality, with all the divine gloom and depression that invariably accompany them The former, mercurial in temperament, race across Europe, dip here and there in some antique fountain of art or literature, but instantly shake off the dreaded beads of too much thought; attend great ceremonies; enjoy the three-hours' dinner at some palatial hotel, are noisy and communicative, and happy. They return fresh from their travels to tell their acquaintances· "We have been there! Really, now, you must go!" The others, if they can shake off the physical inertia which always accompanies and balances mental irritability, glide softly through Europe, linger over the spots sanctified by genius, spend quiet, dreamy hours in cool, shady galleries, avoid the big hotels, watch Nature in silence and the solitude of their hearts, and return to the winter fireside to embody in novel, or poem, their experiences, doubly hallowed in the light of memory. These are the men that make you despair, for they have the second-sight, the vision that rises with the dawn and haunts them till the dusk

LXXV.

This enchantment of memory is really much the same as the enchantment of art. A beautiful picture gives you more pleasure than the beautiful reality it represents You dare not say it is greater, or more perfect, or more true than Nature, but you feel greater pleasure in the contemplation of it than in the vision of the reality Why? Because you are not a part of it. You see it from the outside Your personality forever jarring with itself and more or less out of tune, is not projected athwart it. You are a something apart; and you see it as a something that has no connection whatsoever with you. Hence its peace, its calm, its truth, are soothing and restful Or, if there be figures in the picture, or something dramatic and striking, for terror or for pathos, they do not touch you with any emotion but that of curiosity and pleasure. You are in a theatre, and this is the stage; but the drama cannot touch you. That picture-frame, like that drop-scene, cuts you away from the representation You are a spectator, not an actor. But in real life you cannot remain a spectator. Would to Heaven you could! You will have touched the great secret of all human philosophy when you have brought to your mind, in its daily and hourly action, the conviction that "Life is a stage, and all men players and actors thereon." But this is impossible and undesirable. You must play your own part, and it is mostly a tragic and solemn one.

LXXVI.

This is the great secret of the happiness of childhood. Children are unconscious of themselves They refer nothing to themselves. They hear of life, its vast issues, its tragedies, its trials, its weight of sorrows, but they can never for a moment believe that such things can affect themselves. The little things that do trouble them, they pass lightly over and forget The little injustices that are done them they immediately condone. They have not as yet begun to refer all things in heaven and earth to themselves. They regard them as no part of their personality. Life is a picture— a pretty picture in a gilt frame. It is a gorgeous drama, where they can sit in the pit, or the boxes, according to their position in life, and look on calmly at Blue Beard and his wives or the madness of Ophelia, or the smothering of Desdemona, while they crunch their caramels, or smear their faces with sugared fruit. Life is a pretty spectacle, created specially for their amusement. If any one were to say: "There are Blue Beards yet in the world, and you may yet be a wife, or, you may yet be an Ophelia, and carry around you bundles of rue; or, you may encounter your Iago, and have your handkerchief stolen;" that child would laugh incredulously into your face. Unconsciousness and unbelief, or rather, all-trusting faith in its immunity from sin and sorrow, are the glorious charters of childhood, as they are also symptoms of perfect, unbroken health.

LXXVII

The first moment of unrest, or subjectivity, or reference to ourselves, is the first moment also that marks our entrance on the stage of life ; and it marks also the first step towards our failure. The unconscious actor is the greatest and the most perfect   Is it not a maxim of the stage   Lose your own personality in the person you represent ?   If you are introspective, or self-examining, or curious to know what the audience is thinking of you, you will soon hear hisses and tumultuous condemnation   Just as in spiritual life, the secret not only of sanctity but of happiness, is abandonment of self, and repose in God, so in our mere earthly life we must abandon ourselves to our inspirations, or fail   The poet who tries to be a poet, will never be a poet.   He may be an artist, or polisher, or filer of sentences and phrases ; but he will always lack the higher afflatus   The saint who thinks he is a saint, ceases to be a saint   The patriot who begins to ask, how the welfare of his country will affect himself, ceases then and there to be a patriot.   All great work is unconscious, and above all, unegotistical.   The moment it becomes conscious, it becomes mechanical , and you can never turn a mechanic into a creator. Hence when critics say that Tennyson was an artist before he became a poet, they imply that he never became a poet   For there never was a truer saying than the old trite one · *Poeta nascitur.* He may bury his gift, and stifle his creative powers, and become a *Poëtes apoïetes ,* but his is a birthright that can never be bought or sold

LXXVIII.

There is another great advantage in this reserve of foreign travel   Something as yet remains unrevealed   Remember that ennui is the disease of modern life ; and that ennui is simply the repletion of those who have tasted too speedily, or too freely, at the banquet of life   Unhappy is the man who has parted with all his illusions , and such is he in a most special manner, who has seen all things, and tried all, and found all wanting   For the first view, the first experience, is the poetry of existence   And poetry, like reverence, will not tolerate familiarity. You won't rave about Alps, or Apennines, the second time you see them. You have acquired knowledge, and lost a dream. Now, the dream forever remains for one who has not seen but believed. The mystery, the wonder, the charm, are yet before him. He may yet see and be glad. Earth and sea hold all their miracles in reserve for him. He cannot sit down in middle age, and say: " I have seen all things beneath the sun; and lo! all is vanity!" No! he will not say that, so long as the bright succession of the world's wonders may yet file before him. He has always a reserve; and sinks even into his grave with all the hope and fascination, all the glamor and straining eyes of inexperience.

LXXIX

To one living at a distance from railways, the whistle of the engine gives a thrill of novelty, and a sudden pleasure. There is a romance, and even a poetry in railways. At least, to one unaccustomed to leave home, a railway journey is a rare enjoyment. He cannot see the great, smooth engine rolling into the platform, or behold the faces at the windows, or take his seat, without a certain excitement, or nervous thrill, that is utterly unknown to the experienced traveller. The comfortable, cushioned seat, the electric light overhead, the mirrors all around him, the new, strange faces, each with its secret soul looking out, anxious, hopeful, or perplexed, the very isolation of his travelling companions and the mystery that hangs around their unknownness, the quiet that settles down on the carriage as it glides out so smoothly from the station; the rapid succession of scenes that move across the field of vision—all is novel, all unexperienced, all delightful! He would give the world to know who, or what, is that old gentleman who has pulled his rug around him and is buried in his papers; or that young, pale fellow, who is so much at home, he must be a much travelled man, or that young girl, who is gazing so steadfastly through the window. And the real pleasure is, that all is mystery, and wonder, and the unknown, even to the end.

LXXX.

Twenty-five years ago I thought that a Cunard, or White Star liner, outward bound, was the most interesting sight on earth   I think so still.   The silence of its movements, its obedience to the slightest touch, the risks and hazards before it, when it is but a speck on the illimitable deep, and the moonlight is all around it, or when it is rocked from billow to billow, like a cork, but, above all, the strange, mysterious faces that look from behind their veils at you, and the stranger drama that is being enacted there— all conspire to make that floating caravenserai one of those objects of interest and wonder that carry with them always the glamor and mystery of another world.   That is, to the inexperienced.   I dare say, that commercial traveller who has crossed the Atlantic twenty times, and who seems so much at home there upon the sloping deck, thinks otherwise.   Probably, he is calculating how much he will win at poker or euchre ; or what seat he shall have at table   That lady, too, who has just done Europe, and who looks so tired and *blasée*, is just hoping that the beastly voyage may be soon over, that she may plunge once more into the glorious whirl of New York excitement.   But to the untravelled, the inexperienced, all is wonder and mystery, from the mysterious being up aloft who is the master of our destinies, to the grimy fireman, who comes up from the Inferno, to catch one breath of fresh salt air.

LXXXI.

If the untravelled is wise, he will speak to no one but in monosyllables, and preserve his own incognito and inexperience to the end.   Thus, he, too, will be a mystery, and somewhat interesting to others, who will be dying to penetrate behind his mask.   And all around will bear the glamor of unknownness to his imagination.   It is horrible—that disillusion about people, around whom you have woven your own webs of fancy.   Now, if you accost that commercial traveller, you will, you must, reveal the fact that you are crossing the Atlantic for the first time ; and down you go several degrees in his esteem   Or, if you are happy enough to get acquainted with that young lady in the canvas chair, blue veiled, and with infinite rugs about her, she will probably tell you "she has just done Yurrup, and is tired of the whole show." And the airy web of fancy is rudely torn asunder. Or, if you should come to know the officers, and they, with their usual kindness, tell you all about their vessel, and their experiences, or gossip about the passengers, or show you the tremendous mechanism that is the heart-throb and life-pulse of the ship, you will have to come down to the standpoint of commonplace; and before you step ashore at New York, your nerves will have cooled down, and you will regard the ship of fancy as a black old hulk, with a hideous brass kettle in its centre.

LXXXII.

There is a great deal more than we are accustomed to think in this habit of reticence and reverence. Touch not, taste not, if you would keep fresh the divine fancies that spring from a pure imagination, excited by pure and inspiring literature. It was the irreverent curiosity of our first parents that opened their eyes to unutterable things. They touched, tasted, and saw. Better for them and their posterity had they kept the reverence due to the behests of the Most High, and with it their unsullied innocence and blessed want of knowledge. There was a tradition of our childhood that the mother bird would desert a nest once breathed upon by others. The place was profaned and she would haunt it no longer, even though the blue or speckled eggs should never come to maturity. Even so with the spirit. It refuses to go back to places once dishallowed by knowledge. It prefers to hover over lonely heights, and to haunt unpeopled solitudes; and there to keep the virginal freshness of its inexperience unsullied by knowledge that opens the eyes of mind and body, but blinds the vision of the soul.

LXXXIII

But, coming back under the umbrage and gloom of great trees from the illimitable expanses of sea and sky, I ask myself why I experience a sudden narrowing and contraction of spirit, although my mind is as free and untrammelled as before. And why do the people, sick of their prison houses and the narrow limitations of daily life, seek for freshness down there as close to the sea as they can go? For they will not look at the sea from afar, nor from safe vantage grounds, but they creep down and sit on rocks that overhang the tremendous depths; and imperil their lives by going lower and lower still, until their feet are washed by the incoming, irresistible tides. What do they want? What do they seek? It is not pure air alone. That they can have on mountain summits. Yet they never go to the mountains. But the most unpoetic, unromantic, prosaic people will seek the seashore, and remain there the whole day long, and tear themselves away from it with difficulty, and even when it is only a memory and a dream, will speak of it the whole winter long, and bear the worries and work of the year in the hope that they shall seek and see the sands and waves and the far horizon again.

LXXXIV.

I experienced a similar sense of imprisonment and freedom once in a brief, very brief holiday abroad. I never saw the Alps from their summits, and therefore must not speak disparagingly of them. But I passed through gorges and ravines, and lonely valleys, several thousands of feet above the sea, but everywhere felt, even on the highest altitudes, as if I were walking the flagged courtyard of a prison, with impassable, unscalable granite walls around and above, grinding and crushing the spirit. Perhaps if I had stood on the St. Bernard, or Monte Rosa, and looked around on the white cold crests that capped the undulations of crags and peaks without number, my sensations would have been different. But I well remember drawing a great breath of relief when the train steamed out from beyond Interlaken, and we passed by Fribourg, and saw in a moment the Lake Leman, unbounded in that direction but by the sky. It was just as if a person, half-asphyxiated by the thick air of a prison cell, had been suddenly summoned to life, liberty, and pure, sweet, wholesome breathing again.

LXXXV

I cannot explain it, except by the theory of our universal and insatiable craving after the unbounded, the Infinite. You imprison the soul, when you limit its aspirations It must be in touch with the universe. It is the one thing on earth, the only thing, that cannot make its home here All things else are content to do their little work, perform their little part, and die Winds arise and blow, and pass away; seas come and go, and scatter themselves on the sands, leaves bud and develop, and fall, animals are born, pass on to maturity, and return to the inorganic state. Man alone looks out and beyond this planet Here he hath no lasting dwelling-place His soul is with the stars. And therefore it chafes at its imprisonment in the body ; and even the accidental environments of place and scenery affect this strange, homeless exile, that is forever pining after its own country. How sweetly the Church interprets this feeling in the beautiful Benediction Hymn :

> Qui vitam sine termino
> Nobis donet in patria

And that is the vision we look for when we strain our eyes across the sunlit sea, and dream of things beyond the visible horizon, but not beyond the horizon of our hopes

LXXXVI.

Hence, the secret of the *Welt-Schmerz*, the dreary, hopeless pessimism that has sunk like a thunder cloud on the minds of all modern thinkers, and blackens every page of modern literature is, that these unhappy unbelievers deny their destiny and vocation, and denying it, refuse to pursue it, and sink down into mere denizens of earth The moment they yield to the sordid temptation of disbelieving their own immortality, they excommunicate themselves from the universe They are no longer part of the great, stupendous whole. Life becomes a wretched span, limited on both sides by the gulf of nothingness, instead of being the prelude to the vast eternity of existence that is connoted by immortality.   Man is a clod, a senseless atom, an inorganic substance, galvanized for a moment into an organism.   He is but a self-conscious yet insignificant part of the chemistry of Nature, with no relations, least of all eternal correspondences, with the vast spirits of the universe.

LXXXVII.

I cannot help thinking that mad Lear upon the moorland, whipped by the storm, disowned by his daughters, and accompanied only by a fool, is the type of such unhappy beings   For irreligion is insanity.   Just as the latter is but the partial and distorted view of the diseased mind that looks out at Nature; so the former is the half-vision that refuses to see the perfect whole, rounded into unity and uniformity under the Almighty Hand. And forth the discrowned victim goes, " the king walking in the mire," as the Wise Man saw him, the storms of life and tempestuous thought are around him, the children of his genius execrate him for his alienation of their birthright, he has with him as " guide, philosopher, friend," a fool—shall we say, his own darkened and stammering intellect ?   And the gloom and desolation grow deeper and deeper around him, for he sees no hope or prospect of the dawn ; but only the night, and the night, and the night !

LXXXVIII.

It is true there is a certain strange luxury in this intellectual melancholy and depression.   But the motive is not sane ; the experience is not wholesome. However much we may pity the loneliness, or admire the genius of all these modern pessimists, " and their name is legion," they are undoubtedly a wretched and degenerate lot.   Sadness is their portion ; life has a dreary outlook to them ; the heat of battle is not in their veins, the cry of victory is not on their lips.   Life is all a hideous drama, until death tears down the curtain, and the lights are extinguished ; and with tears on their pallid faces, the spectators pass out into the night. How that dreary, dull undertone of sadness rolls through all modern literature !   Never a note of triumph, never a psalm of hope, never a glorious prophetic pæan about the future that is to be, where man shall touch his real spiritual evolution, and reach his finality amongst his brethren of the skies But a low deep wail, musical enough, if you like, echoing along the minor chords of human misery, and sobbing itself away into silence, unless the wind moaning among the tangled grasses and nettles above the deserted and forgotten grave, can be taken as the echo in nature of the threnodies that wailed from such desolate and despairing lives.

LXXXIX.

"Our desires went beyond our destinies," they say, "and thus were we unhappy." Nay, it was not your desires, but your powers, that reached beyond your imagined and narrowed destinies, and hence you were unhappy. You would not recognize facts. You stretched yourselves on a Procrustean bed, and sought a comfort that would not come. You were made other than you thought. You disputed the very laws of Nature when you contended that those faculties of reason, imagination, affection, were limited in their development and enjoyment to the transient objects of the senses and of this lower life. You refused to believe in the infallible proportion of things, the rigid, inexorable law that destiny must proportion itself to nature, and that the eternal harmonies that govern all things demanded an infinity for cravings that were infinite, an eternity for love that was stronger than death. But this you refused to accept. You made yourselves monsters, anomalies in creation Like the barbarians of old, you proved to yourselves that the destiny of the sun was to sink in the sea, and be extinguished You could not understand how to-morrow, and to-morrow, and to-morrow, he is destined to rise, and "exult again, like a giant, to run his destined course"

XC.

And so we have, especially in France, all those *rêveurs* and *penseurs*, and moralists, and soliloquists, fleeing from practical life, and with heads bent and drooping eyes, wandering through

the solitudes of Nature, and talking to trees, and trying to catch
in the murmur of the stream, or the whisper of the wind, some
answer to the eternal questionings of weary and dispirited minds.
The rush from society to Nature is a curious phenomenon of our
age. It is a symptom of the strange morbidity that has come
down upon the world, since philosophers and poets first disturbed, then broke up, the healthy equilibrium of Christian teaching in the minds of their disciples The return to Nature, the
elimination of its omnipresent, beneficent Creator, the searching
everywhere for the great god, Pan, the disappointment, the unrest, the self-disgust and weariness, are visible everywhere in
those pages that interpret emotions and thoughts, which probably
the eyes of men would never have seen, if all this solitariness and
introspection and reverie were not tinged with that species of
affectation and vanity which is at once the cause and effect of all
that eccentricity, which drives men from the orbit of their species,
and compels them to an existence, unhappy and alone.

XCI.

How different the eternal hope, the far visioning, the ever
exultant pæan that rises from the Christian heart! It is always
childhood and morning, and great peace, and eternal, invincible
faith in the ultimate perfection of all feeble and unstable things
Nature, the sombre and veiled companion of the children of un-
faith, becomes the revealed and laughing nurse of the children of
belief. She, too, is but the beloved servant in our Father's house
where we are the children. She puts on no Sibylline airs, utters
no phrenetic prophecies, conceals no subtle meanings, speaks no
mysterious language All the occult mysticism that unbelief
affects to see beneath her phenomenon, resolves itself into the
sweet simplicities of one who is a handmaiden to the great Lord
of all things. And hence, we are not frightened by her power,
nor terrified by her magic, nor awed by her sublimity All her
motions and signs we refer to a Cause and an End We appreciate
their beauty and holiness; but rest not there. All things in her
and about her round to perfection—that final perfection which is
God!

XCII

From summer maturity and splendor, the year is moving steadily onward to the decline and ashen grayness of winter again. The garden beds, shorn of all their blossoms through the slips that are to be reserved for next summer, look mutilated of all their ripened strength and beauty, their strong stalks having developed into wood, the especial horror of a gardener There is a smell of frost in the early evening, as the fogs rise ghost-like from the valleys, and the sun has sunk down from the imperial heights of summer and taken humbly a lower arc in the heavens. How swiftly has the summer gone ! It seems but yesterday that so late as nine, or half-past nine o'clock, I watched the trees blackening against the saffron sunset. Now, it is pitch dark at eight o'clock. The swallows are training their young for the autumnal flight, and holding more frequent conclaves in the skies and on the roofs. The hum of the threshing machine comes mournfully from afar off I see the rich produce of the harvest flung into its gaping mouth to come forth seed and grain The stags are belling in yonder forest The first patch of gold is seen on the chestnut. Nature is winding up her little affairs in view of her approaching demise And the winds are beginning to rise, and practise their winter requiems over a dead and silent world.

XCIII.

The great transatlantic liners are filled, every berth, with "travelled men from foreign lands," rushing homewards to the little roof that shelters them, and the little lives which are linked with theirs The equinoctial gales are blowing in their teeth, yet the home-comers speed onwards. Home and love await them across the white breakers of the angry seas. Everywhere the turbulent riotousness of summer is giving way to the rigid order of winter. The hatches are being fastened down, and everything must be snug and tight before the rain, and the snow, and the storm. The time is coming for the merry fire, and the beloved book, and the tea-urn, and the curtained and carpeted luxuries of home.

And outside—housed, too, for evermore against all the dangers and vicissitudes of life—the beautiful, mysterious dead sleep on in their silent cities   The moonlight throws black shadows of shrub or cross athwart their graves   The seasons come and go, and they are swept round and round in the swift diurnal march of Mother Earth   But they are at rest.   Theirs is the peace of eternity.   Theirs, the fruition.   Ours, still the faith and the hope— in God, in His eternal laws, in our own souls.

> I trust in Nature, for the stable laws
> Of beauty and utility—Spring shall plant,
> And Autumn garner to the end of time.
> I trust in God,—the right shall be the right,
> And other than the wrong, whilst He endures.
> I trust in my own soul, that can perceive
> The outward and the inward,—Nature's good
> And God's.

THE END.